Crybaby Rebellion

Crybaby Rebellion

Ossie Vitt and the 1940 Cleveland Indians

GARY WEBSTER

McFarland & Company, Inc., Publishers

Jefferson, North Carolina

ISBN (print) 978-1-4766-9705-5
ISBN (ebook) 978-1-4766-5766-0

LIBRARY OF CONGRESS CATALOGING DATA ARE AVAILABLE

Library of Congress Control Number 2026002010

Front cover image: Cleveland Indians players Ken Keltner and Rollie Hemsley, with coach Luke Sewell and manager Oscar Vitt (26), argue with umpire Lou Kolls during a 1940 game in Municipal Stadium (Cleveland State University).

Printed in the United States of America

McFarland & Company, Inc., Publishers
Box 611, Jefferson, North Carolina 28640
www.mcfarlandpub.com

Table of Contents

Preface   1

1. Graveyard of Managers   5

2. It Would Be All About Oscar   14

3. Déjà Vu All Over Again   21

4. Shaping Up   25

5. Zeroes in Chicago   51

6. What's with the Yankees   62

7. Calm Before the Storm   81

8. Please, Mr. Bradley   87

9. Bottles, Buggies and Bonnets   109

10. Taking Charge ... Briefly   124

11. Floyd Who?   146

12. California, Here He Comes   177

Chapter Notes   189

Bibliography   193

Index   195

Preface

This book might be considered a bit of revisionist history, because in my research for this narrative, I learned that history needed a bit of revision ... or should I say correction? That will be explained in the pages that follow.

Some 76 years after it was published, in 1949, and reprinted in 2005, Franklin (Whitey) Lewis' book *The Cleveland Indians* remains the definitive work regarding the first half-century of the team's existence. It will be referred to frequently in the pages that follow. It may have been the first baseball book I ever read. I remember borrowing it from the library of my elementary school. I didn't know at the time that Lewis had been the sports editor of the *Cleveland Press*, the city's afternoon newspaper to which my family subscribed.

Like many sportswriters, Lewis occasionally stretched the truth, and thus my introduction to the unprecedented events of the 1940 baseball season was somewhat skewed. Specifically, Lewis wrote in his book that the Indians entered the season "national favorites," to use his own words, to win the American League pennant. As I grew older and became immersed in the history of not just the national pastime but also of my favorite team, that statement intrigued me. It also didn't make sense.

Entering the 1940 season, the New York Yankees were the defending World Series champions. They'd made a mockery of the American League pennant race in 1939, winning 106 games and finishing 17 games ahead of the runner-up Boston Red Sox. The Indians placed third, 20½ lengths in arrears. It was the Yankees' fourth consecutive pennant and world's championship. The juggernaut seemed to be clicking on all cylinders. Most of the national sports columnists, in their articles written immediately after the Yankees had polished off the National League champion Cincinnati Reds in a four-game sweep, offered no reason to believe New York could be stopped in 1940.

The Yankees returned their entire starting line-up intact in 1940. That included the pitching staff, which, as 1940 would prove, was beginning to show the effects of age. The Indians made no significant additions during the off-season, but they had strengthened their infield considerably in the middle of the 1939 season when second baseman Ray Mack and shortstop Lou Boudreau had been promoted from the minor leagues and helped the Tribe finish strong, winning 34 of its final 54 games, and 19 of its final 26. With the Yankees and Indians returning the same personnel in 1940, why was a team which had choked on New York's dust while finishing 20½ games behind the previous season considered the "national favorites" to de-throne the defending champs? Determining the reasons was one of my inspirations for writing this book.

The other reason was researching the importance and impact of the unprecedented player rebellion that occurred on June 13. As noted in the book, the history of baseball, and in subsequent years, of all major league sports, had and has been littered with instances of players unhappy with the manager or head coach, and seeking a method of effecting a change at the top. These methods were always clandestine. Only the Indians of 1940 took the ultimate step: they met with ownership, and demanded it fire manager Oscar Vitt immediately, insisting they couldn't play winning baseball as long as he was in command. They presented a laundry list of grievances to the team president, which they felt justified their demand. No other major league sports team, before or since, has taken such a drastic step, no doubt in part because the tactic failed.

Since I began studying sports history, baseball in particular, I've been fascinated by the saga of the "Cleveland Crybabies," as the Indians of 1940 have come to be known. Who was involved in the rebellion? How did Vitt respond to the knowledge that many of his players disliked, even hated, him, and had demanded he be replaced? How did he carry on under the circumstances? Were the players mocked and ridiculed in ballparks around the league, as legend has us believe? What did the writers who covered the Indians on a daily basis think of all the chaos that engulfed the team for the rest of the season? How did the local fans react? And how, in spite of all the turmoil, did the Tribe stay focused enough to chase the Detroit Tigers down to the last weekend of the season in the league's closest pennant race in 20 years?

At times during the 1940 season, at least in Cleveland, what transpired off the diamond was more interesting, and more important, than what transpired on it.

1

Graveyard of Managers

It's appropriate that the events chronicled in this book took place in Cleveland, which has been the home of a star-crossed franchise in the American League since the league was founded in 1901. Such a bizarre turn of events as those of June 1940, and, to a lesser extent, the entire 1940 baseball season, would've seemed out of place had they happened anywhere else.

To understand why the unprecedented events of the summer of 1940 seemed almost normal for the Cleveland Indians, it's necessary to examine the team's history, at least as it pertains to managers.

Cleveland was among the eight cities former sportswriter turned baseball executive Byron Bancroft (Ban) Johnson selected for his new American League in 1900. Johnson had been president of the minor Western League since 1894, and his secret intent from his first day on the job had been to elevate the league to major status, to compete with the National, which enjoyed a monopoly on major league baseball since the collapse of the American Association, then a major league, in 1892. First, Johnson built the Western League into the strongest minor league in the sport. He knew the National League would eventually buckle under the weight of its 12 clubs, and that happened after the 1899 season, when four teams (Louisville, Baltimore, Washington, and Cleveland) were lopped off. Johnson had no interest in Louisville, Baltimore or Washington (at least not immediately) but grabbed Cleveland, despite its history of not supporting its National League team, for his American League.

The American retained the Western League's minor league status, as well as a few of its teams, for the 1900 season. By 1901, Johnson was ready to do battle with the National League. He began by eliminating Buffalo, Minneapolis, Indianapolis, and Kansas City. Cleveland was retained, despite lackluster attendance in 1900. The departing franchises were replaced by Boston, Philadelphia, Baltimore, and Washington. On April 24, 1901, Cleveland visited Chicago for the first game ever played in the American League ... as a major league. All eight teams were scheduled to open the season that day, but the other games were rained out.

Cleveland's status in the American League was shaky from the start. The team's attendance of 131,380 was the lowest in the major leagues. Understandably, the city's fans didn't flock to League Park on Cleveland's east side to watch a seventh place team that posted a 54–82 record and finished 28½ games out of first.

In what could be considered his "State of the American League" address on July 30, 1901, Johnson spoke to reporters and looked ahead to 1902. The big news was that the American League would place a club in St. Louis the following season. Johnson had planned to move Milwaukee's team to St. Louis in 1901, but the owner Johnson had hand-picked to buy the Brewers backed out at the 11th hour, forcing the team to play an essentially lame duck season in Milwaukee. Johnson announced on July 30 that the American League would definitely put a team in St. Louis in 1902, with Milwaukee being the most likely candidate to relocate. However, Johnson warned that "Cleveland or Baltimore may be shifted."

Ultimately, the Brewers moved to St. Louis to become the woebegone Browns. The Orioles were shifted, in 1903, to New York to become the Highlanders, who became the Yankees. Cleveland kept its team, but lost its manager. Jimmy McAleer, who starred through the 1890s in centerfield for the National League's Cleveland Spiders, announced his retirement from baseball late in the 1901 season. Trying to coax victories out of the talent Cleveland had assembled for its first American League season proved to be more aggravation than McAleer could stand. He wasn't retired long. Johnson recruited him to manage St. Louis in 1902. He guided the Browns to a second-place finish.

McAleer became the first in a long line of managers who couldn't deal with the rigors of managing in Cleveland. Bill Armour replaced McAleer in 1902, and submitted his resignation late in the 1904 season. The team, known as the Bronchos in 1902, and the Naps in 1903, following the acquisition of the league's first superstar, second baseman Napoleon (Larry) Lajoie, improved steadily. Still, by the end of the 1904 season, Armour was weary and disgusted. He told owner Charles W. Somers that he couldn't manage a ball club that didn't want to be managed. Armour managed Detroit in 1905 where, late in the year, he found himself with a rookie outfielder named Ty Cobb.

As was the custom in that era, Somers decided to name his team captain his manager. Lajoie ran the Naps through the middle of the 1909 season, losing the 1908 pennant to Detroit (no longer managed by Armour) by a half game. The Naps were expected, at least in Cleveland, to finish one notch higher than they had in 1908. Instead, the team was playing .500 ball in mid–August when Lajoie stepped down. He was succeeded by "Deacon" Jim McGuire, who'd resigned … one step ahead of the posse … as manager of the Boston Red Sox in 1908. Lajoie was relieved to be rid of the pressure of managing, and McGuire fared no better in the Naps' dugout than he had in Boston's.

Following a slow start to the 1911 season (11 losses in 17 games), McGuire resigned, to be replaced by the Naps' first baseman, George Stovall. The club responded to Stovall's leadership and finished third. Cleveland's winning percentage of .544 under Stovall (74–62) was the second highest in the league, bettered only by the eventual champion Philadelphia Athletics. The players, who liked Stovall, expected him to be re-hired. So did the fans, and so did Stovall. Instead, Somers hired former Athletics first baseman Harry Davis to manage the Naps in 1912. The agreement with Connie Mack for Davis's services had been reached shortly after McGuire's resignation. Stovall had been a lame duck all season, but didn't know it. No one knew except Somers, Mack, and Davis.

Somers thought Davis, having played most of his career for Mack, might bring some of Mack's baseball acumen to Cleveland. The players took an immediate dislike to Davis, partially because he'd replaced the popular Stovall, and partially because he tried to instill the kind of discipline in the Naps that Mack used to run the Athletics. Stovall was then traded to the Browns, angering the players further. Davis never stood a chance, and resigned after a 6–3 loss to St. Louis, which was then managed by Stovall, dropped the Naps' record to 54–71, on September 1. Cleveland was in sixth place, 33½ games out of first. Mack was glad to welcome Davis back to Philadelphia, and intimated Cleveland's players had laid down in order to get Davis fired. Somers replaced Davis with outfielder Joe Birmingham, and the Naps won 21 of their final 28 games, including a nine-game winning streak. Does that closing rush lend credence to Mack's charge? Who knows?

The Naps contended in 1913, but faded late (a nasty habit copied by many future Cleveland teams) and finished third. Cleveland finished last in 1914, losing 102 games (a club record that stood for 77 years), and when the 1915 Naps got off to a slow start, Somers fired Birmingham and replaced him with coach Lee Fohl. Shortly afterward, Somers was forced by financial reverses to sell the club to "Sunny" Jim Dunn. Dunn made a huge splash by acquiring star centerfielder Tris Speaker from the Red Sox, and together, Dunn, Fohl and Speaker rebuilt the club, by then, with the departure of Lajoie after the 1914 season, re-named the Indians. Fohl called the shots from the Tribe's dugout until mid-way through the 1919 season, when he resigned with the team in second place (44–34) but not mounting a serious challenge to the league-leading Chicago White Sox. Dunn convinced a reluctant Speaker to assume the reins, and the rejuvenated Indians posted a 40–21 record for their new boss. They failed to catch the White Sox (how different might the 1919 World Series have been if they had?), but were poised to capture their first pennant, and World Series championship, under Speaker's leadership in 1920. That was followed by a near miss in 1921, when Babe Ruth and the New York Yankees weren't to be denied. The Indians trailed the Yankees by just percentage points in mid–September, but lost three out of four in the Polo Grounds and finished second, 4½ games behind.

After leading the Indians to a surprising second place finish, three games behind the Yankees, in 1926, Speaker abruptly resigned under mysterious circumstances. He was replaced by one of his coaches, Jack McAllister, under whom the team flopped in 1927. McAllister was dismissed after one season. Native Clevelander Roger Peckinpaugh, the American League's Most Valuable Player in 1924 with the pennant winning Washington Senators, was the Indians' new manager. Despite the fact the Tribe played worse for Peckinpaugh than it had for McAllister, the new ownership, which purchased the team from Dunn's widow after the '27 season, exhibited patience. Peckinpaugh was retained for 1929, and former umpire Billy Evans, who was hired by the new ownership as general manager, quite possibly baseball's first as we define the job today, started the re-building process.

Led by a group of owners known as "the millionaires," Evans, and Peckinpaugh, the Indians became a good, but not great, team. They didn't challenge the dynastic Athletics of 1929, '30 and '31, nor did they put up much of a fight as the Yankees won the 1932 pennant. When they didn't give the Senators much resistance in 1933, at least through the first third of the season, co-owner and club president Alva Bradley decided a change was in order. The Indians had a record of 26–25 when Bradley, declaring the team was performing lackadaisically, fired Peckinpaugh and shocked everyone by replacing him with former Washington pitcher and manager Walter Johnson. The Indians had been in second place just a week earlier, but then lost five in a row and nosedived to fifth, eight games out of first.

Johnson had retired to his Maryland farm after being fired by the Senators following a strong third place finish in 1932. He'd posted a winning record (350–264) managing the Senators from 1929 to 1932, including a second place finish with 94 victories in 1930. However, according to *The Cleveland Indians Encyclopedia*, Johnson had "developed a reputation for impatience" while managing the Senators.

Ironically, or perhaps not so ironically, Johnson clashed with some of the Tribe's pitchers during his brief tenure. Again, according to *The Cleveland Indians Encyclopedia*, Johnson suffered from a problem many superstar players who became managers were plagued by: he couldn't accept the fact that not every pitcher ... in fact, none of his pitchers ... could perform up to the standard Johnson had achieved during his Hall of Fame career.

Although the Indians had been mediocre during Peckinpaugh's not quite 5½ seasons in charge, his dismissal wasn't well received by the fans. Even though Bradley insisted (with considerable justification) throughout his nearly two decade long term as team president that it was ultimately the fans, and not ownership, who fired the manager, few fans were calling for a change in 1933. And no one expected Peckinpaugh to be replaced by Johnson ... who was Peckinpaugh's closest friend in baseball, following their years as teammates. Although Johnson was one of baseball's all-time nice guys, Cleveland's media, fans, and, most importantly, players (many of them, anyway) took an immediate dislike to him. The Indians showed no more spark for Johnson than they had for Peckinpaugh, winning 48 games and losing 51 to finish fourth with a record of 75–76.

The 1934 Indians improved from fourth place to third with a record of 85–69. That didn't impress the *Cleveland Press*, which editorialized about the situation late in the season. The editors determined the Indians had failed to challenge for the pennant due to a lack of leadership from the manager, and suggested a change was in order. Actually, the editorial did more than suggest Johnson be replaced. It was a demand. Bradley responded quickly and decisively. He signed Johnson to a contract for 1935. It proved to be a mistake, and the events of 1935 may have been a precursor to the events of 1940.

Early in 1935, Johnson claimed to have uncovered what he termed an anti–Johnson bloc among his players, supposedly led by third baseman Willie Kamm and catcher Glenn Myatt. Johnson insisted Kamm and Myatt were poisoning the minds of the team's young players with their attitude and rhetoric. Both players denied trying to undermine their manager, but Johnson insisted they be released, and they were. Kamm retired and became a scout. Myatt, who'd been with the Indians since 1923, signed with the New York Giants. He finished his career with the Detroit Tigers in 1936. Myatt's release further infuriated the fans. The *Plain Dealer* reported on June 4 that a group of fans had gathered 500 signatures on a petition stating "we believe Johnson should be removed as manager of the Indians at once."[1] The Tribe was floundering in the standings, and Bradley felt compelled to step in before a bad situation got worse.

Bradley composed a statement, which the players were required to sign (whether it represented their true feelings or not) declaring their loyalty to their team, and their manager. The statement was displayed for the fans in full page advertisements purchased in each of Cleveland's three daily newspapers on June 6 and 7.

The statement included a headline: SOME INSIDE STUFF DIRECT FROM THE CAMP OF THE INDIANS. Beneath it was written, "we, the members of the Cleveland baseball club, want the fans to know we are not a team split wide open by dissension, arrayed against our manager. On the whole, we are a group of 21 contented athletes. We … feel we have a very good ball club. We are positive we are a pennant contender. We firmly believe in our manager, Walter Johnson. We are 100 per cent loyal to our public, manager Walter Johnson, and president Alva Bradley."[2] The statement contained some other flowery prose, but that was the gist of it. It was signed by all 21 players.

While glad to accept the ball club's money to provide it with the space to distribute its propaganda, the *Plain Dealer*, in the same June 7 edition, questioned the statement's authenticity. An article lacking a by-line reported that after the Indians' game in Detroit on June 2, long-time club secretary Walter McNichols had been dispatched by Evans to the team's Navin Field clubhouse to gather player signatures. Each player was told Evans had "requested" his signature. The story claimed the players hadn't seen the statement to which their signatures were affixed until they read it in the city's two afternoon newspapers on June 6.

The statement, which may have done Johnson's cause more harm than good, convinced no one. The Indians were a team torn apart by dissension, with many players harboring a seething resentment against their leader. It paled in comparison to the contempt in which the fans held Johnson. By early June, Bradley had instructed the team's concessionaire to abandon the common practice of selling beer and soft drinks in bottles, in favor of paper cups. Bradley feared angry fans would hurl the bottles at Johnson when he set foot outside the League Park dugout. But Bradley's support of his beleaguered manager remained steadfast, and in spite of the chaos, the Indians surged as spring turned into summer. The Tribe moved into second place on June 17, getting as close as 2½ games behind the front-running Yankees after a 3–2 victory over the White Sox in the first game of a League Park doubleheader on June 30. That was where the surge ended.

The White Sox won the nightcap, 8–0, starting the Indians on an eight-game skid which included a five-game sweep at the hands of the defending champion Tigers, who were poised to make their move after languishing in fourth and fifth places for much of the year. Cleveland fell to fifth place on July 17, rallied briefly to move up a notch on the 24th, then slumped back to fifth, assisted by the Tigers, who arrived in Cleveland on the 26th, shortly after wresting first place from New York, and proceeded to win three of four. The game of Saturday, July 27, was attended by 5,000 fans, most of whom cheered on the visitors, who pounded Tribe pitching for 14 runs. The Indians won the final game of the series, but still trailed Detroit by 9½ games. Only 2,000 patrons had attended the final game of the Detroit series. Despite his personal admiration for Johnson, Bradley couldn't justify supporting him any longer. He summoned Johnson to his office on July 29 and fired him. Or, more accurately in Bradley's opinion, Cleveland's fans had fired him. The poor attendance for the Detroit series led Bradley to believe the fans had resolved to stay away from League Park as long as Johnson was manager. He'd be replaced by one of his coaches, Steve O'Neill.

Ever the gentleman, in spite of the abuse, justified or unjustified, he'd received since the day he arrived in Cleveland, Johnson didn't want O'Neill to get off to a rough start. With the team in a tailspin, he told Bradley it was likely to lose quite a few games on its brief western trip to Chicago and Detroit. Johnson asked permission to stay in the dugout until the team returned to Cleveland, at which time Bradley could announce his resignation. Bradley agreed. The Indians lost five of the six games. Johnson resigned on August 5, with the Tribe in fifth place with a 46–48 record, 13½ games out of first.

The Indians responded to O'Neill, winning 36 of their remaining 59 games. There was no hope of salvaging the 1935 season, but enthusiasm ran high for 1936. O'Neill was a popular choice among the fans, most of whom remembered him as the starting catcher on the Tribe's 1920 World Series championship team. However, in spite of the spurt O'Neill presided over during the final two months of 1935, he wasn't able to do any more with the Indians than Johnson had, or Peckinpaugh before him. In fact, they played worse for O'Neill than they'd played for Johnson in 1934. The 1936 Indians finished fifth (80–74). The 1937 Indians finished fourth (83–71). At one particularly frustrating juncture of the 1937 season, the *Cleveland Press* pleaded with the manager to read the riot act to his underachieving players. But ranting, raving and cracking the whip weren't part of O'Neill's repertoire. He was fired by Bradley after the 1937 season.

For the record, O'Neill's two and a fraction seasons in Cleveland were the start of a highly successful managerial career. He guided the Tigers to the 1945 American League pennant and World Series title. He also managed the Red Sox and Phillies, and never endured a losing season. O'Neill's teams compiled a record of 1,040–821 (.559) with three second place finishes. In this author's opinion, that's a record worthy of Hall of Fame consideration. But O'Neill couldn't take the Indians where their fans, and Bradley, desperately wanted them to go.

The events of May and June of 1935 were a mere tempest in a teapot compared to what would transpire five summers later.

Bradley ... and, most likely, most of the Tribe's fans ... hungered for a rip-snortin' fire breathing dragon of a manager, who'd light a fire under a group of perennially underachieving players, and hold their feet to it.

They found him in Newark, New Jersey.

2

It Would Be All About Oscar

On Sunday, August 8, 1937, the Indians lost to the World Series-bound New York Yankees, 6–5, in Yankee Stadium. The loss dropped Cleveland 22 games behind the defending World Series champions. Cleveland had won 43 games and lost 50. It was the low point of the season for Steve O'Neill's warriors. From that point on, the fifth place Tribe caught fire, winning 40 and losing 21. Unlike 1935, however, when the Indians went on the warpath after O'Neill replaced the much- despised Walter Johnson as manager, leading to what proved to be unfounded optimism for 1936, the hot streak fooled no one. It was a mirage. The pressure was off. The Indians improved one notch in the American League standings, from fifth place to fourth. But fourth place, which represented an improvement over the Tribe's fifth place finish of 1936, wasn't what club president Alva Bradley envisioned when he elevated O'Neill from coach to manager. Cleveland's record of 83–71 was good, but not nearly good enough to scare the Yankees. Or the other two teams ahead of it.

Throughout the 1930s, the Indians, under the ownership of Bradley and a group of wealthy Clevelanders known as "the millionaires," had been good, but not nearly good enough. That was wearing thin not only with Bradley, but with the fans, who weren't swarming the ticket windows at either tiny League Park, or mammoth Municipal Stadium, to watch the Indians win more than they lost, but not nearly enough more. O'Neill became the fourth manager Bradley would dismiss since assuming the club presidency in 1928. "Changing managers is the most unpleasant feature of my job," he said after firing O'Neill. "It's just one of those things. The show must go on."[1] O'Neill rejected Bradley's offer of a scouting position. He'd re-emerge as a manager in Detroit; in Boston with the Red Sox; and

14

in Philadelphia with the Phillies. His teams would never experience a losing season.

Bradley and general manager Cy Slapnicka set to work finding a manager who was the opposite of the easy-going O'Neill. Both men were convinced the Indians had the talent to give the Yankees a run for their money, but needed a manager who'd put his foot on the accelerator and keep it there.

Oscar Vitt had spent the 1937 season managing the Newark Bears of the International League, who may have been the best minor league team ever assembled. The Bears were the Yankees' top farm club, and were loaded with talent. Every Newark player, save for Jack Fallon, would eventually reach the big leagues, either with the Yankees or another team. Some baseball historians believe the '37 Bears had a more talented roster than some major league clubs, such as the sad-sack St. Louis Browns, who won only 46 games against 108 losses.

Vitt led the Bears to the best record in the International League at 109–43. The Bears cruised through the International League playoffs, winning eight straight games, but then appeared to meet their match in the American Association champion Columbus Red Birds, the top farm club of the St. Louis Cardinals. Columbus won the first three games of the "Little World Series" before the Bears clawed back, winning the next four and the championship of minor league baseball. That got the attention of Bradley and Slapnicka, who began a thorough investigation of Vitt's background. They were mightily impressed with what they heard and saw.

According to the *Cleveland Plain Dealer*, Bradley and Slapnicka zeroed in on Vitt "after a thorough examination of the qualifications of minor league managers from coast to coast. Having chosen him as an outstanding man, they asked the opinions of many baseball men, both in the majors and minors, and the former Tiger was enthusiastically recommended."[2]

Sports columnist Gordon Cobbledick noted that a ringing endorsement from the front office of the International League's Buffalo team, which had a working agreement with the Indians, and which O'Neill would wind up managing in 1938, may have put Vitt's candidacy over the top. Cobbledick wrote that Buffalo "paid Vitt a glowing tribute, declaring no better man could be found in or out of the big leagues."[3]

Cobbledick, in introducing the Tribe's new manager, didn't indicate whether Vitt had been under contract to the Yankees for 1938. He did say Bradley and Slapnicka were concerned the Yankees wouldn't let Vitt leave his Newark post, so they bypassed the Yankees and approached Vitt directly. Vitt visited Cleveland in the middle of October, and a contract was hammered out. It was a two-year deal, the first multi-year contract Bradley had given a manager since purchasing the team nine years earlier.

No press conference was held to introduce Vitt, but when contacted by the *Plain Dealer* at his home in Oakland, California, Vitt noted that "all I have to do is beat the New York Yankees to be successful. That's funny, isn't it, after I worked for the Yankees the past three years?"

Of his historic contract, at least as far as the Indians were concerned, Vitt said, "I have a two-year contract, and the terms are satisfactory." Those terms weren't released to the public. "This job is a great opportunity, and I think I have a good ballclub with which to work. The Indians have pitching, and that's 70% of the battle."[4]

Cobbledick informed readers who were scratching their heads wondering "who is this guy?" that "in New York, the name is well, and probably favorably, known. On the Pacific Coast, it is known perhaps even better. In Detroit, many fans still remember it. But to the rest of the country, save for those whose baseball memory goes back twenty years or more, it means nothing."[5]

Cobbledick noted that Vitt had a fond memory of Cleveland, as it was the site of his first game in the major leagues. Detroit Tigers manager Hughie Jennings wrote Vitt's name in the starting line-up in left-field on opening day of 1912 in League Park. Vitt played for the Tigers from 1912 to 1918, and the Boston Red Sox from 1919 to 1921. He compiled a lifetime batting average of .238, with four home runs and 296 RBI in 1,065 games. He turned to managing in the Pacific Coast League, first at Salt Lake City in 1925. When that franchise was moved to Hollywood in 1926, Vitt went with it, and managed the Stars until 1934. Yankees general manager George Weiss hired Vitt to manage his Oakland farm club in 1935, and then sent Vitt to Newark in 1936. That may have been the most significant endorsement of Vitt's ability as a manager. Newark was loaded with players almost ready for the major leagues ... players whose job it would be to keep New York on top. The Yankees weren't about to entrust their prize prospects to any old manager.

People who knew baseball knew Vitt, and thought highly of him. That was what mattered to Bradley and Slapnicka. Cobbledick wrote that veteran baseball people, the type of people Bradley and Slapnicka consulted as they conducted what they believed was a thorough search for O'Neill's replacement, spoke glowingly of Vitt, describing him as a major league caliber manager stuck in the minors, inasmuch as there were only 16 big league clubs. Ironically, in June of 1940, when his players were rebelling against him, *Cleveland Press* sports editor and columnist Whitey Lewis would refer to Vitt as a minor league caliber manager mis-cast in a major league dugout.

On the personal side, Cobbledick described the new manager as "a genial character with a ready smile and a quick wit."[6] Vitt's "quick wit" would prove to be part of his undoing.

The day after Vitt's hiring was announced, sports columnist James E. Doyle of the *Plain Dealer* published an interview with pitcher Steve Sundra, who had toiled for O'Neill at Toledo, and for Vitt with Newark in 1937. Sundra posted a 15–4 record for the Bears, and would eventually be promoted to the Yankees. Doyle wanted an answer to the question, "what does Vitt have that O'Neill lacked?" The consensus was O'Neill, while as tough a player as they come, wasn't tough enough to be a successful manager. Doyle asked Sundra, "does Vitt have the needles so many people seem to think the Indians need?"

"He's a good manager, all right," replied Sundra of his former boss at Newark. "But, so far as needles go, he does that so kind of quiet and easy-like, that a ballplayer doesn't realize he's taking on the extra hustle that Oscar wants out of him. Yeah, he's pretty smart."

Doyle asked Sundra if Vitt was "all hustle" himself. "Yeah, he's got just enough of it himself so that his slogan was '23 runs today, boys.' And every day."[7] Sundra added that Newark's fearsome line-up was almost good enough to score 23 runs every day. That wouldn't be the case with the Indians.

Vitt hadn't even donned a Cleveland uniform before Cobbledick warned of his probable demise. After all, this was Cleveland, the legendary graveyard of managers. If Tribe fans demanded a pennant, Vitt would probably be judged a failure, as Cobbledick didn't think the team possessed enough talent to win one. If the fans would be satisfied with a manager who squeezed maximum production from the players on his roster ... which it had been determined O'Neill had failed to do ... then Vitt would be judged a success.

Cobbledick may have been asking his readers, and all of Cleveland's baseball fans, to go easy on Vitt. He knew full well Tribe fans wanted a pennant, having experienced just one in the team's 37 years in the American League. He knew the knock on O'Neill had been failing to drive his players hard enough. And he knew all managers were ultimately judged by championships. As Colonel Jacob Ruppert, frustrated owner of the Yankees, had, according to legend, informed his manager, Joe McCarthy, after finishing second in 1933, '34 and '35, he hadn't been hired to be a bridesmaid. McCarthy got the message and led the Yankees to four straight pennants and world's championships.

Bradley wasn't nearly as blunt as Ruppert, but Vitt hadn't been hired to finish second, either.

That Vitt was entering a hornet's nest was addressed by two of the country's most respected sportswriters in articles composed shortly after his hiring. Wrote Shirley Povich in the *Washington Post*, "if there was an Alcatraz in baseball, the Cleveland club would certainly qualify ... the Indians are seemingly confirmed violators of baseball laws. Their faculty for getting into trouble is amazing."[8] Povich's low opinion of Cleveland may have been colored by the shabby way the city, its fans, and its players, had treated the beloved Walter Johnson, the greatest player in Senators history, and possibly the greatest pitcher of all time, during his two seasons as the Tribe's manager.

In March of 1938, under the headline SUGGESTS AWARD OF VALOR FOR MANAGER OSCAR VITT: MAN WHO GAVE UP SOFT BERTH IN NEWARK TO TAKE PRECARIOUS JOB OF PILOTING CLEVELAND CLUB SHOULD BE GIVEN MEDAL FOR BRAVERY,[9] legendary scribe Grantland Rice expressed his misgivings about Vitt's decision.

Oscar Vitt starts in Cleveland, where some good men have failed. Cleveland's baseball temperament is unstable. The hopes of fans are riding high one day and coasting to the depths the next. Frequently, the manager is caught in the middle. Sharply critical scribes, noisily articulate fans, and, too frequently, ballplayers who huddled in cliques in clubhouse corners have wrecked the careers of managers who tried desperately to win in Cleveland. Oscar knows all this, of course. He walked into the job with his eyes wide open, and against the warnings of some of his friends. He knew it was a hard job, but didn't hesitate to tackle it.[10]

The circumstances in which Vitt took over the Indians were hardly unusual. A new manager usually replaces a manager who had failed. Successful managers rarely get fired. O'Neill hadn't failed to win, but he'd failed to win enough. His teams didn't seem to click on all cylinders until late in the season, after the issue had been decided. When the pressure of a pennant race no longer existed. Vitt wasn't going to oversee a complete re-build of a losing ballclub. The Indians had the talent to compete, though possibly not with the powerhouse Yankees. Bradley, and the team's fans, firmly believed the Tribe had underachieved for O'Neill, and required a stronger leader with a firmer hand to, as we'd say today, take the team to the next level. A manager who would, as the *Press* had implored O'Neill to do, give the hired hands a chewing out when necessary.

As for walking away from a "soft" job managing Newark, a position Vitt probably could've kept for years and excelled at, with the Yankees continuing to supply him with top notch talent, any manager

Centerfielder Roy Weatherly (left) and first baseman Hal Trosky during a practice at League Park. Weatherly declined to participate in the player rebellion against Oscar Vitt. Trosky was thought to be the ringleader.

with any kind of competitive spirit wants a shot at the major leagues, and believes he can succeed where others have failed. Vitt may have had many faults, but lacking competitive spirit wasn't among them. There were only 16 major league managing jobs in 1937. Cleveland's was open. Vitt wouldn't be taking over a train wreck. He'd be taking over a fourth place club that won 83 games the previous season. He'd be joining a team with financially stable ownership, and the ability to spend money to improve the club. Though pundits such as Povich and Rice, and even Cobbledick, were quick to point out the pitfalls of managing the Indians, the job had its positive aspects.

Still, Vitt's three-year tenure would prove to be a bumpy ride. Especially in 1940.

3

Déjà Vu All Over Again

Through the first two months of the 1938 season, Alva Bradley's decision to install Oscar Vitt as a replacement for Cleveland icon Steve O'Neill, whose contributions to the 1920 World Series champion Indians hadn't been forgotten by the team's fans, despite the passage of nearly two decades, appeared to be a stroke of genius. Vitt's Tribe stormed out of the starting gate, winning eight of its first 10 games. The Indians moved into first place on April 22 for two weeks, slipped to second and then third briefly, then surged back into the lead on May 18, and remained there through July 12, leading the pack by as many as 4½ games on June 8.

As Cleveland fans knew all too well, however, baseball seasons weren't two months long. They were 5½ months long, and the Indians had perfected the art of teasing their supporters by starting quickly, then fading as the summer progressed. The 1938 season would be no different than so many others, in spite of the presence of Vitt in the dugout. From a record of 44–26 on the 12th of July, the Tribe won 42 and lost 40 the rest of the way. They were caught and passed by the Yankees and the resurgent Boston Red Sox and finished third, 13 games out. A slight improvement over O'Neill's final season, but not a significant one.

The 1939 season resembled O'Neill's two full seasons at the helm. The Indians started slowly, not reaching the .500 mark until Memorial Day weekend. They wouldn't slip below the break-even point again, but never seriously challenged the Yankees. Then again, nobody seriously challenged the Yankees in 1939. The Indians flip-flopped between third, fourth and (briefly) fifth places from Memorial Day through September 18, when they moved into third place to stay. A late-season surge (an O'Neill trademark) saw the Tribe win 19 and lose seven between September 6 and the end of

21

Catcher Frankie Pytlak signs his 1938 contract in the office of Indians president and co-owner Alva Bradley. Pytlak wasn't so easy to sign in 1940.

the year. Cleveland finished third again at 87–67, 20½ games in back of the pennant winners. The 87 victories represented a one-game improvement over 1938.

Vitt's contract would expire at the end of the 1939 season, and his status quickly became a topic of conversation among fans and media ... which, in 1939, pretty much consisted of newspapers. When asked, which was frequently, Bradley insisted he'd made no decision about 1940, and wouldn't until after the season. However, a report in a newspaper 500 miles from Cleveland may have forced his hand.

During the first week of August, according to Gordon Cobbledick in the *Plain Dealer*, a New York paper he declined to identify claimed to have learned from "an unassailable authority" that Vitt's days in Cleveland were numbered. He'd soon follow O'Neill, Walter Johnson and Roger Peckinpaugh out the door of the League Park clubhouse. Possibly to put an end to the rampant speculation, and to save Vitt the agony of twisting in the wind for nearly two months, Bradley signed his manager to a one-year deal on August 11. As had been the case with Vitt's first contract, financial terms weren't announced.

Said the club president, "I have been more than pleased with the results Oscar has obtained in the last two seasons, and I hope he will be with us for a long time. After all, our team had certain weaknesses of which we were all aware, and to blame the manager for failure to win a pennant with such a team would be extremely unfair. We didn't expect him to win the pennant, and we feel that he has done an excellent job keeping the Indians in the first division."[1]

The 49-year-old Vitt was pleased to know where he stood for 1940. "I'm glad I'm going to have a chance to carry out some of the plans we've made for next season. We're going to have a better ball club, and I think we may go places with it."

Vitt addressed the rumors of dissension on his team, due mainly to the fact several players reportedly didn't like him. "Well, I guess that can't be helped. I'll just go along doing the best I can, just as I've done for the past two seasons, and the boys will have to like it."[2] Vitt had no intention of pandering to his players, and neither did Bradley.

"They've got to know who their boss is, and they may as well know now Vitt will be giving the orders again next season," said the club president. "I will back him up in whatever action he may see fit to maintain discipline."[3] In order to maintain discipline during the 1939 season, Vitt had fined temperamental outfielder Jeff Heath $50 for speaking to him in a threatening manner after Vitt had accused Heath of failing to hustle during a game against the Browns in St. Louis. It was a criticism that was probably warranted, as Heath himself would admit in the spring of 1940. He'd docked outfielder Julius (Moose) Solters $250 for breaking training rules when the Indians played an exhibition game in Wilkes-Barre, Pennsylvania. What sort of mischief Solters had engaged in while in Wilkes-Barre wasn't specified.

Cobbledick claimed the Indians weren't any more rambunctious than an average major league baseball team. "For the most part, the players have respected Vitt's authority, even when they didn't like it, and his relations with them have been generally amicable." The Tribe's fans may have been more unhappy with Vitt than his players. Cobbledick added, "Cleveland fans have been noted throughout the league for their wolfishness."[4] Any group that could run the universally admired Johnson out of town had to have a bit of wolf in it.

Bradley may not have expected Vitt to win the pennant in 1938, or 1939, but Cleveland's "wolfish" baseball fans did. And they weren't pleased that he'd failed to do so. Many weren't pleased with Bradley for giving Vitt another chance in 1940.

As to what effect, if any, Vitt's re-hiring had on his players, the Indians were in fourth place with a 53–47 record on August 11. They were 16½ games behind the rampaging Yankees, who were on their way to 106 victories, in a 154-game season. The Tribe posted a 34–20 record the rest of the way, including the aforementioned 19–7 spurt in September.

It was a situation reminiscent of the 1934 season, when an infuriated *Cleveland Press*, after determining Johnson hadn't provided the necessary managerial leadership, demanded Bradley fire him. Bradley responded by signing Johnson to a contract for the 1935 season, a decision that would seem to be justified since Johnson had improved the Tribe's record from 75–76 to 85–69. Some of that improvement, however, had to be attributed to Bradley's decision to move the team's home games back to tiny League Park from massive new Municipal Stadium, whose outfield was roughly the size of the Grand Canyon. Babe Ruth had joked that outfielders should be allowed to ride horses to patrol Municipal Stadium's huge pasture. Cleveland's lefthanded batters ... as well as those on visiting teams ... had become accustomed to pounding League Park's short right-field wall, which was just 290 feet from home plate. Johnson was also in the midst of an alleged player insurrection, which may or may not have existed only in his mind. Again, Bradley felt compelled to show the *Press*, and possibly the hired hands, who was in charge.

Such were the perils of managing in Cleveland.

In two seasons as the Tribe's bench boss, Vitt had compiled a record of 173–133. The Indians finished a total of 33½ games behind the Yankees. In other words, a continuation of the same old, same old that Clevelanders had grown tired of.

Vitt's Indians, like O'Neill's Indians, and Johnson's Indians, and Peckinpaugh's Indians, were good, but not nearly good enough. He'd be given an opportunity to change that in 1940.

Ironically, on the same day the Indians re-hired Vitt, Detroit owner Walter O. Briggs re-hired his manager, Del Baker. Vitt and Baker would spend the next season matching wits in the closest American League pennant race in two decades.

4

Shaping Up

The 1939 American League pennant race hadn't been much of a pennant race. Joe McCarthy's New York Yankees had withstood the devastating loss of their first baseman, Lou Gehrig, who was forced to retire in early May by the disease which now bears his name and would take his life two years later, to post 106 victories and finish 17 games ahead of the second place Boston Red Sox. Oscar Vitt's Indians finished third, 20½ games back. The Yankees then disposed of the National League champion Cincinnati Reds in a World Series sweep. It was the Yankees' fourth consecutive world's championship, and after the final out of the fourth game of the World Series was recorded, there appeared to be no reason to believe the Yankees would be challenged in 1940.

Before Vitt got on the train which would take him from his home in the San Francisco Bay area to Cleveland, where he'd consult with his bosses before departing for spring training in Fort Myers, Florida, he sounded a note of caution for McCarthy and the defending world's champs.

"The Yankees can be beaten," Vitt said. "The Yankees are going to have their ears pinned back more frequently this season than last. The Red Sox, Detroit and Cleveland will give New York plenty of trouble. From all indications, every club in the league will be better balanced. Come to think of it, I didn't find any clubs last season that could be called pushovers. We beat the St. Louis Browns in all three games of one series, but we had to go extra innings each time." Everyone beat the Browns in 1939. St. Louis won just 43 games and lost 111. Connie Mack's Philadelphia Athletics finished seventh at 55–97, and the Washington Senators placed sixth with a record of 65–87. Five of the American League's eight clubs posted winning records in 1939. The managers of the two clubs that finished directly behind

25

the Yankees in 1939, Vitt and Boston's Joe Cronin, spoke confidently during the spring of expecting New York to decline in 1940. But would the Yankees decline sufficiently to be overcome by the Indians or Red Sox? Or both? Deficits of 17 and 20½ games, respectively, would be quite a mountain to climb.

Vitt wasn't making any predictions about his team … at least not in late February … other than to say the Tribe would be "plenty O.K."

Vitt told reporters at the train depot that his 1940 outfield figured to be Jeff Heath in left, Roy Weatherly in center, and Ben Chapman in right. He said first baseman Hal Trosky would not be converted to the outfield, and young infielder Oscar Grimes wouldn't replace Trosky at first base. Vitt said Grimes would compete with another youngster, Ray Mack, for the second base job, and he lauded his young shortstop, Lou Boudreau, as the second best shortstop in the American League. He ranked New York's Frank Crosetti at the top.

Indians radio broadcaster (and former player) Jack Graney presents pitcher Johnny Allen with a proclamation in honor of his 15-game winning streak in 1937. Manager Oscar Vitt looks on.

Of his pitching staff, Vitt said the key was the performance of two veteran stalwarts, Mel Harder and Johnny Allen. Both had suffered arm injuries in 1939. "If Mel can get his winning streak started early, and if Allen's repaired arm holds up, we should do plenty of scalping."[1]

Facing more reporters, and more questions, when he arrived in Cleveland, Vitt reiterated his belief that the Yankees were vulnerable. "The Yankees aren't going to have any picnic this year. Several clubs will give them their share of trouble, and we'll be one of 'em."

Vitt denied saying his starting outfield was already set. "Whoever wrote that piece about me picking Heath, Chapman and Weatherly as my starters made it up out of his own head. Every job in the outfield is open, and I'm looking for Beau Bell to have something to say about it." Bell had been obtained from Detroit a month earlier in exchange for outfielder Bruce Campbell. "And maybe that young Clarence Campbell, too. He's a cocky kid, and that won't hurt him any." Vitt knew a little something about being cocky.

Vitt said he didn't want to trade catcher Frankie Pytlak, who was embroiled in a salary dispute with the front office. "Me want to get rid of Frankie? No, sir! The only way to get rid of him would be by a deal that would benefit the ball club plenty, and that would mean getting somebody mighty good." Vitt's boss, general manager Cy Slapnicka, didn't value Pytlak as highly. Slapnicka had offered Pytlak and Allen to the Athletics for catcher Frank Haynes and been turned down. Vitt and Slapnicka would have many disagreements in 1940.

It was probably no coincidence that Slapnicka sought to unload Allen and Pytlak in the same trade as Allen, too, was unhappy with the contract he'd been offered and was holding out as training camp approached. Vitt said of Allen, "I'd be disappointed if he doesn't win 12 games. And pitchers who can win that many are hard to find."

Vitt said he'd allow Harder to establish his own training regimen as he recovered from arm miseries. "Mel can get in shape in his own way. I'm not going to ask him to pitch an inning in the spring until he tells me he's ready. And if he doesn't tell me he's ready all spring, it will be all right with me. I want him to take it slow, so he won't have any more of that early season arm trouble." Harder had won at least 15 games for the Indians each season since 1932.

Vitt talked about the Tribe's prized young infield prospects, Mack and Boudreau. Of Mack, he said, "who says I've got my mind

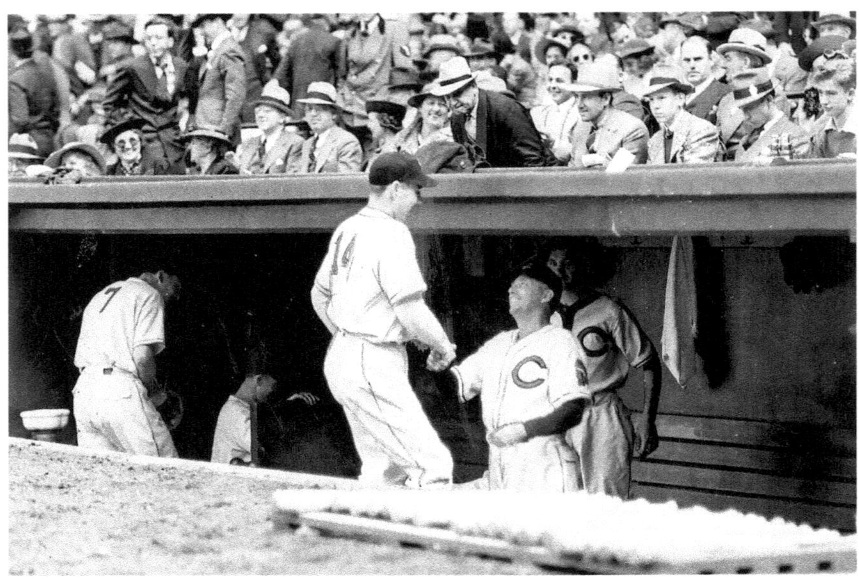

Oscar Vitt greets Bob Feller in the Tribe's League Park dugout during a 1938 game. Feller wasn't yet wearing his famous uniform number 19.

Oscar Vitt (left) and New York Yankees manager Joe McCarthy at a post-season banquet. Vitt was the manager of the Yankees' top farm club before being hired in Cleveland.

made up to farm him out? Say, all he's got to do is show me he can hit just a little bit. I know what he can do around that sack [second base], and what he can do is enough to keep him in this league." Mack saw action in 36 games in 1939, batting an anemic .152 with six runs batted in.

Vitt called Boudreau "a sweetheart, and no flash in the pan, either. He made the difference in our ballclub last fall. I wanted him to come down to Florida with the first squad, but he had a chance to pick up a hundred bucks refereeing a couple of basketball games, and I told him to take it." A hundred bucks meant a lot to a young player such as Boudreau, who'd starred in basketball at the University of Illinois. He'd fared better than Mack in 1939, batting .258 in 53 games with 19 runs batted in.

Vitt was asked about Heath, the outfielder with the volcanic temper who'd threatened him physically after Vitt had accused him of lackadaisical play during a game against the Browns in 1939. "His troubles are behind him. He'll go into this season with a new mental attitude. You watch and see. I'm looking for him to do a complete comeback."[2] Heath batted .343 and led the American League with 18 triples in 1938. His average plummeted to .292 in 1939.

The Cleveland entourage's train bound for Fort Myers left at 3:05 p.m. on the afternoon of February 26. It was given a hero's reception upon its arrival, as Fort Myers hadn't hosted a major league team's spring training in four years. The Clevelanders were greeted by a high school band and majorettes, the mayor of Fort Myers and the chamber of commerce, and hundreds of residents.

"This is the best team I have ever taken south," Vitt announced. "I'm not going to have to worry about second base. This year's team will give 'em all trouble, and this goes for the Yankees."[3]

The Yankees were experiencing a minor problem as their spring activities commenced. Star pitchers Red Ruffing and Spud Chandler, and star catcher Bill Dickey were all holding out. Their salary disputes were expected to be resolved quickly, but star players seeking more money for their services was the price of winning.

The Indians conducted their first spring workout on February 29. All players weren't yet required to report. There were 15 pitchers, three catchers, and a few position players present for the initial workout. The *Plain Dealer* reported that unlike most managers, Vitt put his troops through just one workout per day, and it was held in the morning. Sports columnist Gordon Cobbledick, who made the trip to Fort Myers to send daily dispatches back to Cleveland, described the first session as short but snappy. It started at 10:30 and concluded shortly before noon. Cobbledick said the players were thoroughly exhausted.

Possibly not Bob Feller, the Indians' ace pitcher. Vitt wanted Feller to cut back on his workouts. "He probably needs less work than any other man in the camp," Vitt said. "He always keeps himself in good condition, and as far as excess weight is concerned, I'd like to see him carry a little more poundage than he has now. It would come in handy in July and August. I've tried to cut him down to a little running to keep his legs in shape, but he thinks he isn't getting any good out of exercise unless it leaves him dripping sweat. And I know that as soon as he begins to throw, we'll have to watch him to see that he doesn't throw too much. If he had his way, he'd warm up for an hour every day."[4] Throughout his career and beyond, Feller expressed a firm belief that pitchers didn't wear out, they rusted out. Feller had

Opening Day, 1938, in Cleveland Municipal Stadium. It was Oscar Vitt's first game as Indians manager. They lost to the St. Louis Browns, 6-2.

reported to Fort Myers weighing 193 pounds. He felt his optimum playing weight was 190.

Allen, Pytlak and pitcher Willis Hudlin continued to hold out as February became March. Cobbledick said the Tribe's payroll was second in the American League to the champion Yankees, and was particularly critical of Allen, who'd been paid $19,000 in both 1938 and 1939. Allen had electrified Cleveland with his pursuit of Smoky Joe Wood's American League record of 16 straight victories in 1937. He finished the campaign at 15–1, and won 14 games in 1938. His record slipped to 9–7 in 1939, and his best years were behind him. Allen was 35, and recuperating from a sore right arm. Cobbledick didn't think Allen was worth the salary he was seeking in 1940, and neither did Slapnicka. On March 3, Slapnicka said he was finished negotiating with Allen by mail, and would meet with him in person in an effort to reach an agreement.

"I don't know whether we'll have any better luck with a personal meeting, but it's worth trying," said the general manager. "We feel that Allen's demands are out of reason, but if he thinks he can change our minds, we'll listen."[5]

The other veteran pitcher Vitt was depending heavily on, Harder, said his right arm was feeling much better. "I throw every day until it gets to feeling loose and free, as if I could keep on throwing for another hour, and then I stop. It's like getting up from the table when you're still hungry. I think if I stick to that program, I'll be all right."[6]

Vitt's coaches were Johnny Bassler, Oscar Melillo, and former Tribe catcher Luke Sewell. Rather than throwing batting practice, as coaches often do, Sewell was taking it. He wanted to be prepared in case he was pressed into service in an emergency. That was a possibility, as Pytlak was still holding out.

In an effort to improve the Tribe's baserunning, Vitt brought a sliding pit to camp. Ben Chapman, described by Cobbledick as the team's only competent baserunner, was going to coach his teammates on proper sliding techniques. "I know of two games in one series that Chapman won for us by knowing how to slide," Vitt explained. "If he can impart some of his knowledge to other fellows on this club, he'll help us win a few more."[7]

Uncharacteristic south Florida weather for early March ... chilly, windy and rainy ... led to the cancellation of the intra-squad game scheduled for March 8. The weather relented the next day, and the rookies, referred to in the newspaper as the "Yannigans," defeated the regulars, 4–2. Cobbledick described the contest as well-played on both sides, despite a stiff breeze that made every fly ball an adventure. The game was only six innings.

The regulars evened the score with a 3–1 victory on March 10, in another six inning game. Lefthander Al Smith surrendered all the regulars runs in the first inning, on doubles by Hal Trosky, Roy Weatherly and Jeff Heath, and singles by Ray Mack, Ken Keltner and Rollie Hemsley. The Yannigans plated their only run in the second off Harry Eisenstat on singles by Del Jones and future Tribesman Jim Hegan, and a sacrifice fly by Packy Rogers. Jones had been the 1939 Three-I League (as in Illinois, Iowa, and Indiana) batting champion. Bill Zuber took over for Eisenstat in the fourth inning and held the Yannigans scoreless the rest of the way. After the game, the fans were treated to a barbecue on the field hosted by the Fort Myers Kiwanis Club.

Also on the 10th of March, the formation of a six club, class C minor league circuit was announced. All the teams were located in Michigan, and the Indians would be affiliated with the franchise in Flint.

Allen's holdout ended on March 11. He met with Bradley and Slapnicka and agreed to a contract which contained no performance bonus clauses. Terms weren't announced, but it was speculated Allen got a slight raise over his 1939 salary.

"Allen is on straight salary," said Bradley. "A bonus clause was not discussed when he signed. He didn't want a bonus clause. However, it is the club's policy to do something for players who have exceptional years."[8] Allen wouldn't have an exceptional year in 1940.

Pytlak didn't figure to be as fortunate as his batterymate. In what would have been an even-up swap of holdout catchers, the St. Louis Browns offered the Indians Joe Glenn for Pytlak. Bradley wasn't interested. "Pytlak will have to accept our terms or stay out of baseball," fumed the team president. "I wouldn't trade him for Joe DiMaggio of the Yankees until he signed."[9]

Added Slapnicka, "I wrote to Frankie more than two weeks ago, and he hasn't given me the courtesy of a reply. The next move is his. He knows where we are (Pytlak was at home in Buffalo, New York), and if he wants to talk to us, he will have to come to Fort Myers."[10] Pytlak departed for Florida, then had a change of heart and returned to Buffalo.

"I'm not going to make any more attempts to get in touch with the Cleveland club," he announced. "I'll stay out of baseball all season rather than accept the ridiculously low salary the Indians expect me to play for. If they don't think I'm worth any more than that, why don't they trade me?"[11] Pytlak reportedly had been paid $9,500 in 1939. He claimed the contract the Indians mailed him cut that salary by a whopping 35 percent. Bradley denied that, although he admitted Pytlak had been offered a pay cut. Sewell continued to take batting practice in the event he was pressed into emergency service.

Cobbledick described Pytlak as Cleveland's last holdout, even though Hudlin was still haggling with Slapnicka over his contract. According to Cobbledick, Hudlin hadn't convinced anyone he really intended to retire and predicted the pitcher would report to Fort Myers within a week.

The regulars defeated the Yannigans, 6–0, in another six inning practice game on March 11. Joe Dobson and six-foot-five-inch righthander Mike Naymick each tossed three shutout innings for the veterans. Some observers were convinced Naymick's fastball was the equal of Feller's, but Naymick lacked Feller's devastating curveball. Naymick lacked a curveball entirely, a deficiency Harder and Eisenstat would try to correct.

"I know of several clubs he can beat right now, without ever showing them a curve," said outfielder Beau Bell.[12] The Yannigans had proven to be no match for him. The regulars collected 12 hits off two rookies named Earl Center and Floyd Stromme. Center would never pitch in the major leagues. Stromme had pitched in five games for the Indians in 1939, losing his only major league decision with an earned run average of 4.85.

The intra-squad games concluded on March 13, with the Yannigans beating the veterans, 2–0. Feller started for the regulars and allowed both runs on one hit in three innings. He didn't strike out anyone. Cobbledick reported Feller didn't bear down with his fastball. The regulars reached Yannigans Cal Dorsett and Johnny Broaca for six hits in the seven inning game. Dorsett pitched in one game for the Tribe in 1940, five in 1941, and two in 1947. He served in the military from 1942 to 1945. He lost his only major league decision, in 1941, with a career ERA of 11.85. Broaca was no rookie. He'd pitched for the Yankees from 1934 to 1938, and for the Indians in 1939, winning 44 games (four with Cleveland) with a career ERA of 4.08. He wouldn't earn a spot on the Tribe's 1940 pitching staff. To emphasize the informality of the Yannigans versus veterans practice games, Sammy Hale pinch-hit for both teams.

Facing someone other than themselves for the first time on March 14, the Indians ventured to Fort Lauderdale and defeated the Syracuse Chiefs of the International League, 6–1. The Chiefs were managed by former Tribe outfielder "Twitchy" Dick Porter, who compiled a .308 batting average with Cleveland from 1929 to 1934. Weatherly, Trosky and Heath were the only regulars to see action for the Tribe. Ken Jongels, Dobson, and Naymick handled the pitching chores.

The Indians took on major league competition for the first time on March 15 and squeezed past the Washington Senators, 2–0, in Fort Myers. Eisenstat, Zuber and Johnny Humphries combined for the shutout. Cleveland managed six hits off three rookies: Bucky Jacobs, Gilberto Torres, and Early Wynn. Tribe fans would become very familiar with Wynn many years later, when he was traded to Cleveland and became one-third of one of the best starting pitching staffs ever assembled.

Cleveland had little trouble topping Vitt's old team, the Newark Bears of the International League, 7–2, on March 16. Vitt sent Smith, Al Milnar, and Don Pulford to the mound. The Indians managed 11 hits off Newark pitching.

Heath, the outfielder accused of not hustling by Vitt in 1939, but who Vitt was convinced would report to camp with a new attitude in 1940, admitted to Cobbledick on March 17 that his manager had been right. Heath accused the entire 1939 team of failing to hustle. "I think you'll see a hustling ballclub this year, because we feel we have something to hustle for," said Heath. "I mean we think we've got a chance, and we didn't feel that way last year. We looked at that infield [minus Mack at second and Boudreau at shortstop] and we knew we had weaknesses that put us out of the running before we started. I doubt if there was a man on the team who could honestly say at the end of the season that he had put out every ounce of hustle in his body throughout the year. I know I couldn't. It was simply impossible. The incentive wasn't there. But this year we've got an incentive. We haven't a weakness left in the infield, we ought to get good pitching, and we've got plenty of punch. We're liable to fool people who think the Yankees can't be beaten."[13]

The Indians continued their tour of the International League on St. Patrick's Day, beating the Rochester Red Wings, 2–1. As Cobbledick had predicted, Hudlin reported to Fort Myers the same day, and appeared, according to the *Plain Dealer,* to be in peak condition.

Cleveland's 11–4 trouncing of the Philadelphia Phillies in Fort Myers on March 18 was a costly victory. Boudreau injured his ankle running the bases and, according to Dr. B.H. Reed, would need crutches for at least two weeks, and would be unable to exercise for at least three weeks. Russ Peters would play shortstop in Boudreau's absence.

The Indians started playing the New York Giants in exhibition games in 1934, when they trained in New Orleans. The rivalry resumed on March 19, with the Giants prevailing in Winter Haven, 4–2. Eisenstat allowed three of New York's runs. Zuber and Humphries held the Giants in check the rest of the way.

Boston Red Sox manager Joe Cronin, who'd managed the Senators to the American League pennant in 1933 at the age of 27, thought his team had the stuff to vault from second place to first in 1940. Noting that Boston had swept the Yankees in a five game series in July of 1939, Cronin claimed "we can out-hit the Yankees, and we've proved it the past two seasons. Last season we batted .291 to the Yankees .288, and the year before .299 to .274. It's my guess that the two men the Yanks will miss most are Red Ruffing and Bill Dickey. Ruffing is 36 and has been having arm trouble lately. Dickey has been in the harness 11 years, catching more than 100 games a year."[14] An expert analysis? Or wishful thinking?

Two runs had been enough to beat the Senators the first time the Tribe met them, but not the second. Washington prevailed in Orlando on March 20, 7–2. It seemed that Vitt's pitching philosophy was to use three pitchers for three innings in exhibition games. Pulford, Milnar and Naymick faced the Senators and allowed 11 hits. The Tribe managed seven.

John Lardner, of the legendary Lardner sportswriting family, revealed on March 21 that Feller had set a goal of 30 victories for the 1940 campaign. The last major league pitcher to win 30 had been Dizzy Dean with the 1934 World Series champion St. Louis Cardinals. "If I get the work, and Mr. Vitt says I will, I think I can win 30. It's easier said than done, especially in a league where almost every hitter is tough, but I did things wrong that I'll do right this year, enough to make the difference."[15] Lardner said his money was on Feller reaching his goal.

The Indians got some good news on March 21. Boudreau was back in camp. His ankle was in a cast, but he was able to do some throwing. Speculation was that Boudreau had aggravated an injury he'd sustained playing basketball in college, but wasn't aware of.

Cleveland's losing streak reached three with a 5–1 loss to Rochester in West Palm Beach on March 22. Bearing down for the first time in spring training, Feller pitched four shutout innings on two hits, walking one and striking out eight. Stromme allowed two runs in his three innings. Center pitched one inning and allowed three runs. Rochester's pitchers held the Tribe to five hits, two of which came with two out in the ninth inning.

The Indians beat the Giants in Fort Myers, 2–1, on March 23. Humphries, Smith and Zuber held New York in check. The Tribe managed just five hits off Hy Vandenberg and Cliff Melton. The next day, Cleveland lost to Indianapolis of the American Association, 8–4. The minor leaguers reached Naymick for an unearned run in the fifth inning, and five earned runs in the sixth. The miserable performance didn't damage the rookie's chances of earning a roster spot.

The Tribe topped the Phillies, 3–1, in Miami Beach on March 25. The game dragged on for 12 innings. Eisenstat became the first Cleveland hurler to pitch five innings, allowing four hits. Mack drove in the winning run with a triple.

In a column published by the *Plain Dealer*, John Lardner asked Red Sox manager Cronin to expand on his comments in *The Saturday Evening Post* earlier in the spring that the Yankees were vulnerable. "We can win this pennant, and I think we are going to," said Cronin.

> We were never afraid of the Yankees. We just couldn't match 'em up until now. Anybody who thinks they have us buffaloed should take a look at the record last summer, when we went into their ballpark and beat them five times in a row at the top of their stride. None of my players has been very respectful of the Yanks since then.
>
> Naturally, it's going to be a hard club to beat. The Yanks have strength at every position, and they won't crack all of a sudden. But I think they'll play a little slower from here on. In other words, they're going and we're coming.[16]

Cobbledick polled the Cleveland clubhouse for its reaction to Cronin's comments. The reaction was that if Cronin was correct, the

Yankees would have to settle for third place, behind the Tribe and the Red Sox.

Feller became the second Tribe pitcher to work five innings on March 26. He held the Cardinals to a pair of hits and a run as the Indians won, 3–2. Cleveland's inconsistent offense banged out 10 hits.

As April approached, Pytlak's holdout continued. Bradley said he was willing to let his reluctant catcher "sit all summer. If he thinks we'll finally get disgusted and trade him, he's making the biggest mistake of his life," said the club president.[17]

Bradley wasn't budging, and neither was Pytlak. "I'm waiting to hear from the club, and unless they boost the ante, I'll keep waiting. I'm in good condition from working out at the YMCA. If they won't meet my terms, I guess I can get another job."[18] The standoff between Bradley and Slapnicka on one side, and Pytlak on the other, turned out to be a break for a young catcher who'd play a prominent role in Cleveland's baseball history.

The Indians broke camp on March 29. They'd take 30 players north to open the season, one of which, to the surprise of most observers, was 19-year-old catcher Jim Hegan. With Pytlak temporarily, and possibly permanently, out of the picture, Vitt thought it was necessary to keep Hegan as insurance in the event of an injury to Hemsley or his back-up, Hank Helf. Hegan would be the starting catcher on two Tribe pennant winners, in 1948 and 1954.

One other rookie earned a roster spot. Twenty-two-year-old Don Pulford pitched his way onto the club with a strong spring performance. Pulford had been barely an afterthought as training camp opened, after an unimpressive 1939 season during which he'd won six games and lost 12 for New Orleans. Cobbledick noted that Pulford had the emphatic endorsement of Hemsley, who knew a pitcher when he saw one.

The other players who'd be wearing Indians uniforms for the first time in 1940 were outfielders Beau Bell and Clarence Campbell, pitcher Al Smith, and shortstop Russ Peters.

The roster broke down as follows:

PITCHERS: Johnny Allen, Johnny Broaca, Joe Dobson, Bob Feller, Mel Harder, Willis Hudlin, Johnny Humphries, Ken Jungels, Al Milnar, Mike Naymick, Pulford, Smith, and Bill Zuber.

CATCHERS: Hemsley, Helf, Hegan.

INFIELDERS: Lou Boudreau, Oscar Grimes, Sammy Hale, Ken Keltner, Ray Mack, Peters, Hal Trosky.

OUTFIELDERS: Bell, Campbell, Ben Chapman, Jeff Heath, Roy Weatherly.

Following their departure from Fort Myers, the Indians embarked upon a spring tradition: the barnstorming tour. They'd work their way north playing exhibition games in mostly small towns, playing mostly against the Giants. The Indians and Giants would do battle 14 times as both teams prepared for their regular season openers.

The barnstorming began in Columbus, Georgia, against the Columbus Red Birds. Vitt had mistakenly thought the game was to be played in Columbus, Ohio. The Tribe trounced the Red Birds, 8–1, before a crowd described by Cobbledick as small and unappreciative. He called the lopsided contest an example of exhibition games which had no value to either club. The minor leaguers were hopelessly outclassed, and the major leaguers just wanted to get the game over with, and performed like it. He didn't understand why big league teams wasted their time scheduling such games.

Cobbledick's game account noted it had been a poor spring for slugging first baseman Trosky, whose last 25 at-bats had produced two harmless singles. Trosky had been held hitless in the game in Columbus by minor league pitching, and minor league pitching of poor quality at that.

On March 30, the Indians beat the Atlanta Crackers of the Southern Association, 8–2, in Atlanta. The game drew a crowd of about 700 spectators. The next day's game drew a crowd of 7,000, with the attraction being Feller. The Tribe topped the Crackers again, 2–0. Feller's spring numbers to date were: 15 innings pitched, seven hits allowed, 17 strikeouts. Vitt had already named Feller his starter for the season opener on April 16 in Chicago's Comiskey Park.

"My chief interest on this trip is to see that the boy is ready to pitch that first one in Chicago," said Vitt. "Mel Harder will probably pitch the opener in Cleveland if everything goes right."[19] Feller appeared to be ready. Harder didn't.

From the moment I began researching this book, I looked for evidence to support Whitey Lewis' statement, made in his 1949 book *The Cleveland Indians*, that "the Indians were national favorites to win their first pennant since 1920 when the '40 campaign got underway." I found none.

With the season two weeks away, the prognostications began. The bookies had established the Yankees as prohibitive favorites to win what would've been their fifth consecutive pennant in 1940. New York was a 1 to 3 favorite, meaning bettors would have to put three dollars on the Yankees to get one dollar back. The odds on the Indians were 8–1. The odds on the Detroit Tigers were 10–1. The odds on Cronin's Red Sox were 9–2.

In the National League, the St. Louis Cardinals were 2–1 favorites to unseat the Cincinnati Reds as champions.

I also looked for reasons to believe the Yankees would decline in 1940. Otherwise, why would a team which had finished third, 20½ games behind and had made no significant personnel changes during the off-season, be established as "national favorites" to dethrone a team which had won 106 games the previous season, then swept the National League champs in the World Series, and had won four consecutive world championships? Again, I found none.

Despite the brave talk coming from the Cleveland and Boston camps, the Yankees, on paper, didn't appear to be vulnerable as the 1940 season began. The entire starting line-up returned intact. That line-up consisted of first baseman Babe Dahlgren (.235, 15, 89), second baseman Joe Gordon (.284, 28, 111), shortstop Frankie Crosetti (.233, 10, 56), third baseman Red Rolfe (.329, 14, 80) right fielder George Selkirk (.306, 21, 101), centerfielder Joe DiMaggio (.381, 30, 126), leftfielder Charlie Keller (.334, 11, 83) and catcher Bill Dickey (.302, 24, 105). Dahlgren and Crosetti appeared to be the weak links, but Dahlgren faced the impossible task of succeeding the legendary Lou Gehrig, who was forced to the bench on May 2 by the illness that would take his life just two years later. Dahlgren's 15 homers and 89 runs batted in paled in comparison to the numbers Gehrig routinely accumulated season after season, but would've looked good on many other teams. And Crosetti's value to the Yankees was with his glove. Anything he produced offensively was a bonus.

If there was cause for concern, it was New York's pitching ... which, admittedly, isn't a good thing to be concerned about. The 1939 starting rotation was Red Ruffing (21–7, 2.93), Lefty Gomez (12–8, 3.41), Bump Hadley (12–6, 2.98), Atley Donald (13–3, 3.81), Monte Pearson (12–5, 4.49) and Oral Hildebrand (10–4, 3.06). The relief corps was essentially Johnny Murphy (19 saves, despite an ERA of 4.40), and long relievers Steve Sundra (11–1, 2.76) and Marius Russo

(8–3, 2.41). Any hope on the part of the Indians and Red Sox that New York might struggle was probably due to the age of its starting rotation. Among the starters, only Donald was under the age of 30, and he was 28. Ruffing and Hadley were 35 in 1940, Hildebrand was 33, Pearson and Murphy were 31, and Sundra was 30.

The 1939 Yankees team batting average was .287, and it produced 967 runs, or 6.4 per game. The team earned run average was 3.31, and the pitching staff had allowed 556 runs, or an average of 3.7 per contest. The roster remained virtually intact during the off-season. Granted, the players, particularly the pitchers, were a year older. Based strictly on the numbers, Lewis' claim that the Indians were "national favorites" to win the pennant makes no sense. And it isn't supported by the evidence.

Bradley shrugged off the bookies lack of confidence in his team. "We have a good ball team. It's a vastly better club than the one we brought north last year. I won't make any predictions as to where we'll finish, as many things can happen over a 154-game schedule, but I'm satisfied that the club will give a good account of itself in the pennant race."[20] There'd be no pressure from ownership on Vitt to produce a pennant in his third season at Cleveland's helm. At least not publicly.

The Giants pounded the Tribe, 10–3, in Jacksonville, Florida, on April 2. Harder and Allen pitched for the first time all spring. Allen pitched three scoreless innings. Harder was hammered for seven runs in his three innings of work. That didn't discourage Tribe coach Johnny Bassler.

"I was tickled to death with the way he looked," said Bassler. "Give him one or two more starts to get accustomed to the pace, and he'll show you he's ready. There's only one thing we have to worry about. That's the possibility that his arm and shoulder might stiffen up when he gets into the cold weather."[21]

Bassler was bullish on the 1940 Tribe. "The Indians might be battling for the top this year," he said. "They have the three elements necessary to make them contenders—good fielding, good pitching and good hitting. Good fielding makes for good pitching, and the boys will start to hit. We know they can hit."[22]

Harder's poor performance against the Giants in his first spring appearance may not have discouraged Bassler, but it discouraged Vitt. "Mel hasn't got a thing," assessed Vitt bluntly. "It was all he could do to get the ball up to the plate. It would be a shame to ask him to go out there and take a beating, to say nothing of the danger of damaging his arm permanently, when he isn't ready. It's a tough case, all right. Mel looked swell in Fort Myers, and was tickled to death at the way his arm felt. It still feels all right. But he can't put anything on the ball. I guess we'll just have to wait for time or summer weather to fix him up as it has in the past."[23] Vitt didn't say so, but he'd undoubtedly scratched Harder from his scheduled start in the home opener on April 19.

On April 3 in Waycross, Georgia, the Indians beat the Giants, 9–5. Milnar, making liberal use of his curveball, allowed one run in five innings. The next day, his elbow ached. But he wasn't complaining. "It only means one thing to me," said the pitcher. "I'm snappin' off that curve better than ever. It's the first time I can ever remember having a sore elbow. I like it. I've always felt in the past that I had a pretty good fastball, but now I've got a curve that'll make them fall back. I'm not predicting anything for this year, but I feel twice as confident as I did last spring. I'm not afraid of anybody, especially the Yankees."[24]

In his game story, the *Cleveland Press* baseball beat writer, Frank Gibbons, expressed surprise Milnar wasn't concerned about his sore elbow, and described baseball in 1940 as an era of hair trigger surgery, in which players went under the knife at the drop of a hat. What would Gibbons think of the prevalence of surgery, and the way baseball coddles pitchers in the 21st century?

As the Indians made their way north, an article in the *Cleveland News* quoted Yankees general manager Ed Barrow as declaring the Indians "the team to beat" in the American League. "The Indians have a great infield this season," Barrow said. "Good catching, and there is nothing wrong with their outfield. They also have Feller, and their pitching should be at least as good as Boston's." That was hardly a compliment, as pitching was considered Boston's weakness.

Barrow put in a good word for his employer. "I'd say only the Yanks have a better infield than the Indians."[25]

On April 4 in Augusta, Georgia, Feller pitched seven scoreless innings and the Indians nosed out the Giants, 1–0.

Pytlak's holdout was back in the news in early April. "The $8,000 contract is our final offer," Bradley said when asked again about the catcher. "I believe this is fair on the basis of Pytlak's showing last year when he hit only .268 in 63 games and twice during the season wanted to retire for the balance of the campaign. In mid-summer he asked to be excused for the second time, and we prevailed upon him to stay. As a matter of fact, I believe Pytlak has now retired from baseball. His requests of 1939, and the fact he has refused to answer our last two letters certainly indicate that. Why, we haven't heard from Pytlak in several weeks. He sent back a letter with the contract he rejected, but pointed out nothing constructive to make us re-consider the figures. Now, he won't even answer. Frankie knows where the League Park office is. If he decides to sign for $8,000, we have the contract ready."[26]

Pytlak wasn't ready to sign for $8,000, which represented a cut of $3,500 from his 1939 salary, which had earlier, and erroneously, been reported as $9,500. He told *Press* sports editor Franklin (Whitey) Lewis he wanted to play elsewhere in 1940. "I haven't come right out yet and said I wanted to be traded, although I've hinted at something like that," Pytlak told Lewis. "But I might as well tell you straight out that I'd prefer to be traded. I know I can catch good baseball. I know I can hit. I know as long as Hemsley is with the Indians, I won't get the chance to catch regularly. So, honestly, I want to be traded."[27] The impasse would drag on.

New York clobbered Cleveland, 15–5, in Cordele, Georgia, on April 5. Pulford endured his first rough outing of the spring, allowing six runs in four innings. Eisenstat's outing was rougher. He allowed eight runs in just three innings.

The Indians announced on April 5 that they'd play the American League's two top drawing cards, the Yankees and Red Sox, seven times apiece in huge Municipal Stadium, anticipating the large crowds a pennant race would produce. Municipal Stadium had 76,000 seats. Tiny League Park, in a residential section of Cleveland's east side, seated just 22,000 spectators. The season's 77 home contests would be split almost evenly, with 40 games to be played at League Park and 37 at Municipal Stadium. Those arrangements could be changed at a moment's notice. The Indians had posted a 21–10 record at Municipal Stadium in 1939, but just 23–23 at League Park. Cleveland players of the era between 1932 and 1946, when the Indians played in both ballparks, often complained that they had no true home field advantage and felt as if they were always on the road. A team with two homes actually has no home.

On April 6 in Macon, Georgia, the Indians topped the Giants, 3–2. Hudlin has his best outing of the spring, holding New York scoreless on two hits over six innings.

The Tribe and Giants played another 3–2 game in Gadsden, Alabama, on April 7, with New York prevailing. Milnar allowed two runs in two innings and left the contest with a sore arm. Milnar may not have been concerned with his aching elbow, but the Indians were. An X-ray examination was scheduled which the pitcher insisted he didn't need. The X-ray revealed no damage. Milnar simply had a sore arm. He wasn't expected to pitch for at least two weeks.

Infielder Sammy Hale's arm had been sore for three years. "Sammy visited the Fountain of Youth, took special baths, and consumed huge quantities of mineral water this spring, but to no avail," said Slapnicka. "He is through as a regular, but we are counting on him for utility work and plenty of pinch-hits this season."[28] Slapnicka also said Sewell would open the season on the Tribe's active roster if Pytlak still hadn't signed.

Harder's sore arm wasn't responding as he'd hoped, but, like Milnar and his sore elbow, Harder wasn't worried. His manager was. "I'm 100% better than I was last year at this time," he insisted. "The muscles in the front of my shoulder are a little stiff, but I think I can work that out without much trouble. Last year it was the back of my shoulder that bothered me, and I couldn't do anything about it. Oscar is worrying more than he needs to about this." Harder had pitched only once all spring, and Vitt decided he wouldn't pitch again until the regular season started. Harder planned to protest that decision.

"I'm not so sure that's true," he said. "If we get a good warm day this week, and I can get loosened up, I'm going to ask to be allowed to pitch."[29] The weather failed to cooperate, and Harder didn't pitch.

The Tribe's exhibition game in Anderson, South Carolina, on April 8 was rained out. Cleveland romped over the Giants, 14–1, in Salisbury, North Carolina, on April 9. Boudreau played five innings in the field, his first action since suffering an ankle injury in mid–March. Just as Boudreau returned, it appeared Trosky may have been lost for a significant amount of time. Early in the victory over the Giants, Trosky was hit on the hand by a pitch from Harry Gumbert. The hand swelled up immediately, and a broken bone was suspected. X-rays revealed the injury to be only a bruise, and Trosky was expected to be back in the line-up in a few days.

After exploding for 14 runs the previous day, Cleveland was limited to one run by former Giants ace "King" Carl Hubbell, who allowed just four hits and struck out eight in a 4–1 victory in Tarboro, North Carolina, on April 10. Although the game accounts in the Cleveland papers didn't indicate whether Hubbell had pitched a complete game, a reference to "breaking" his shutout would seem to indicate he did. The next day in Danville, Virginia, the Giants prevailed again, 5–2. "Prince" Hal Schumacher did pitch a complete game for New York. A pitcher hurling a complete game in spring training is a development major league baseball will never see again.

Among this author's reasons for researching the 1940 baseball season was the apparently mistaken impression I'd been given by baseball history books, particularly Lewis' book *The Cleveland Indians*, that the Tribe entered the season as the favorite in the American League, despite the fact the Yankees had won four straight world's championships and 106 games the previous season. That wasn't the case. The Yankees were solid favorites, although the Indians were accorded dark horse status by most of the prognosticators. Even the writers who covered the Tribe on a daily basis didn't give it much of a chance to dethrone the defending champions. On April 12, Cobbledick made his predictions in the *Plain Dealer*. He picked New York, followed by the Indians, followed by the Red Sox. As for the rest of the league, he saw the order of finish being Chicago, Detroit, Washington, Philadelphia and St. Louis.

Perhaps referring to Cronin's bravado, Cobbledick noted the surprising amount of chatter about the Yankees being ripe for the picking among the players in spring training. He didn't agree. He picked New York to win a fifth straight pennant in 1940, with the Indians second, assisted by what he termed helpful additions. Notably, Boudreau at shortstop and Mack at second base, although the pair had been summoned from Cleveland's Buffalo farm club in late July of 1939, and seen considerable action during the season's final two months. They were still considered newcomers. The Tribe's deficiencies in the infield in 1939 were mentioned repeatedly throughout the spring of 1940.

Cobbledick didn't think the Yankees would waltz to the pennant by a 17 game margin, as they'd done in 1939, regardless of who the runner-up turned out to be.

Gibbons, Cobbledick's counterpart with the *Press*, predicted the American League's order of finish to be New York, Cleveland, Boston, Detroit, Chicago, Washington, St. Louis and Philadelphia. Gibbons said the Indians would be an improved club, but probably lacked the offensive firepower they'd need to give the Yankees a run for their money, he told his readers on April 12.

Gibbons' boss, Lewis, picked the Indians to come home third, behind the Yankees and Red Sox. He termed the Tribe's outfield unstable, and said it lacked a power threat to compliment Hal Trosky. Without more punch, Lewis predicted the Indians wouldn't pose a threat to either New York or Boston.

In the *News*, Tribe beat writer Ed McAuley's first division in the American League consisted of New York, Cleveland, Boston and Detroit. Making his prediction for 1940 on April 12, McAuley said a second place finish was in the cards largely because of the presence of Feller in the Cleveland pitching rotation.

McAuley was certain Feller could be counted on ... barring injury ... to win at least 25 games. He thought the rest of the staff could produce an additional 65 victories, and the 90 wins should allow the Indians to finish ahead of Boston. McAuley said Cleveland's staff was the equal or better of any pitching staff except New York's. They had, in Hemsley, the second best catcher in the league ... Bill Dickey of the Yankees being the best receiver in the circuit. The infield defense was sound, but Cleveland's outfield, featuring Heath and Weatherly, was just fair. McAuley said his prediction of a runner-up finish was based on the assumption Harder would shake his arm problems and win at least 15 games, and that Allen would return to his previous form after winning just nine games in 1939. Also that Mack would significantly improve his .152 batting average from the year before. McAuley conceded there were a number of question marks about the Tribe.

Ed Bang, sports editor of the *News*, picked the Yankees to win the pennant, followed by the Indians, Red Sox, and Tigers.

How could the Indians have been "national favorites" to win the pennant, as Lewis wrote in his team history in 1949, when none of the writers who covered them on a daily basis picked them to win? Not even Lewis himself.

Vitt wasn't making any predictions. "I want to see how a lot of things work out before I go poppin' off about how good we are," he said.[30] It was admirable restraint on the manager's part, since he was notorious for "popping off," often with very little provocation.

In an article published in the *Press* on April 16, sportswriter George Kirksey of the United Press quoted the odds ... apparently from different oddmakers than those mentioned earlier in this chapter ... as follows:

NEW YORK: 2–1	CHICAGO: 15–1
BOSTON: 9–2	WASHINGTON: 30–1
INDIANS: 8–1	PHILADELPHIA: 50–1
DETROIT: 10–1	ST. LOUIS: 100–1

A few brief comments followed each team's odds. The comment regarding the Browns' chances of winning their first pennant said, simply, "doomed." While the Browns were never a factor in the pennant race, they emerged as the most improved ball club in the American League, and would be a major thorn in the side of the Indians in particular.

In the National League, Kirksey quoted the following odds:

CINCINNATI: 11–5	NEW YORK: 7–1
ST. LOUIS: 11–5	PITTSBURGH: 10–1
CHICAGO: 5–1	BOSTON: 50–1
BROOKLYN: 5–1	PHILADELPHIA: 100–1

The Phillies' chances for a pennant, which would've been their first since 1915, were summed up in one word: hopeless. It was going to be a long season for Philadelphia's baseball fans, regardless of which team they rooted for.

Kirksey's personal prediction was that the Yankees would win their fifth straight pennant, with the Indians third.

Gibbons asked no less of an expert than Giants manager Bill Terry, a three-time pennant winner and one-time world's champion, for his impression of the Indians, noting that New York and Cleveland had been exhibition opponents since 1934. Terry had seen a lot of the Indians through the years. He'd gotten a bird's-eye view of the current club as the two teams barnstormed north from spring training. He called the 1940 edition one of the most promising.

"I have seen more powerful looking Indians teams, but this one is about the best balanced," Terry told Gibbons. "It has lost power, but it has gained the equivalent in defense. After all, it is a well-known fact that to keep the other fellow from scoring a run is the same as scoring one yourself."[31] The consensus among the so-called "experts" appeared to be another season of the same for Cleveland's baseball fans. The Indians would be good, but not good enough to unseat the Yankees. The players, saying what players are supposed to say, felt differently.

Chicago White Sox manager Jimmy Dykes announced on April 11 that Edgar Smith would match pitches with Feller in the season opener in Comiskey Park. Smith had split four decisions against the Tribe in 1939.

A mixture of rain and snow canceled the exhibition game between the Indians and Giants scheduled in Bluefield, West Virginia, on April 12. Snow in Cleveland canceled the game scheduled for League Park on April 13. The Giants headed for New York; the Indians worked out amid piles of snow in League Park on April 14. The preliminaries had been completed.

Tribe catcher Rollie Hemsley (left) and pitcher Bob Feller inspect the snow-covered playing field of Chicago's Comiskey Park on the day before the 1940 season opener.

On April 15, the Indians sold the contract of pitcher Johnny Broaca to the Jersey City club of the International League. That Broaca, described by the *Press* as eccentric, had made the 30 player roster was a surprise to many. He'd pitched sparingly, and not very well, for the Indians in 1939, then had the gall to hold out for a better contract into spring training. The holdout was so inconsequential it was ignored by the newspapers. He'd pitched mostly batting practice in the spring. How much money the Indians received for Broaca's contract wasn't announced.

Lewis devoted a full column to Vitt's two seasons as the Tribe's manager on the 15th of April, the day before the regular season opened. He conceded that the ebullient Vitt liked to talk. And talk. And talk. He admitted Vitt hadn't exactly ingratiated himself with his players after his hiring by constantly referring to his powerhouse Newark club of 1937, and often comparing his Cleveland players to his Newark players ... usually to their detriment. The players got tired of hearing about how great Vitt's Newark team had been. They felt he was demeaning them.

Lewis claimed Vitt's players thought he belittled them, making critical comments to reporters he could be sure would print them in their game stories and columns. Lewis reminded his readers that much had been written about the players' dislike for their manager as far back as 1938. Vitt seemed to get the message, at least to an extent, and toned down the rhetoric somewhat in '39. He talked less, but still had problems with Heath, Hemsley and Pytlak. Vitt's players were less vocal in their criticism of him, and Lewis said even those who didn't like him respected his baseball acumen. That represented an important point, as it is often noted that players don't necessarily need to like their manager or head coach personally, but it is imperative they respect him. Apparently, at least in Lewis's opinion, the Indians respected Vitt, even if they did so grudgingly.

As far as Lewis was concerned, Vitt had done a good job with the '39 Indians. He said they had third place talent, and Vitt had brought them home in third place. No one had expected a miracle, not even Cleveland's extremely demanding fans, who, according to Lewis, felt Vitt had done a first class job in his first two seasons. These were the same fans Cobbledick had called wolfish, and had run the universally admired Walter Johnson out of town. Lewis said the fans liked Vitt because he wasn't afraid to disagree with the front office, notably Cy

Slapnicka, when he found it necessary. Since the fans liked Vitt, and the owners liked him, and the players admitted that he did a capable job, Lewis determined he was the right guy to manage the team in 1940.

Lewis may have thought so, but others ... most of them players, but also, at least occasionally, Slapnicka ... disagreed. The fact Lewis felt compelled to dedicate a column to an analysis of the relationship between Vitt and his players was an indication the water had been choppy during the previous two seasons, and that rough seas may lie ahead. They did. Rougher than anyone could've anticipated.

Following the Tribe's workout in freezing weather on April 14, Hemsley became the latest to express the opinion the Yankees weren't invincible. "They're all human, just like us. Those Yankees have the same number of arms and legs, too. Why should we feel anything's impossible?"[32]

Feller expressed confidence in his readiness to open the season.

Possibly the first device created to measure a pitcher's velocity, on display at League Park in 1939. The park's infamous 40-foot-high rightfield wall is in the background.

Infielders Oscar Grimes (left) and Lou Boudreau flank manager Oscar Vitt in 1939.

"I feel just as good as I ever felt in my life," he said. "It should be a good year, but I've seen a lot of corn crops that looked good in the spring end up being pretty sick by harvest time."[33]

Feller would never look better than he'd look on the mound in Comiskey Park on April 16, when the games started to count.

5

Zeroes in Chicago

If Oscar Vitt's primary purpose in spring training had been to fully prepare his young ace pitcher, Bob Feller, for the season opener in Chicago's Comiskey Park, he succeeded spectacularly.

The Indians worked out in chilly League Park on Sunday, April 14, in preparation for the opener. They had known for several days, when White Sox manager Jimmy Dykes announced his starting pitcher, that they'd be facing lefthander Edgar Smith. According to Gordon Cobbledick, Dykes had decided Smith had what it took to baffle Cleveland's batters when he and Feller were locked in a scoreless tie that extended into extra innings in Comiskey in August of 1939. The White Sox managed just one hit off Feller through 11 innings, but Smith matched the Tribe's ace pitch-for-pitch, and won when his teammates scratched out a run in the 12th frame.

The Indians ... most of them ... departed Cleveland on a train leaving Union Station at midnight. Vitt wasn't with them. He'd been asked to participate in a nationwide radio broadcast heralding the opening of a new baseball season emanating from Chicago, and left Cleveland 12 hours ahead of his players. The ebullient Vitt and a radio microphone were a natural combination. Also leaving early were Lou Boudreau, Bill Zuber, Ken Jungels, and coach Oscar Melillo, who each had family and friends in the Chicagoland area they'd asked for, and been granted, permission to visit before the game.

Also not on the train were Mel Harder and several other pitchers, who stayed in Cleveland and would work out under the watchful eye of coach Johnny Bassler until the team returned to open the home season against Detroit on April 19. Harder hadn't seen much action in the spring, and was still trying to get his arm into shape.

According to the Associated Press, the largest opening day crowd was expected to gather in Detroit's Briggs Stadium, where it

51

was anticipated 40,000 fans would watch the Tigers and St. Louis Browns. The smallest crowd was predicted to be in Boston's Bee Hive (AKA Braves Field), where only 10,000 were expected to watch the Bees, as the team was known in 1940, tangle with the Brooklyn Dodgers.

Cold and windy weather limited the crowd in Comiskey Park to 14,000, less than half the anticipated attendance, on April 16. Those who braved the elements witnessed history.

The last time Feller and Smith squared off in Chicago, the White Sox had won, 1–0, in 12 innings. Smith almost matched Feller zero for zero again, weakening only in the fourth inning, when Jeff Heath singled with one out and Rollie Hemsley tripled with two out, driving in the game's only run. They were two of the Tribe's six hits.

The White Sox didn't have any.

Feller pitched the first and, to date, some 85 years later, the only no-hit game on the opening day of the baseball season. It may have been easy for the crowd … and, for that matter, the players … to lose sight of the fact Feller hadn't allowed a hit. He struggled through the first two innings, permitting four baserunners. Three Chisox walked. Taft Wright reached base when centerfielder Roy Weatherly dropped his routine fly ball. When Joe Kuhel coaxed Feller's fourth base on balls leading off Chicago's third inning, Feller stopped trying to fight the elements. The chilly weather prevented him from gripping the ball well enough to throw his curveball, so he and Hemsley decided to stick with the fastball. After walking Kuhel, Feller threw nothing but heat the rest of the way. He retired the next 20 consecutive batters.

By the ninth inning, in spite of the early traffic on the bases, everyone in the ballpark, and on both teams, knew Feller was flirting with history. Mike Kreevich opened the home half of the ninth by popping a fastball to second baseman Ray Mack. Julius (Moose) Solters, Feller's teammate briefly in 1939, took a ball, sent a routine groundball to shortstop Boudreau, who threw him out easily. White Sox shortstop Luke Appling then did what he was notorious for doing: fouling off pitches he didn't like. Feller quickly got Appling in an 0-and-2 hole. Appling fouled off the next four offerings. The next four pitches were wide of home plate, and Appling had received Feller's fifth walk of the contest. Wright took a first pitch fastball out of the strike zone, then slapped a hard grounder to Mack's left. The ball appeared to be headed for rightfield, but Mack stopped it with a dive. The ball glanced off his glove and into short rightfield. He retrieved it and threw it to first baseman Hal Trosky, beating Wright to the bag by half a step. At least, in the opinion of the umpire. Wright and his teammates thought otherwise, but had no recourse other than to accept the verdict.

It was the first no-hitter of Feller's Hall of Fame career. He'd toss two more, in 1946 and 1951. He walked five and struck out eight.

"Thanks, everyone, for the congratulations," Feller said in the Tribe clubhouse afterward.

> Don't forget the support I had out there today. The important thing was not pitching a no-hitter but winning the game. I wasn't sure I had a no-hitter until it was announced over the loudspeaker after the game. That ball Weatherly had trouble with, he had to run for it and I thought it might have been scored as a hit. No kidding, I didn't think about it at all. I knew, of course, the ball Weatherly dropped had been scored as an error, the White Sox hadn't made any hits, but the idea of going all the way without giving a hit, well, I just didn't have time to think about that.
>
> I'll admit I would have enjoyed the prospect of a no-hitter if it had been a one-sided game. But with a one run lead, I knew that every batter who got on base represented the tying run. I was thinking about getting them out, that's all.[1]

"I'd rather beat the Yankees consistently," Feller added as he discussed his opening day gem. "My part in the All Star game last year was more thrilling to me than today's game. You've got to be lucky to pitch a no-hit game."[2]

Feller almost had to share his historic moment with Lefty Grove of the Red Sox. Pitching in the presidential opener in Washington's Griffith Stadium, Grove retired the first 21 Senators he faced. An error by Ted Williams ruined Grove's bid for a perfect game, and he eventually settled for a two-hit, 1–0 victory.

A 1–0 victory, achieved thanks to the first opening day no-hitter in baseball history. An omen for the rest of the season, perhaps?

Rain, which had threatened the opener, arrived in Chicago the following day. The second and third games of the season opening series were washed out.

The Indians arrived at Union Station at 8:30 on Thursday evening, April 18, and found 5,000 fans waiting for them. Most were waiting to greet Feller. The *Plain Dealer* reported that the Tigers, who'd provide the opposition for the home opener the following afternoon, pulled into Cleveland just ten minutes later, but had been warned to "lay low" and avoid the pandemonium.

The mob included Cleveland's mayor, Harold Burton, and a band that serenaded both Feller and his teammates. A microphone was set up for Feller to address the crowd.

"We're very glad to be back, and I want to thank you for myself and all the Cleveland players for this welcome," he told the gathering. "I'm certainly glad to be playing with them, and with Cleveland. We will give you all we've got, and we want you to stay behind us."[3]

The previous day, addressing a Knights of Columbus luncheon, Tribe president Alva Bradley had predicted, "Bob Feller will be the greatest pitcher in baseball history, if he doesn't experience any bad accidents."[4]

Bradley faced a near mutiny (a preview of coming attractions) when he spoke to Vitt by phone after the second weather postponement in Chicago. Aware of the civic welcome planned for the Tribe Friday morning, Bradley told Vitt the players would have to stay in Chicago until the midnight train. Vitt responded that he wasn't concerned about any civic welcome. The players wanted to come home, and Vitt wanted them to get a good night's sleep in their own beds the night before the home opener. He didn't want them being forced to hang around Chicago for half a day with time on their hands. Bradley relented, and allowed the team to depart on the two o'clock train. The civic welcome was hastily re-scheduled for Thursday night.

Cobbledick praised the 1940 Indians in his column of April 19. He told his readers they'd see a Cleveland team loaded with self-confidence. A team possessed with the spirit of all for one, and one for all. In other words, the 1940 Indians would be a big, happy family, each player pulling for his teammates on a daily basis to an extent rarely seen in the major leagues. The Indians wouldn't have the sluggers they'd employed in the past, but they'd be vastly improved defensively. Cobbledick said it was this family atmosphere Vitt wanted to preserve by insisting Bradley allow the team to leave Chicago early in the afternoon of April 18.

Doesn't sound like the ogre the players would demand Bradley fire two months later.

The Tigers arrived in Cleveland having split their season-opening two game series with St. Louis. Manager Del Baker said he expected his team to contend.

"With Hank Greenberg and Rudy York in the line-up every day, and Charlie Gehringer pounding the ball, we'll be plenty tough to beat." Baker was pleased with the production the Tigers were getting from a pair of former Cleveland outfielders, Earl Averill and Bruce Campbell. Both had been traded to Detroit in 1939, Averill during the season, and Campbell afterward. "My only regret is that I can't keep them in the line-up at the same time," he moaned.

Baker conceded the Yankees were the favorites ... probably heavy favorites ... to win another pennant in 1940. But he didn't expect New York to enjoy the kind of cakewalk it had in 1939, when it finished 17 games ahead of second-place Boston. "A few injuries would practically ruin the Yankees," he noted. "Even if the Yankees don't lose any of their key men, I don't expect them to out-class the rest of the league, as they did in each of the past four seasons."[5]

Just as had been the case in Chicago, typical Midwestern spring weather held the crowd down at Municipal Stadium on April 19. A feature reporter for the *Plain Dealer* ... which noted with great pride before the contest that the Indians were the only team in major league baseball which hadn't allowed either a hit or a run ... spoke with the first fan to arrive in the centerfield bleachers. The fan called it "the coldest ball game I've ever been to." The game-time temperature was 39 degrees. A gathering of 26,529 in the massive concrete ballpark on the shore of Lake Erie watched Johnny Allen tame the Tigers, 4–0, surrendering only three hits. The Tribe scored all its runs off Henry Pippen in the sixth inning. Boudreau led off with a line drive up the middle that nearly separated Pippen from his head. Weatherly bunted him to second, and he scored on a double down the leftfield line by Ben Chapman. Trosky walked, and both scored on a home run by Heath into the rightfield seats through a stiff wind. Allen took it from there. Weatherly ended the game with a diving catch of a drive off the bat of Pinky Higgins for the final out.

Through two games and 18 innings, Indians pitchers had allowed just three hits and no runs.

"If I ever pitched on a colder day, I don't remember it," said Allen in the victor's clubhouse. "I didn't get tired, but my arm kept tightening up. After pitching last season, my arm and shoulder became very painful. It's a little stiff now, but that's to be expected. There isn't any pain, however, and that's what convinces me I'm going to make a big comeback."[6] Mindful that Allen had pitched sparingly in exhibition games, Vitt sent Johnny Humphries to the bullpen in the sixth inning to have him available in case Allen faltered. He didn't.

Heath said he had a feeling the pitch he hammered into the rightfield seats in the sixth inning would be one could handle. Pippen had walked Trosky ahead of him, and he didn't want to issue a free pass to Heath to load the bases. "I had a hunch that Henry Pippen was going to get that 3-and-2 pitch over the plate in the sixth, and I got ready to meet it."[7]

In the happy clubhouse following the game, Vitt issued a tongue-in-cheek warning to his pitchers. "You boys were great out there, and I'm proud of you. But I think you are getting a little too confident, so I'm going to issue a warning. The first pitcher who permits the opposition to score a run is going to be fired."[8]

Harry Eisenstat, who'd been obtained from Detroit in 1939 in exchange for Averill, took his manager's comment in the spirit in which it was intended. "I'm ready to pitch under those terms. I may not be able to blank those Tigers, but I'm more than willing to take a crack at the job. Just send me out there, boss, and I'll take care of my part of the assignment."[9] Vitt's tongue-in-cheek warning had been directed at Willis Hudlin, who was scheduled to start the following day. But weather postponed the second game of the series. The miserable early season conditions caused the postponement of six of the eight scheduled games on April 20. The hurler Vitt sent to the mound on April 21 failed to extend the club's shutout streak.

He wasn't fired.

Feller had beaten the Tigers six times without a loss in 1939. Detroit got a measure of revenge in the season's third game. After holding the White Sox without a hit in the opener, Feller was hammered by the Tigers, allowing six hits and five runs in three innings. Eisenstat relieved and failed to take care of his part of the assignment, which was to keep the Tigers at bay and give his teammates a chance to mount a comeback against Lynwood (Schoolboy) Rowe, Detroit's starter. Eisenstat permitted six hits and four runs in three innings. Jungels finished up, and the Tigers romped, 12–2.

Feller was asked how he could pitch so well in the season opener in Chicago, and turn in such a poor performance four days later. "I wouldn't give you an alibi if I could think of one," he admitted. "I warmed up the same length of time and the same way. I wasn't nervous, and if there was any strain about pitching another no-hitter, remember the first batter removed that. If there is a reasonable answer, it must be that my control was bad. That's the way it goes."[10]

All told, cold, wet, and windy weather had resulted in 28 postponements during the season's first week, costing club owners an estimated half million dollars. The Associated Press reported Tigers owner Walter Briggs had grown weary of trying to open the season in mid–April, when winter was struggling to hang on in the middle west and northeast, where all 16 major league clubs were located. Briggs wanted to reduce the season from 154 games to 140, which would've moved the season openers into early May. The last 140 game season had been in 1919, due to uncertainty as to whether baseball would be played at all following the end of World War I. Briggs held a minority viewpoint, and the baseball season would not be shortened.

The Indians opened the season's second road trip ... if a single game in Chicago could be considered a trip ... in St. Louis on April 22. Hudlin was staked to a quick 5–0 lead by his teammates in the first inning. The Tribe knocked Browns starter Howard Mills out of the game before Mills recorded a single out. The big blow was Heath's bases loaded triple. The Browns reached Hudlin for a two-run home run off the bat of Harlond Clift in the second inning, which concluded the scoring for the day. Hudlin went all the way, allowing seven hits.

The second game of the series was rained out, the Tribe's third postponement in seven days. Cobbledick took advantage of the unscheduled off-day to write a column urging Bradley to reach contract terms with Frankie Pytlak, who was still at home in Buffalo. The Indians had Hemsley and Hank Helf on the roster, with coach Luke Sewell having spent spring training getting into playing shape in the event he'd be pressed into service due to Pytlak's absence, which with every passing day appeared more likely to be permanent. Cobbledick accused Bradley of holding a grudge against Pytlak, and cutting his salary as a matter of spite. Next to Cobbledick's opinion was an Associated Press story quoting Pytlak as saying he was ready to report to the Indians for any salary in excess of the $8,000 the club was offering.

The weather relented on April 24, enabling the Indians to sweep their abbreviated series with the Browns with a 6–4 victory.

Cleveland scored single runs in each of the first three innings, then added three more in the ninth. Those proved to be crucial when starter Al Milnar tired after pitching seven strong innings. The Browns scored three in the eighth, assisted by a double play the Indians failed to turn. Milnar staggered through the eighth and gave way in the ninth to Joe Dobson, who retired two batters, and Al Smith, who recorded the final out. Cleveland touched four St. Louis hurlers for a dozen hits.

The Indians returned to Cleveland for a quick two game series against the White Sox at League Park. For the second time in barely more than a week, Feller opposed Edgar Smith in the first game on April 26. Neither pitcher was quite as effective as in the season opener, but the Tribe plated three runs against Smith, and Feller allowed only one. Hemsley and Heath clouted home runs, which were much easier to come by in tiny League Park, whose 40-foot-high rightfield wall was a mere 290 feet from home plate, than in spacious Municipal Stadium, which lacked an outfield fence until 1947, when Bill Veeck installed one. Babe Ruth once joked that outfielders should've been allowed to ride horses to patrol the wide open spaces in Municipal Stadium.

Off the field, Pytlak was reported to be in Cleveland on April 26 to re-open contract negotiations with Cy Slapnicka. He was expected to sign quickly.

The Indians wrapped up their brief homestand with an 11–1 loss to the White Sox on April 27. Just as Feller had been brilliant in his first start of the season and ineffective in his second, Allen was routed by Chicago in his second start. The White Sox scored three in the first, one in the fifth, and seven in the seventh to put the contest out of reach. Dobson and Zuber finished up. The Indians were held to four hits by White Sox lefthander Thornton Lee, who hadn't pitched since an exhibition appearance on March 30, but showed no signs of rust due to the long layoff.

In the meantime, Pytlak didn't show up at the team's League Park office on April 27, and no one seemed to know his whereabouts. Allen, Pytlak's former roommate, said it was his understanding Pytlak had returned to Buffalo. Whoever answered the telephone at Pytlak's residence said he wasn't there, and wasn't expected. The value of his services may have increased during the loss to Chicago. Hemsley had to leave the game after being hit on the bare hand by a foul tip.

Helf caught the rest of the game. Hemsley's injury wasn't serious, but it was enough to throw a scare into the front office, which was frightened by the prospect of Sewell having to catch in an emergency.

Although the Indians had until May 14 to reduce the roster to 25 players, they chose to do some trimming in late April. Pitchers Cal Dorsett, Don Pulford and Earl Center were farmed out. Dorsett was sent to Milwaukee of the American Association. Pulford and Center were assigned to Wilkes-Barre.

The very early returns indicated the defending champion Yankees were having trouble with lefthanded pitching. Vitt didn't want to read too much into a late April shutout hurled by Philadelphia southpaw Chubby Dean at New York's expense, but he had noticed the trend. "I have a sneaking hunch that I have two lefthanders who may cause the Yankees a load of grief," he said. "We all know that Al Milnar did well enough against them last year. Well, Al Smith figures to do even better in my opinion. Yep, I just might give Smith a shot or two at those babies. It should be interesting to watch."[11]

The Indians opened the first extended road swing of the season in Detroit on April 27. Hudlin wasn't able to start due to a back ailment, so Vitt turned to big Mike Naymick, the pitcher whose repertoire consisted of a fastball and nothing more. It was enough for Naymick to dispatch the Tigers, 4–2. His control left something to be desired as he walked six, and allowed four hits. Trailing 4–1 in the bottom of the ninth, the Tigers made things interesting, chasing Naymick and loading the bases with two out and one run in. Vitt called on Humphries, who retired Hank Greenberg on a line drive to Weatherly for the last out.

The Cleveland offense did its damage against 18-year-old rookie southpaw Hal Newhouser. Boudreau drove in three runs with a pair of home runs and a single. They were Boudreau's first homers as a big leaguer.

Hudlin's sudden injury wasn't Vitt's only problem. Milnar, who'd insisted during spring training that he wasn't worried about the pain in his pitching elbow, and actually welcomed it as it meant he was snapping off his curveball, continued to be plagued by pain in his pitching elbow. He was expected to miss his start against the Tigers on April 29. He didn't.

Milnar was on the mound and appeared to be cruising to an easy victory when his teammates battered Rowe for six runs in less than two innings. Two more runs in the seventh increased Cleveland's lead to 8–1. Detroit reached Milnar for single runs in the seventh and eighth innings, then launched an all-out assault on Tribe pitching in the ninth. Cleveland had added a ninth inning tally to build its lead to 9–3. The Tigers wiped out the deficit out with a six run ninth against Milnar, Humphries, Zuber and Smith, who managed to record the final out and keep the contest tied at nine apiece.

Luther Thomas retired the first two Cleveland batters in the 10th, but Chapman singled and scored on Trosky's first home run of the season. Detroit threatened against Smith in the bottom of the frame, but didn't score.

Vitt reacted to the loss of a six-run lead by clapping his hands to his head and falling back off the dugout steps against a supporting pole. The players, who were just as distressed as Vitt over the sudden collapse of the pitching, didn't appreciate the manager's histrionics. They'd seen such emotional outbursts often in the past two seasons.

Feller started the final game in Detroit and was tagged for three first inning runs. He settled down from that point and kept the Tigers off the scoreboard while his teammates plated three runs against Pippen, whom they'd beaten in the home opener. Feller's wildness cost him the game when he hit a batter and issued three walks in the eighth, the last of which forced home what proved to be the winning run in a 4–3 Tiger triumph. Pippen allowed 10 hits but picked up the victory. Al Benton retired the last two Tribesman in the ninth.

Through the first two weeks of the season, the Indians had experienced some difficulty hitting lefthanded pitching. That didn't concern Sewell, who hoped the rest of the league would keep sending lefties to the mound against the Tribe. "If they insist on pitching lefthanders against us, they'll have to use inferior pitchers," said the Cleveland coach who, as a former catcher (and possibly a future catcher if Frankie Pytlak didn't sign) knew a little something about pitching. "There aren't more than two or three good southpaws in the league. We'll beat the poor ones. I'd rather they use a poor lefthander any day than a good righthander."[12]

Sewell, who'd spent spring training getting into playing shape in the event Pytlak continued to hold out, said he was prepared to catch as many as 30 games if necessary. It wasn't.

From Detroit, it was on to Philadelphia for the Indians, and they wrapped the first half month of the campaign with a 10–5 victory over the Athletics in Shibe Park on April 30. Cleveland's 13-hit attack on two Philadelphia hurlers, rookie Herman Besse (a lefty) and Bill Beckman, included two home runs by Trosky, and two more by third baseman Ken Keltner. Trosky's first homer struck a three-year-old child playing in the street behind Shibe Park's right-field wall, but the girl wasn't seriously injured. His second blast landed on the roof of an apartment building across the street, an estimated 450 feet from home plate. Hudlin was touched up for 12 safeties by the Athletics, six coming in the eighth and ninth innings, when he seemed to ease up with a 9–2 lead. Philadelphia scored three times in the eighth, but Vitt didn't go to his bullpen.

Cobbledick noted in his final column of April that the Indians were quite amused by a story in a Philadelphia newspaper pointing out that Vitt had compiled a .190 batting average one season. A prankster clipped the story from the paper and taped to it the manager's Shibe Park locker.

The American League's standings as of the close of business on April 30:

INDIANS	8–3	.727	--
Boston	7–4	.636	1
Detroit	6–5	.545	2
Washington	6–5	.545	2
St. Louis	5–5	.500	2½
New York	4–6	.400	3½
Philadelphia	4–8	.333	4½
Chicago	3–7	.300	4½

The Tribe was off to a strong start. All appeared to be well in Cleveland.

What's with the Yankees

The month of May opened with a dull defeat in Philadelphia. Nelson Potter of the Athletics held the Indians to a single run (a 400 foot homer by Ray Mack) while Johnny Allen again lacked the form he showed while shutting out Detroit in the home opener, and Cleveland fell, 5–1.

In his May 2 column, Gordon Cobbledick advised his readers not to be fooled by the Yankees slow start. Ten games and a record of 4–6 were far too small of a sample size to declare the New York dynasty on the rocks. Cobbledick noted that while the Yanks' offense wasn't producing, they were still getting championship caliber pitching.

Rain washed out the final game of the series in Philadelphia. More than two weeks into the season, the Indians had managed to play only one full series—the three gamer with the Tigers in Detroit. Rain had wiped out at least one game of every other series on the schedule to date. That would mean a lot of make-up contests later in the summer.

Cobbledick's column of May 3 included this quote, which he attributed to Oscar Vitt: "if we were 20 games ahead of the Yankees with 21 to play, I'd still be scared." If Vitt was trying to be funny, Cobbledick failed to get the joke. He found the comment not the proper way to boost the confidence of a ball club. Team president Alva Bradley would hear the same complaint from the players the following month.

It was too cold and wet in Washington to play baseball on Friday, May 3, but not too cold and wet to practice, and the practice session Vitt held proved to be costly. Tribe utility infielder Oscar Grimes was struck in the face by a line drive off the bat of Sammy Hale. According to Dr. W.E. Meloy, who examined Grimes, had the ball struck him just one inch higher, it probably would've killed him.

Cleveland baseball fans still remembered all too well the death two decades earlier of beloved shortstop Ray Chapman, when his skull was crushed by a pitch in a game against the Yankees during the feverish pennant race of 1920. Grimes' picture, on the front page of the *Plain Dealer* on May 4, appeared above the caption "Escapes Death." Grimes was hospitalized, and his wife flew to Washington to be by his side in the hospital. Ironically, Mrs. Grimes used a ticket that had been reserved for Hal Trosky, who'd left the team in Philadelphia to return to Cleveland, where his infant son required emergency surgery. Trosky reported his son was doing as well as could be expected, and he planned to re-join his teammates in Washington.

Vitt called a halt to the practice after Grimes' accident. Grimes was expected to be hospitalized for at least a month.

The Tribe scored three runs in the third, three more in the sixth, and added five in the eighth to pummel the Senators, 12–4, on May 4. That concluded what turned out to be a one-game series in the nation's capital.

Rookie Tribe infielders Ray Mack (left) and Lou Boudreau.

The postponements in Philadelphia and Washington enabled Vitt to juggle his pitching rotation and lead with his ace in the first game of a series in Boston's Fenway Park on Sunday, May 6. The Red Sox were in first place and the Tribe in second ... until Bob Feller got through with them. According to Cobbledick, Fenway Park was Feller's "jinx" ballpark, and the Red Sox were his "jinx" team, but Feller shook that off, and pitched Cleveland to a 6–1 victory, which boosted the club into first place. It was only Feller's second victory in Fenway Park. He'd been pitching for the Tribe since 1936. The Indians scored five times in four innings off rookie lefthander Mickey Harris, who'd won his first two decisions for Boston.

Tribe coach Luke Sewell could breathe easy when it was announced Frankie Pytlak had ended his holdout and signed a contract. Pytlak would share the catching duties with Rollie Hemsley and Hank Helf, so Sewell wouldn't be needed in an emergency. Unless the Indians should somehow lose the services of all three receivers.

Just as important ... and welcome ... as the news of Pytlak's return was the announcement by Mel Harder that he was ready to pitch. Vitt had made it clear in spring training that Harder would decide when he'd pitch, and for how long, as he recovered from arm trouble which had plagued him in 1939. Harder took his time, and informed Vitt while the Tribe was touring the East that he felt his right arm was ready for regular duty.

Red Sox manager Joe Cronin had expressed his doubts about the Yankees winning a fifth straight pennant in 1940, and with the Indians in town in early May, Boston coach and former major league catcher Moe Berg agreed with his boss. "The Yankees are cracking," Berg said. "This is the year for one of us to move in—either the Red Sox or Indians."[1] Berg's preference, of course, was that the Red Sox unseat New York as American League champions. Cobbledick didn't think they would.

Noting that Berg's opinion of the Yankees was gaining traction around the league, Cobbledick expressed the opinion that if Berg knew whereof he spoke, the Indians had their best chance to win a pennant since 1920. Cleveland's pitching was far superior to Boston's, and pitching won pennants. Particularly if Harder was healthy, and returned to the form that had made him one of the league's best hurlers since 1932.

The Indians' stay in the American League's penthouse was brief. The Red Sox tallied six times in the fourth inning of the second game of the series against Willis Hudlin and Johnny Humphries, and held on for an 8–5 victory, re-gaining first place. Cleveland pecked away at Boston starter Emerson Dickman, scoring a run in the second, two in the fourth and two in the sixth. Jack Wilson relieved Dickman in the seventh and slammed the door over the next three innings.

Pytlak's return to the Indians was delayed for an extremely unusual reason. American League President Will Harridge said he needed formal assurance from Pytlak that he hadn't played for any other team at any level of professional baseball during his extended holdout. Until he got it, Pytlak was ineligible.

Cleveland mashed 13 hits in the series finale but fell, 6–4. Boston reached Mike Naymick for three runs in his two innings of work. Allen relieved and allowed two more runs in the third. Lefty Grove started for Boston and worked 7⅓ innings, allowing a dozen hits and all four Tribe runs. The game marked the season debut of Harder, who was the fourth of five pitchers employed by Vitt. Harder worked one-third of the eighth inning, allowing a hit and a run. One of the Tribe's hits off Grove was Trosky's fifth home run of the season. The loss dropped Cleveland into third place.

Feller, who'd beaten the Red Sox in the first game, pitched batting practice before the third, and caught the attention of manager Cronin. "What a kid. What a kid he is!" Cronin gushed. "That's what makes him great. He isn't satisfied with a marvelous natural talent. He works to better himself. I wish there were more like him in the game."[2]

When the Indians arrived in New York to finish their road trip, they found the Yankees in an unusual spot: seventh place. After connecting for 13 hits (but still losing) their previous game in Boston, the Tribe stroked 14 hits off Yankee pitching and coasted to a 10–4 victory. The assault included homers numbers six and seven by Trosky. Al Smith worked the first eight innings for Cleveland before allowing a leadoff single in the ninth and giving way to Al Milnar. The victory boosted the Indians back into second place and dropped the Yankees into the cellar ... although just a half game behind Washington.

United Press columnist George Kirksey addressed the question "what's wrong with the Yankees" on the seventh of May. "To state the case plainly, the Yankees definitely aren't what they used to be," he wrote. "Overnight, a fighter, a ball club, or a racehorse can go sour. The Yanks have lost that keen fighting edge, that extra something that made them champions. And with it went their psychological edge over the other American League ball clubs. The Yanks are too good a ball club to be counted out of the 1940 pennant race for keeps at this early date, but they are going to face a harrowing fight to battle their way back up the ladder."

Cobbledick's column of May 8 told of a conversation in the Tribe's New York hotel between Vitt and sportswriter John Kieran, who wasn't particularly impressed with Vitt's ball club. Kieran pointed out ... correctly ... that the Indians had just dropped two out of three to the Red Sox.

"They left me hoping they're the only team we have to beat to win the old gonfalon," Vitt said. Did he really refer to the pennant as "the old gonfalon"? It sounds more like a quote a sportswriter would concoct. Anyway, Vitt told Kieran, "if ever a club looked bad winning, they did. Why, they started their best three pitchers against us, and we knocked every one of them out of the box—Harris, Dickman and Grove. How are they going to win with a pitching staff like that?"

Kieran reminded Vitt about the previous day's 6–4 loss to the Red Sox. "Yeah, they sure beat our brains out yesterday," Vitt snorted. "They got four runs on two pop flies in the second and third innings. We got nothing on 10 line drives. I'd like to play that ball game over 100 times, and we'd win 99."

Kieran told Vitt of a recent conversation he'd had with White Sox manager Jimmy Dykes, whose club had split its four games with the Tribe to date. Dykes suggested the Indians had only one legitimate starting pitcher, a guy named Feller. "Dykes! Dykes! Everywhere I go, somebody tells me what Dykes said about this or that. Next time you see Dykes, you better tell him to button up that lip, and not keep reminding people he's in this league. First thing he knows, somebody is going to notice where the White Sox are [tied for sixth place with St. Louis at that moment], and Dykes will wish he hadn't popped off so much."

Kieran persisted. Who'd pitch for Cleveland on the days Feller didn't?

"Harder'll pitch, and Allen, and Milnar, and a few others that are better than the best Dykes has got," Vitt responded. Kieran told Vitt Harder, in the opinion of Dykes, was washed up. "I'll tell you how good Harder is. He's so good that for the last two years, he has won 15 games in half the season. Only this time, he's going to be ready in May instead of waiting till July. He'll be starting in a week, then look out!"

Vitt's final words to Kieran were "we'll get by. Don't worry about our pitching."

Those don't sound like the comments of a manager who was constantly undermining the confidence of his players, which was one of the grievances the Indians had against Vitt. What he said in public, and what he said to his players in private, must've been very different things.

Feller pitched in Yankee Stadium on May 9, and the home team was sorry he did. Feller held New York to three hits and no runs, and the Tribe completed a two-game series sweep with a 4–0 victory. It was the Yanks' sixth straight defeat, their longest losing streak since 1930. Many of the 15,000 fans booed Joe DiMaggio when he legged out an infield hit to break up Feller's bid for a second no-hitter in the seventh inning.

The Indians finished the trip with a record of 5–3, and two postponements. They returned to Cleveland to open the first true homestand of the season in second place, trailing Boston by a game and a half.

Before leaving New York, Cobbledick devoted a column to the numerous reasons the Yankees, winners of 106 games the previous season, found themselves in last place with one-third of the month of May in the books. He wrote that he based his analysis on conversations with many baseball experts, but not with Yankees manager Joe McCarthy. He claimed anyone asking McCarthy what was amiss with his team risked a punch in the nose, or worse.

According to the experts, the Yankees were struggling mightily because 11 seasons of catching 150 games or more had left Bill Dickey a mere shell of his former self. They were struggling because right fielder Charlie Keller's defense left something to be desired. They were struggling because leftfielder George Selkirk was on the downside of his career. They were struggling because DiMaggio had a knee injury. They were struggling because shortstop Frank Crosetti and first baseman Babe Dahlgren (who faced the unenviable task of succeeding the immortal Lou Gehrig) couldn't hit. They were struggling because pitcher Red Ruffing had reached the end of the line, and pitchers Lefty Gomez and Monte Pearson (who'd been roughed up by the Indians in the first game of the series) were suffering from various aches and pains.

Cobbledick made it clear he didn't necessarily agree with all the opinions, or even most of the opinions, regarding the Yankees demise expressed by the unidentified experts he spoke with. Cobbledick still felt the Yanks were plenty dangerous and would have to be dealt with as the season progressed.

By the time the Indians arrived home to face the St. Louis Browns, Pytlak had satisfied Harridge that he hadn't played any professional baseball during his lengthy contract dispute with the Tribe, and was restored to the roster.

The Browns were the American League's most improved team in 1940. It would've been difficult not to be improved. A team which lost 111 games the previous season, as St. Louis had, couldn't have gotten much worse. The Browns weren't contenders, but they'd win 24 more games in 1940 than they won in 1939. They were slowly building the team that would win the franchise's only pennant five years down the road. And they'd given the Indians trouble in 1939, at least in one series in which the Tribe needed extra innings in all three games to achieve a hard-earned sweep. Browns manager Fred Haney called the Indians the best of the American League's western clubs (Cleveland, Detroit, Chicago, St. Louis). But he hadn't called them the best team in the league.

Vern Kennedy of the Browns blanked the Indians in six of the seven innings he pitched in League Park on Friday, May 10. In the fifth inning, they exploded for five runs, which was all they needed in a 9–4 victory. Four eighth innings runs, plated against reliever Howard Mills, were icing on the cake. Milnar earned his third win despite leaving the game trailing, 4–0. He was the pitcher of record when his teammates scored five in the fifth. Zuber and Eisenstat held St. Louis scoreless the rest of the way.

An injury to right fielder Roy Weatherly required Vitt to make his first significant line-up change of the season. Weatherly pulled a muscle in the second contest at Yankee Stadium and was replaced by Beau Bell, who contributed a hit to the fifth inning outburst.

The victory increased the Tribe's lead over the Yankees to seven games. It isn't often that a game story notes the second place team's lead over the last place team, but the Yankees weren't any old last place team. They were the YANKEES, the four-time defending World Series champions, and everybody was keeping a close eye on them. The truth is, had New York not stumbled badly early in the season, had it come even remotely close to duplicating its overpowering form of 1939, it would've left Cleveland and Detroit choking on its dust and fighting each other for second place.

In a column titled "It's News to Most of You," written by *Plain Dealer* sports editor Sam Otis and featuring little known sports trivia, it was noted on May 10 that Herman Franks, the catcher for the Brooklyn Dodgers, once retired from baseball briefly while playing for the Hollywood Stars of the Pacific Coast League in 1933, at the suggestion of his manager. Franks' manager was Oscar Vitt. Franks would become a successful major league manager himself in the 1960s, with the San Francisco Giants.

Allen's season to date had been either feast or famine. He'd been either very good, or very bad. On May 11, he was very good against the Browns. And he had to be. The Indians scored just one run off Emil Bildilli, and they waited until the bottom of the ninth inning to do it. Rollie Hemsley's line drive single off League Park's 40 foot high metal wall in rightfield with the bases loaded plated the game winner as the Tribe triumphed, 1–0. Allen allowed five hits, and no runner reached third base.

The Yankees lost to the Red Sox for their eighth consecutive defeat. They trailed the Indians by eight games. The headline above the game account in the *Plain Dealer* read SAME OLD STORY: YANKS LOSE AGAIN. When was the last time such a headline had been seen in a newspaper?

The Indians had scheduled most of their Sunday home games for Municipal Stadium, which could accommodate 76,000 fans as compared to League Park's seating capacity of 22,000. The final game of the St. Louis series was contested on the lakefront on May 12. It drew a crowd of 10,518, which would've looked good in League Park. It made Municipal Stadium look practically deserted.

Hudlin started and got a quick hook from Vitt after allowing five hits and two runs in two innings. Vitt took advantage of the chance to get an extended look at Harder, who pitched seven innings and was charged with the loss. After pitching five scoreless innings, Harder ran out of gas (he'd pitched only one-third of an inning all season, and just once in the exhibition season) and allowed a run in the eighth and two in the ninth as the Browns broke a 2–2 tie and won, 5–2. Despite the loss, Harder appeared to be ready to give the Tribe's starting rotation a much-needed boost.

The Yankees snapped their losing streak with a 4–0 victory over the Red Sox.

The oddsmakers weren't at all fazed by the Yanks' slow start. The revised odds, as of May 12, still had New York as the prohibitive favorite (4–5) to win the pennant. The odds on the Red Sox were 2–1. The odds on the Indians, originally established at 8–1, had been shaved to 4–1. The *Plain Dealer*'s story made no mention of the odds on the Tigers.

The landmark ruling by arbitrator Peter Seitz, which struck down baseball's draconian reserve clause and created free agency, was 35 years in the future in 1940. But the inequity in player contracts had been a topic of discussion since it had been instituted in the early 1880s, and it was addressed by Cobbledick in his column of May 12, inspired by Pytlak's long holdout against the Indians. The team held all the cards in the dispute. Thanks to the reserve clause, major league baseball considered Pytlak Cleveland's "property" even though his contract had expired. Alva Bradley and Slapnicka controlled his fate. They chose not to trade him, or release him. They also chose not to meet his salary demand. Pytlak had no recourse but to stay home in Buffalo, or find work in another profession. Cobbledick ... who didn't face a similar situation is his chosen profession ... had no problem with that.

Sounding very much like the lawyers who represented the club owners in the 1975 arbitration case of Andy Messersmith and Dave McNally, Cobbledick went into painstaking detail explaining why the end of the reserve clause would mean the end of professional baseball. Wealthy clubs such as the Yankees would corner the market on the best players, leaving the less affluent teams to pick over the dregs to stock their rosters. Cobbledick's point was no more baseball would throw 400 major leaguers, and thousands of minor leaguers, out of work, in addition to depriving tens of millions of fans of the national pastime. He made a number of valid points, and the current financial inequity between large market, medium market, and small market teams is a significant point of contention today, which ultimately needs to be addressed. But history has shown when what he feared ... the demise of the reserve clause ... came to pass in 1975, it didn't mean the end of baseball. Far from it.

The Indians enjoyed their first scheduled day off of 1940 on Monday, May 13. The eastern clubs the Tribe had visited on its road trip would return the favor beginning on May 14.

Hudlin's unsuccessful two inning stint against the Browns was his last appearance in a Cleveland uniform. He was handed his unconditional release on May 14, a development that reportedly shocked his teammates. Hudlin had pitched for the Tribe since 1926, winning 18 games in 1927, 17 in 1929, and 15 in 1931, '34, and '35. But he was clearly on the downside of a distinguished career in 1940, and departed Cleveland with a record of 2–1 and an earned run average of 4.34. Fifteen major league seasons had taken a toll on Hudlin's right arm. He knocked around for the rest of the 1940 season, pitching in eight games for the Senators (1–2, 6.51), six for the Browns (0–1, 11.12) and one for the New York Giants (0–1, 10.80). He'd pitch once for the Browns in 1944, when ballplayers, due to the manpower shortage caused by World War II, were literally recruited off the scrap heap. He lost his only decision with a 4.50 ERA. Hudlin won 158 games and lost 156 with an ERA of 4.41. All but one of his victories were earned in a Cleveland uniform.

"It was either Hudlin, or one of our younger pitchers," Vitt explained. "We have a pretty tough situation right now, trying to cut the squad down to the required 25. Remember, too, we can't put Oscar Grimes on the retired list even though he won't be able to play for a couple of months maybe. I wish Hudlin all the luck in the world. It's a tough break, but we all expect those things in this racket."[3]

Feller, like Allen, had been either very good or very bad early in 1940. He was very bad when he faced the Athletics at League Park on May 14. He allowed five runs in the second inning (after striking out the side in the first) and two more in the fourth, after which Vitt went to his bullpen. Joe Dobson kept Philadelphia off the scoreboard until the ninth, while his teammates rallied to tie the game at seven. The Athletics un-tied it with two ninth inning runs, pinning the loss on Dobson.

Connie Mack, the 76-year-old manager of the Athletics, had a message for Cleveland reporters. "Stop being so nice to the Yankees," he urged. "Write that they can be beaten, and that they're just another club. When I spoke at the Philadelphia sportswriters dinner [in January] I said that the Yankees would finish third."[4] Mack said he expected a two-team pennant race between the Indians and Red Sox, and that neither team should slip below second place at any point during the season.

The Athletics visit to League Park was brief. Rain wiped out the second and final game of the series. Rain wiped out all the games scheduled in the American League on May 15. As the raindrops descended on League Park, the Indians trimmed their roster to get to the 25 player limit. They demoted pitcher Ken Jungels to Milwaukee of the American Association. The decision boiled down to whether to keep Jungels or Naymick, who some felt would benefit by being sent to the minor leagues to work on his control. Naymick didn't figure to see much action with the Tribe, but Vitt felt it advisable to keep him around. With Jungels gone, the Indians had 10 pitchers and 15 position players.

Bucky Harris, the former "Boy Wonder" who'd managed the Senators to the 1924 World Series championship at age 24, and was in his second tour of duty at the Washington helm in 1940, brought his club to Cleveland on May 16. The Senators were floundering in sixth place, largely due to a lack of hitting. "It takes more than good defense to win ballgames," he said. "We have been holding teams to low scores but failing to win because we couldn't produce in the pinches."

Harris was asked about Mack's prediction pertaining to the Yankees. "Connie Mack may be right when he says the Yankees will wind up in third place," Harris answered. "But if they do, two other clubs will have to step along at a brisk pace. The Boston Red Sox are nine games ahead of them right now, and that's a sizable lead, but I think the Yankees will start whittling down that margin in the near future. New York isn't as powerful as it was in past years, but it's too good a club to be bogged down in eighth place."[5]

Wet spring weather continued to plague the American League on Thursday, May 16. Three of the four games scheduled that day, including Washington at Cleveland, were rained out. Only the Red Sox and Browns were able to play, and Boston won, 7–5, increasing its lead over Cleveland to three games.

With an off day resulting from the weather, Vitt took advantage of the opportunity to worry about his roster. "I wish the outfielders would start hitting," he mused. "We won't do anything about it yet, though."[6] The front office had until June 15 to make a trade to add some offense.

It was often said of Colonel Jacob Ruppert, the owner of the Yankees, that he enjoyed games in which his team scored 10 times in the first inning ... and then pulled away. The Indians tried that formula on May 17, and it worked to perfection. Cleveland hammered Washington pitching for 10 first inning runs, and never took its foot off the accelerator, cruising to an 18–1 victory. The Tribe collected more runs than hits, banging out 15 safeties. Senators starter Sid Hudson, who'd been pitching in Class D in 1939, faced six batters. He walked five, and allowed a fluke single to Trosky on a bad hop. Things only got worse for Washington from there. Milnar somehow managed to bear down throughout and went the route. The game marked Pytlak's first appearance on the field since ending his holdout.

The Indians should've saved two of those 18 runs for the following day. They scored only twice, and it wasn't enough, as the Senators squeezed out a 3–2 victory.

More concerning than the defeat was the possible loss of Allen from the starting rotation. Allen left the game in the eighth inning with a sore elbow, the cause of which was diagnosed by team physician Dr. M.H. Castle as a strained muscle. Castle said Allen's return depended on how the elbow responded to treatment. He faced the possibility of being shelved for up to six weeks.

The Senators departed Cleveland with a new pitcher: Hudlin. The former Tribesman had been negotiating with a few clubs and rejected Washington's first offer because it lacked a guarantee he'd be with the team the full season. The Senators reportedly relented and met Hudlin's terms. "I had offers from three teams and accepted Washington's proposition because the Nats need pitching and I want to work regularly," Hudlin said as he packed his bags.[7] If the Senators did promise Hudlin he'd be with them all season, they didn't live up to it.

The beleaguered Yankees arrived in Cleveland not quite as beleaguered as they'd been after losing twice to the Indians in New York earlier in May. The Yankees had moved out of the basement on the strength of three straight victories. They failed to extend that streak to four.

Feller's perplexing early season continued. Routed in his previous outing against Philadelphia, he held the Yankees to four hits and won, 5–1. The Tribe scored twice in the first inning off Red Ruffing, then added one in the third and two more in the seventh. Both pitchers went the distance. Not surprisingly, rain delayed the contest in Municipal Stadium by 40 minutes, and the crowd of 27,600 could've been larger except for a traffic cop stationed outside the ballpark, who told hundreds of motorists headed for the game that it had been postponed, and sent them on their way.

As was often the case in 1940, the scene shifted from Municipal Stadium to League Park for Monday's game. Al Smith limited the Yankees to three hits, two of them in the ninth inning with the game long since decided, while the Indians were pummeling three New York hurlers for 17 hits and 10 runs. The 10–2 pasting of the world champs was Cleveland's sixth straight victory over New York, dating back to 1939.

Smith was a reclamation project who'd won 14 games for the New York Giants in 1934. "I haven't got enough stuff to get by unless I have excellent control," Smith said after beating the Yankees. "When I was with the New York Giants, my biggest trouble was wildness. Lack of control also brought my release by the Phillies." A pitcher found wanting by the woeful Phillies didn't figure to have a major league future, but Smith wound up with Cleveland's Buffalo farm team. "With manager Steve O'Neill and coach George Uhle [a former Tribe pitcher who won 200 games in his career] helping me, I gradually improved my control, then I worked on a screwball and enjoyed considerable success." Smith won 16 games and lost only two with Buffalo in 1939, and that earned him a shot with the Indians in 1940. He was making the most of it. Smith said he didn't mind the short rightfield wall in League Park.

"After working in that Buffalo bandbox and some other International League parks, that rightfield wall seems about 100 miles away," he said.[8]

New York returned the favor on May 21, trouncing the Indians, 10–2. It marked the first time all season the Yankees had been able to field the same line-up that had run roughshod over the American League in 1939, and it overwhelmed the Indians. New York scored three first inning runs off Milnar and didn't look back. Still, the Yankees, after losing two of three to the Tribe, left Cleveland in last place, half a game behind the White Sox. The loss dropped the Indians 2½ games behind the Red Sox, who arrived in Cleveland as the Yankees were departing. The Indians were 2½ games ahead of Detroit, which had moved into third place.

"The boys realize that they have an excellent chance to win the pennant, and they intend to make the best of it," Cronin told Cleveland reporters. At least he didn't refer to the pennant as "the old gonfalon." Cronin said the Red Sox batting prowess set them apart from the other contenders. "What other teams can match our power? [Jimmie] Foxx is peppering fans with home run drives, and Ted Williams is just beginning to hit his stride."

As for the pitching, which Vitt believed was Boston's weakness, Cronin said, "don't worry about our pitching. We haven't looked any too strong in the box to date, but there is bound to be an improvement. How can you keep a pitching staff in good condition when you only play two games a week? Weather conditions will be more favorable next month, and I expect a big improvement in our pitching."

Cronin admitted that doubleheaders later in the season, necessitated by the numerous postponements in April and May, would put a strain on his pitchers ... and every other team's. "It won't be possible, of course, to use three and four pitchers a game. Perhaps I'll have to leave the starting hurler in the box regardless of how he's being treated, and trust our power hitters to win the game, 15–14."

As for the pennant race, Cronin said, "four teams have an excellent chance to win this season. Cleveland is a distinct threat. Detroit is loaded with dynamite, and the Yankees can be counted on to make a strong drive. I look for a dogfight down the home stretch, with the ultimate winner taking the flag by two or three games. The American League has been clamoring for a close race for a number of years, and this is the season in which its prayers will be answered."[9]

Boston's batting ability was on full display at League Park on May 22 ... but so was Cleveland's. The two teams combined for 31 hits and 15 runs, including four homers ... three by the Tribe. Cleveland won, 9–6, with the victory going to Harder, who was touched for 12 hits and five runs in 4⅔ innings. Harry Eisenstat and Dobson held the Red Sox to a run on three hits over the final 4⅓ frames.

Despite Harder's poor pitching line, Cronin claimed to be impressed. "Cleveland fans can quit worrying about Harder's arm. We hit him hard, but he looked great. He had trouble with his control and made several pitches too good, but his curves were snapping, and he had plenty on his fastball. I'll be surprised if he doesn't at least equal his record of last season."[10] Harder did manage to strike out Williams twice. The victory moved the Indians to within 1½ games of the Red Sox.

Good news came from the trainer's room. Allen's sore elbow had responded extremely well to treatment. It had been speculated he might miss up to six weeks. He wouldn't even miss six days. Allen was pronounced healthy, and ready to take his next turn in the rotation.

The Indians and Red Sox would face another doubleheader, or at least another make-up game, on their plates later in the season, as rain washed out the second and final game of the series on May 23. That ended the first extended homestand of the year. The Tribe had won six and lost four.

The Indians spent the last weekend of May in St. Louis. The Browns had just fallen into last place, trailing the Yankees. Feller was a one-man gang for Cleveland, pitching a complete game seven-hitter, striking out nine, and driving in the game-winning run with the first home run of his career. An unusually large crowd of 25,562 (it was a rare night game) in Sportsman's Park watched the Browns fall, 3–2. The gathering was, astonishingly, the third largest in the history of the St. Louis franchise, which dated back to 1902. Twice in the 1930s, the Browns had failed to draw 90,000 patrons for an entire season. Management rarely put a product on the field worth supporting. The Browns hadn't finished in the American League's first division since 1929 (fourth place). Cobbledick noted that the crowd was three times the total number of fans who attended the 11 games the Indians played in Sportsman's Park in 1939. Such was the state of American League baseball in St. Louis.

The victory cut Cleveland's first place deficit to one game. There was a downside, however. Feller was supposed to pitch the previous day against the Red Sox, until the rain came. By pitching in St. Louis on Friday, Feller wouldn't be available to start the Tribe's Monday game at home against third place Detroit.

The Indians played the first of their make-up doubleheaders in St. Louis on May 25. Well, they were scheduled to. Nature had other plans. It rained. It was little wonder the Tribe couldn't build any momentum during the first month and a half of the season. They rarely played three consecutive days.

Cobbledick took advantage of yet another weather postponement to note that possibly the main question facing the Indians in spring training was whether Ray Mack would provide enough offense to justify making him the team's regular second baseman. Mack was a vacuum cleaner on defense. But he'd hit just .152 in very limited duty in 1939. As the end of May approached, Mack was leading the Tribe's regular players with a .347 batting average. His teammate, Trosky, thought he knew why.

"At the beginning of the season, other managers got the idea that the way to stop the Indians was to stop me and Jeff Heath, and they thought that the way to do this was to throw one lefthander after another against us," Trosky explained. "Now, Mack had trouble all spring with righthanders curveballs, but lefthanders didn't bother him a bit. He wasn't afraid of a curve that broke in to him. He knew he could hit southpaws. So, while Heath and I were getting a regular diet [of lefties] and not liking it very well, Mack was getting fat on their pitching. The result was his confidence grew, and that was all he needed. Now, he's sure of himself, and I'm not sure whether he knows, or cares, whether a righthander or lefthander is pitching."[11]

Mack wasn't a .347 hitter, but he swung the bat well enough to belong in the starting line-up. There was never any doubt that his double play partner, Boudreau, would hit. Together, they gave the Indians possibly the best keystone combination in the league. Mack's glove had saved Feller's opening day no-hitter.

Cobbledick spent part of a rainy Saturday in St. Louis talking to a local icon: former Cardinals second baseman Rogers Hornsby, who'd managed the Cards to the 1926 World Series championship, and also managed the Boston Braves, Chicago Cubs, and Browns. Hornsby was then operating a baseball school in Hot Springs, Arkansas. He'd always had opinions and was never reluctant about expressing them. Hornsby told Cobbledick he thought the Tribe's reserve outfielder, Beau Bell, who'd played for him with the Browns in 1936 and '37, had the potential to be an outstanding hitter.

"I understand they tried to make a pull hitter out of him in Detroit," said Hornsby, still considered by many to be the greatest righthanded hitter in baseball history. "That alone was enough to ruin him. He can't pull, and he shouldn't try. His power is in right-center, just like mine was. And that ought to be all right with you people in Cleveland. Give that fellow a chance to get in stride, and he's liable to knock down your [rightfield] wall for you."

Hornsby also had praise for Boudreau. "A lot of people are talking about him around the league now, but all they talk about is his fielding. They seem to think the fact he's hitting is just an accident. Don't let anybody make you believe that. The kid's a good hitter. He's got plenty of guts up there at the dish. He may get fooled now and then, but he's never going to be scared."

Hornsby said he thought Mack would develop into a power hitter. "With his strength, he ought to hit 'em out of the park as fast as the factories can make 'em." He also liked catcher Jim Hegan, who was playing for Cleveland's Wilkes-Barre farm club. "I saw Slapnicka the other night, and I told him that if I owned that Hegan, I wouldn't sell him at any price. The kid was down to my school this spring, too, and he's got everything."

As for the Tribe's chance for the pennant, Hornsby said, "this is Cleveland's chance. This is your year to win if you're ever going to have one. And, for my money, it'll be all right if the Yankees finish ninth. Do 'em a lot of good."[12]

The weather cooperated on May 26, and the Indians split a doubleheader with the Browns. Cleveland got a second poor start from Harder and couldn't overcome it with offense, losing the opener, 5–3. St. Louis scored all of its runs in the fourth inning off Harder and Dobson. In the nightcap, Milnar was the beneficiary of an offensive onslaught for the second time in three starts. The Indians plated 13 runs on just 10 hits, one of them being Trosky's 10th homer, and romped, 13–1. The split moved the Tribe to within a half game of Boston.

Cobbledick's column of May 27 contained two interesting observations. Without quoting him directly, he claimed Yankees manager Joe McCarthy had told reporters in St. Louis the Indians were the team to beat in the American League. And, in an anecdote which proved to be chillingly prophetic, Cobbledick said Cleveland's general manager, Slapnicka, wished Feller would get married and father a child ... and soon. Becoming a father would've removed Feller from eligibility for the military draft. World War II, in which the United States wasn't yet involved in the spring of 1940, was raging in Europe.

"If we ever did get into the war, he'd be the first one to want to go," Slapnicka said. And he knew what he was talking about. Following the attack on Pearl Harbor in December of 1941, Feller enlisted in the navy immediately, serving with distinction for four years.

Night games were few and far between in 1940. The perpetually cash-strapped Browns had paid $174,000 to install lights in Sportsman's Park, which they owned and shared with their tenants, the

Cardinals, in the hope of attracting the kind of crowd they attracted against the Indians on May 24. The city of Cleveland, which owned Municipal Stadium, spent $57,000 to install lights to allow the Tribe to play a handful of games after dark. Lights were never installed at League Park.

The first home night contest of 1940 was played on May 28, and the Indians were vanquished by the Tigers, 6–1. Louis Newsom, better known to some as Buck and to others as Bobo, held Cleveland to six hits and struck out nine. Vitt tried to cross the Tigers up by starting Naymick rather than Allen, his reasoning being they may have had trouble catching up with the tall righthander's fastball under the lights. They did, but only until the third inning. A splendid (for a Monday) crowd of 25,718 watched.

Allen started the second game at League Park and didn't last long. Vitt used four relievers, including Naymick, whose arm was relatively fresh since he'd been knocked out of the box early the night before. Detroit won, 8–5. The Indians salvaged the final game of the set, 7–4, behind Feller. The Tigers managed six extra base hits off the Tribe's ace, a homer and five doubles, but fell behind early and couldn't catch up.

Before leaving town, Earl Averill, the former Tribe outfielder who'd been traded to Detroit for pitcher Eisenstat in 1939 because, among other reasons, he couldn't stand playing for Vitt, posed the question, "do you still think the Indians will finish ahead of the Tigers with a pitching staff like that?"[13] Cleveland had surrendered 18 runs to the Tigers in losing two out of three, and even Feller had been hit hard. Cobbledick conceded that, except for Feller, Smith and Milnar, the Tribe's pitching had been among the poorest in the league. He suggested Vitt wasn't making the best use of the talent available, particularly Naymick, whose speed might be valuable out of the bullpen ... even though Naymick's control was shaky, and he had no secondary pitches.

Thursday, May 30, was Decoration Day, the holiday known today as Memorial Day and celebrated on the last Monday of the month. A holiday meant a doubleheader, scheduled for Municipal Stadium in anticipation of a large crowd. The White Sox provided the opposition, and each team started a pair of lefthanders. Cleveland's duo of Smith and Milnar bested Chicago's duo of Edgar Smith and Thornton Lee by identical 3–1 scores. Cleveland's Smith took a shutout into the ninth inning of the first game; Milnar allowed the White Sox a run in the third inning of the nightcap, and then nothing more. For one afternoon and 18 innings, the Indians pitching was more than adequate.

The sweep enabled the Tribe to pick up a game on Boston, which split its doubleheader with the Yankees.

Only one game was scheduled in the major leagues on May 31, and it was rained out. It didn't involve the Indians. The standings at the end of the last day of the month:

Boston	22–10	.688	--
INDIANS	23–13	.639	2
Detroit	20–15	.571	3½
New York	17–18	.486	6½
Chicago	16–21	.432	8½
Washington	16–22	.421	9
St. Louis	14–21	.400	9½
Philadelphia	13–21	.382	10

All still appeared to be well in Cleveland. But appearances can be deceiving.

Calm Before the Storm

The month of June, the events of which would prove to be without precedent in the history of North American major league professional sports, started just as May had started, with the Indians losing a dull game to the Athletics in Philadelphia.

Hal Trosky's 12th home run was all the offense the Tribe could muster in a 6–1 defeat. Lee Ross, who'd been hit hard in all his previous appearances according to the *Plain Dealer*'s game story, held Cleveland to a pair of hits. Johnny Allen started for the Indians, and was pulled after just two ineffective innings.

Looking for additional offense, Oscar Vitt tinkered with his line-up. Centerfielder Ben Chapman was benched in favor of Roy Weatherly, who was able to play for the first time in a week after pulling a muscle late in May. Beau Bell remained in rightfield, having played well in Weatherly's absence. Vitt also moved Ray Mack from the seventh to the eighth position in the batting order. In a totally un-related development, leftfielder Jeff Heath changed his uniform number. Heath wore number 33 on the back of his jersey, but wore jersey number 24 for this game.

In his June 2 column, Gordon Cobbledick noted that baseball attendance had declined across the board, including in Cleveland, despite the fact the Indians were legitimate contenders for their first pennant in 20 years. He attributed the decline to concerns about the war in Europe, which were leaving average folks with little time to indulge in such frivolity as a major league baseball pennant race. When the 1940 season was in the books, however, the Indians would finish third in the American League in attendance, and baseball attendance overall would increase significantly over 1939.

What was becoming a familiar problem was on display in Shibe Park in a Sunday doubleheader. The *Plain Dealer* called it hopelessly inept second string starting pitching. When Feller, or Al Smith, or Al Milnar didn't pitch, the Indians didn't win. Feller pitched the first game and won, 7–2, for his eighth victory of the season. Mike Naymick, Johnny Humphries, Bill Zuber and Joe Dobson worked the nightcap and couldn't hold the early lead the batters gave them. The Athletics rallied for a 12–6 win and a split of the twin bill. Making matters worse, Mack, the Tribe's hottest hitter through May, cooled off once the team arrived in Philadelphia. Mack was held hitless in the first three games of the series, and struck out six times.

The Indians managed a split of the series with a 4–0 victory on June 3. Milnar picked up his seventh victory against one loss. It was the first time the Athletics had been blanked. With the win, Cleveland moved to within one game of Boston for the league lead.

The Yankees had shaken off their early season malaise and moved into fourth place, 4½ games behind Boston and 3½ games behind the Indians. Connie Mack was asked if he'd changed his opinion of the Yankees, given their recent spurt. "Call it a hunch if you like, but I still think this isn't their year," said the Athletics manager. "They're going good now, all right, but they haven't been beating the good clubs. I want to see how they'll react when they run into another bad spell, as they will. If the Indians and Red Sox keep beating them, they'll have plenty of trouble." Mack had predicted the Indians and Red Sox would fight it out for the pennant. Did he still think so?

"I think they should," he said. "They're both great ballclubs with wonderful power and good defense. They have what a club must have to beat the Yankees."[1]

It was another make-up doubleheader, and another split for the Tribe, on June 4 in Washington. Mel Harder pitched poorly again in the opener, and the Senators won handily, 7–2. Smith salvaged the split with a 3–2 victory in the nightcap. The Tribe was the only first division club to win that afternoon, meaning it gained a half game on Boston, which it trailed by a half game; on Detroit, which it led by 2½ games; and on New York, which it led by four.

Feller, Smith, Milnar, and a cast of thousands wasn't going to pitch the Indians to the pennant, and Vitt knew it. He spent 30 minutes on the phone with Cy Slapnicka before the doubleheader split with the Senators. Vitt's job was to manage the talent, Slapnicka's job was to acquire it. Vitt had seen enough of Allen and Harder to know he couldn't count on them for the long haul. Vitt told his boss he needed pitching, particularly starting pitching, and needed it immediately if he was going to keep the Indians in the pennant race. Vitt said he was willing to sacrifice some of his reserve strength if that was needed to acquire pitching. Slapnicka assured Vitt he'd scour the minor leagues in search of pitching, and explore trade avenues. The trading deadline was June 15. In the meantime, the Indians had to hope Allen would shed his maddening inconsistency, and Harder would round into form. He'd had virtually no spring training, and it showed.

Slapnicka had passed on a chance to claim Dizzy Dean on waivers from the Chicago Cubs. So had every other major league team. Dean, who'd won 30 games for the Cardinals 1934 World Series champions, had asked to be allowed to go to the minors to work on a sidearm delivery he hoped would restore him to his former glory. The Indians, in need of pitching, could've claimed Dean for the waiver price of $7,500. They chose not to.

Cobbledick placed the odds of the Indians finding a serviceable veteran pitcher in the minor leagues, or obtaining one via trade, at "50–1."

Vitt, in a bind, turned to Dobson, normally a reliever, to start against the Senators on June 5. Washington countered with a 20-year-old rookie, Walter Masterson. Masterson had all the better of the encounter, holding Cleveland to four hits in a 6–1 victory. The Indians lost more than a game. They lost the services of Weatherly for three days. Weatherly had been thrown out of the first game of the previous day's doubleheader. He wasn't nicknamed "Stormy" for nothing. He was known for his contempt for umpires in general, and George Moriarty in particular. An argument with Moriarty had gotten him tossed from the game in Washington. The American League office suspended Weatherly for three days, and fined him $25.

Allen and Harder pitched well enough to enable the Indians to win the series finale in Washington. Allen started and allowed four runs in seven innings. Harder relieved and shut out the Senators in the eighth, ninth, and 10th. Milnar pitched a scoreless eleventh inning. Mack's two-run home run tied the game at four in the eighth, and Frankie Pytlak's triple plated the winning run in the 11th. Cleveland stayed a half game in back of Boston, and gained a game on the Tigers and Yankees.

As the Indians moved up the coast to New York to continue their eastern trip, nothing in Cleveland's newspapers hinted at any discontent in the dugout or clubhouse. But the clock was ticking, and midnight was about to strike.

Feller took a 4–3 lead into the bottom of the ninth inning at Yankee Stadium on June 7, and with the bottom of New York's order coming up, a Tribe victory appeared likely. Four singles later, Feller trudged off the mound a 5–4 loser. Milnar evened the series with a 3–0 victory the next day, allowing just two hits. The Indians out-hit the Yankees in the rubber match, 9–6, but couldn't match New York's power. Three Yankee home runs made a loser of Smith, 4–3. Just days after Cobbledick had written about poor attendance in both leagues, the Indians and Yankees drew better than 75,000 paying customers to their weekend series. A crowd of 28,659 watched the game on Sunday, June 9.

Cleveland's loss left it in a virtual first place tie with Boston. The Red Sox led by 14 percentage points, by virtue of having played six fewer games than the Indians. Detroit was a game behind, and the fourth place Yankees were three games back.

First place had been at stake when the Indians paid their first visit to Fenway Park in early May, and the American League lead was on the line again when the Tribe arrived in Boston on Monday, June 10. The first game of the three-game set was rained out. In the meantime, Slapnicka responded to Vitt's plea for pitching help by purchasing the contract of righthander Nate Andrews from the Browns. Andrews posted a 17–9 record for Columbus of the American Association, a Cardinals farm team, in 1939. He was drafted from Columbus' roster by the Browns, but failed to make the team out of spring training and was sent to St. Paul, for which he'd won one game and lost three. Andrews' best pitch was an overhand curveball. He'd report to Cleveland on June 14, when the Indians returned from their trip.

Another postponement meant Vitt had another chance to juggle his pitching rotation. It was Allen's turn to pitch on June 11, but Vitt decided to go with Feller on three days' rest. The decision may have had dramatic repercussions. Not only was Feller pitching on short rest, he was less than 100 percent physically. His right side was heavily taped to protect a torn cartilage. He didn't have his best stuff, and the Red Sox pummeled him, 9–2. The loss dropped the Indians into third place, behind Detroit, although they remained a game behind the Red Sox. What happened in the Tribe's dugout may have been just as important, if not more so, than what took place on the field.

Feller allowed five runs in five innings. According to the book *The Cleveland Indians*, written in 1949 by *Press* sports editor Whitey Lewis, a disgusted Vitt was heard muttering to himself in the Tribe dugout during a Boston rally, "there's my star, the great Feller. How can I win a pennant with him?" Other sources report the remark as being "look at him! He's supposed to be my ace. I'm supposed to win the pennant with that type of pitching?"[2] Whatever Vitt actually said, his players ... many of whom disliked him, some intensely ... heard him. Feller may have been the most respected member of the team. He was pitching on short rest, and he was injured. But he was on the mound giving it his best effort, and his manager was belittling him. It wasn't the first time Vitt had made a sarcastic remark about one of his players, and they'd heard enough. But they were about to hear more.

The Indians scored three times in the sixth inning of the final game of the abbreviated series to take a 5–3 lead. But Milnar couldn't hold it. Boston chased Milnar, and his successor, Harder, with a six-run eighth inning for a 9–5 victory. It was Cleveland's third straight loss ... the first time the Indians had dropped three in a row all season. Statistically, the eastern swing hadn't done much damage. The Indians had won five and lost eight. They'd left Cleveland in second place, one game out of first, and returned in second place, two games out. The damage the journey had done psychologically, however, may have been another matter entirely.

The acquisition of Andrews didn't end Slapnicka's effort to add reinforcements as the trade deadline approached. He revealed that Andrews wouldn't report to the Tribe as scheduled on June 14, and possibly not for several days afterward. "Andrews' daughter is ill, and he hasn't yet left St. Paul. He may not join the club for several days. We don't know whom we are going to release to make room for Andrews until the pitcher is officially signed."

The Indians and Tigers had done business twice in the past year. Earl Averill, on the downside of a Hall of Fame career, was swapped to Detroit in June of 1939 for Harry Eisenstat. After the season, the Indians exchanged outfielders with the Tigers, sending Bruce Campbell to Detroit for Clarence Campbell and Bell. It was rumored another deal between Cleveland and Detroit was in the works. "We have discussed several trades with the Tigers this season, but have been unable to reach an agreement. We also have sent out feelers to other clubs," said Slapnicka.[3] The Tigers reportedly had an interest in several of Cleveland's players, but would they be willing to fortify the club they'd wind up fighting for the pennant until the final weekend of the season? And would the Indians be willing to do the same?

The poor eastern trip, particularly the two demoralizing losses in Fenway Park, led to a somber train ride back to Cleveland. Gibbons wrote on June 12 that there were rumblings of discontent in the Tribe's dugout and clubhouse. He told his readers the close harmony displayed by the club in the early stages of the campaign was quickly disappearing. Gibbons said Vitt faced a significant challenge getting the undercurrent of tension under control, and suggested he may not be up to that challenge. He said there was no obvious reason the Indians should continue to struggle, as they were at the moment. He claimed too many players were fighting with forces aside from the players in the opposing uniforms, and a lack of team spirit was the result. A lack of spirit that threatened to derail a promising season.

Gibbons, as a result of a casual conversation with Hal Trosky in a Boston bar, knew something no one except the players knew, but something everyone would find out, and soon.

June 13 was to have been an off day, but the Tigers were in town to make up the game that had been postponed on April 20. The first pitch at League Park was scheduled for 3:00. Before that, however, several of Cleveland's players had another piece of business to attend to.

Please, Mr. Bradley

Thursday, June 13, wasn't going to be just another day at the office for Alva Bradley.

Shortly after arriving at his downtown Cleveland office, Bradley was informed that a delegation of his employees wanted to see him. They represented most of the 25 players who wore Cleveland Indians uniforms. During the meeting, Bradley's phone rang. He took the call and found Hal Trosky on the other end of the line. Trosky had left the team to arrange his mother's funeral. But the matter being discussed in the team president's office was of sufficient importance for Trosky to interrupt his grieving, and make sure his opinion was heard.

"Mr. Bradley, I just want to tell you that I'm 100% in favor of the story you're now hearing. Those are my sentiments without qualification," Trosky said, according to Whitey Lewis' account of the meeting in his book *The Cleveland Indians.* And Trosky knew exactly what Bradley was hearing. He and his teammates had discussed the action taken on June 13 for quite some time. The pot had been boiling for a while, all the way back to the previous season. Oscar Vitt's sarcastic reaction to Bob Feller's and Mel Harder's poor performances in Boston during the recent road trip brought the matter to a head.

Only a few hours had passed since the train carrying the Indians had arrived in Cleveland from Boston. The team had a make-up game to play against Detroit at League Park that afternoon. But the players had decided they could wait no longer to confront Bradley with their list of grievances against their manager.

In the lengthy history of major league professional sports in the United States, which dates back to the founding of baseball's National League in 1876, many teams have had issues with their managers or head coaches. Many teams have schemed to undermine a manager or head coach, in the hope of inducing management to make a change. Only the 1940 Indians, however, were so bold and blatant as to meet with the team president and co-owner, and demand the manager be dismissed immediately. It hadn't happened before, and it hasn't happened since.

INDIANS DEMAND OUSTER OF VITT; CAN'T WIN FOR HIM, ALVA BRADLEY TOLD, screamed the front-page headline of the *Plain Dealer* on June 14. Gordon Cobbledick described the insurrection as an act without known parallel in baseball history, which it was. It remains an act without known parallel in the entire history of American professional sports, 86 years later.

Eleven players met with Bradley, including Feller, Harder, Ken Keltner, Jeff Heath, Oscar Grimes, Sammy Hale and Rollie Hemsley.

The delegation told Bradley that the players, both individually and collectively, couldn't play the kind of baseball needed to win a pennant ... which they firmly believed themselves capable of winning ... as long as they were playing for Vitt. Cobbledick described the players' grievances against their acerbic manager as follows:

> Vitt had ridiculed his players in conversations with newspaper reporters, fans, and players on opposing teams.
>
> Vitt had undermined the confidence and spirit of individual players with sarcastic comments on their poor performances.
>
> Vitt had been insincere and two-faced in his relationships with his players, often praising them to their faces, and criticizing them harshly behind their backs. Such as his biting remark about Feller ... while the pitcher was out of earshot ... in Boston two days earlier.
>
> Vitt was a wild man in the dugout, storming back and forth on the bench during games, making caustic remarks about the team's performance, and passing his jitters on to his players.
>
> Vitt's antics had made him a laughingstock among the rest of the American League, and the low regard in which other teams and players held him had caused the Indians to lose dignity and pride in themselves. He was an embarrassment to the ball club.

Just what was so bad about Vitt? The book *Indians Baseball: 100 Years of Memories*, published by the Cleveland Baseball Club itself in 2000, devotes several pages (66 through 70) to the uprising of June 1940, and the factors that led to it.

According to New York sportswriter Dan Daniel, Vitt once heard Trosky complain about playing on a cold, rainy day in Yankee Stadium, fearing it could lead to pneumonia. Responded Vitt, "well, for all the good you are doing us, you might have pneumonia."

After watching Harder load the bases in a game, Vitt asked no one particular in the dugout, "why doesn't that guy quit baseball? He's through." The book asserts that Vitt often reminisced about his powerhouse Newark Bears of 1937, and wished he had them on the field instead of his current club.

"Vitt would rip his own players apart," said Harry Eisenstat. "Especially Bob Feller. He's the ace of the staff, and Vitt was very negative toward Bob. Then he would apologize afterward."

After serving as third base coach in 1938 and '39 ... where his "clownish" behavior embarrassed his players.... Vitt stayed in the dugout when the Tribe batted in 1940, thus "subjecting his players to a full nine innings of nervous antics and biting comments."

Said Feller, "I think the pressure of the pennant race got to him. He was always nervous and jumpy. Years before, he'd been warned by Alva Bradley about his talking. I remember Bradley saying, 'Oscar, you talk too much. It's going to get you in trouble someday.'"

It did during the fateful series in Fenway Park during which Vitt criticized Feller and Harder. On June 12, with the contest tied at five, Vitt had summoned Harder, who proceeded to allow four runs. The Indians lost. Upon returning to the dugout, Vitt confronted Harder and told him, "it's about time you won one, the money you're getting." Another source reported the remark as "we've been waiting a long time for you to get ready, and now it seems that will be never." Vitt had allowed Harder to set his own pace as he recovered from arm problems suffered the previous year.

Replied Harder, a respected veteran who'd pitched with distinction for Cleveland since 1928, "I gave you the best I had." The players heard Vitt rip Feller. They heard him rip Harder. And they decided they'd heard enough.

While the Indians were in Boston, Trosky invited Frank Gibbons to join him for a beer. He then explained how he'd personally had enough of Vitt, and how most of his teammates shared his feelings. Trosky said the players had decided to meet with Bradley and demand that Vitt be fired. Gibbons had just been handed the greatest scoop in sportswriting history. Instead of writing it, however, he cautioned Trosky to seriously consider the ramifications of the action the players were planning. He suggested the players "wait and see what happens."

They did. But not for long. Vitt's criticism of Feller and Harder pushed them over the edge. They carefully planned their strategy on the train returning to Cleveland from Boston. Lou Boudreau and Ray Mack were excluded from the rebellion, as the veteran players feared being involved in such an unprecedented situation might give them a reputation as malcontents, which could damage their careers. Roy Weatherly opted out voluntarily. He wanted no part of the insurrection.

To his credit, Bradley listened to the delegation's complaints against Vitt. He could've simply told them to get out of his office, stop griping, and do their jobs. They had a game to play that afternoon. Bradley did tell the hired hands that they should've given more thought to the action they'd just taken before taking it, and that when news of their meeting with him broke ... as he knew it would, and it did ... they'd face ridicule not only from Clevelanders, but from fans in every city they visited in the American League for the rest of the season, and possibly for the rest of their careers. He hoped they could handle the abuse they'd be subjected to in every ballpark in the league.

The meeting was meant to have been top secret, but it took only minutes for the media ... essentially newspapers in that era ... to learn of it. When asked, Bradley tried to downplay its significance. "A few of the boys wanted certain things corrected," he said. As to whether he'd make the "correction" the "boys" had asked for ... actually demanded.... Bradley responded, "naturally, I am going to look into the matter, but until I have investigated thoroughly, I can't say what action will be taken."[1] If any.

Vitt claimed to be completely blindsided by the player rebellion against him. He managed that afternoon's game against the Tigers, which the Tribe won, 3–2, in 10 innings, totally unaware that many of the men he shared the dugout with despised him, and had demanded his dismissal. He knew nothing of the meeting in Bradley's office until informed of it by a newspaper reporter seeking comment after the game. Vitt at first thought the reporter was pulling his leg. Assured that the meeting had taken place, and Vitt was in the midst of a full-blown mutiny, he phoned Bradley for confirmation. He got it.

"Mr. Bradley did not tell me about this affair when I saw him after today's game," said a startled Vitt. "When I reached him last night, he said he intended to talk with me about it tomorrow morning." Possibly Bradley felt he needed time to consider just how he was going to explain such an unprecedented event to his manager.

Vitt insisted he had "no reason to believe that any member of the club had any enmity toward me." Although he had admitted, after signing his contract for 1940 in August of 1939, that there may have been players who didn't like him, and they'd simply have to deal with the fact he'd be back for another year at the helm. He had no intention of changing his style to accommodate them.

"Nobody can say that I have not given 100% in energy to the team. I can't imagine what could have impelled them to do this. It looks as if somebody has been stirring up some trouble,"[2] Vitt conceded. "There is more behind it than appears on the surface. There are men on the committee for whom I have done as much as anyone possibly could."

"Grimes and Hale," Vitt continued. "I can't figure that one out. I've always had a strong feeling of friendship for those boys. And Feller. Well, it's all over my head."

Gibbons asked Vitt how he could continue to manage the Indians under the circumstances. "I'm not sure, but Ol' Os will give it a try," he answered.[3]

Gibbons quoted several players he didn't identify, detailing their grievances against the manager. Vitt's constant criticism and sarcasm "has even gotten under Bob Feller's skin. That's really getting to the jumping off place," said one.[4]

"How can we have any confidence in ourselves when Vitt is running up and down the dugout popping off? He's always afraid something is going to happen and he gets us down," said another.[5]

One player said Vitt's game strategy left much to be desired, but "you could overlook those things, but you can't overlook a fellow who is a front-runner. This game is too tough for that, and a manager should always remember there are 154 games to a season."[6]

Gibbons knew the players resentment of Vitt stretched back to the 1939 season, and asked how the club played so well after Vitt had been re-hired for 1940. "That was a bread and butter proposition," said one player. "We knew we had to go through the rest of the season with him and decided to make the best of it. This time, we hope to get some action."[7]

Vitt was neither naïve nor a fool. He knew of the discontent brewing in his clubhouse, and shortly after being re-hired, called a team meeting to address it. Players with grievances against him were invited to speak up. No one did.

"We knew he was set to stay then," explained one player. "No one wanted to stick their neck out."[8]

One player expressed the opinion that Vitt had no choice but to resign. "How can we go on now that this has been brought to light? I know that I could never feel the same way toward Vitt, and that he could never feel the same way toward me."[9]

"I never thought they'd do this," Vitt lamented as he tried to process the chaos swirling around him and his ball club. "Maybe I've hollered a lot, but anyone can get nervous in this game. Why, Mr. Bradley and other officials have heard me because they sit right by the dugout, and they've never kicked to me."

> Vitt acknowledged the sarcastic remark he made to Harder a few days earlier, after he'd failed to hold a 5–5 tie and gave up four runs to the Red Sox. Mel Harder, well, I knew Mel was sore, and I didn't blame him when he failed to stop the Red Sox the other day. I was so darned upset about blowing the game that I made some sour crack as he passed me on his way to the clubhouse. I regretted it later, for after all, Mel was doing the best that he could. But don't other people say things like that, unthinkingly, when they're under pressure. Sure, I've been nervous in the dugout. Certainly I've shown my disappointment and I've pointed out mistakes to the players on the bench.
>
> That's one of the reasons I gave up coaching this season. I wanted to help the fellows in the dugout by calling errors of judgment, as well as smart plays, to their attention. What do the fellows want? A manager who doesn't care whether they win or lose?[10]

While Vitt admitted he regretted his sarcastic remark to Harder, he said nothing about apologizing to the Tribe's elder statesman.

When Vitt was hired in October of 1937, Cobbledick wrote that he'd probably be a failure, if success was defined only as winning pennants. Cobbledick expressed the opinion that all a club could reasonably ask of a manager was that he squeeze the maximum amount of performance out of the players he's given. If Vitt did that with the Indians, he'd be a success. Following the unprecedented events of June 13, Cobbledick declared Vitt "an apparent failure."

"Is Oscar Vitt a good manager?" Cobbledick asked in his column the day after the insurrection. "This question has been asked as frequently as any other since he was placed at the head of the team a little more than two years ago. The answer, in light of yesterday's developments, apparently is 'no.' For the first requisite of a good manager is that he convince his players of his qualifications for the job. And Vitt has failed in that."

Cobbledick closed his column by conceding one of the points made by the players against their manager. He considered it a case of what goes around, comes around. Vitt had spent nearly 2½ seasons constantly criticizing his players. Those players, Cobbledick wrote, were repaying him with interest.

Lewis expressed his opinion ... and Lewis never lacked an opinion ... in a scathing column in the *Press* on June 14. He cut Vitt a tiny bit of slack, admitting the unprecedented situation was the screwiest that had ever arisen in better than six decades of major league baseball. He conceded that Vitt faced the daunting task of managing one of the rarest aggregations of screwballs ever assembled in a big league dugout. Regardless, Lewis expressed the hope Vitt had managed his last game, and listed the reasons he felt a resignation was in order.

Lewis didn't think Vitt should step down because of player dissatisfaction. He didn't think Vitt should step aside due to his well-publicized disagreements with the business office (i.e., Cy Slapnicka). He didn't think Vitt was too proud to manage a group of players who despised him. In Lewis's opinion, Vitt had out-lived his usefulness to Cleveland's major league baseball team, and should pack his bags and get out of town immediately. Lewis almost defied anyone reading his column to disagree with his conclusion.

Lewis didn't absolve the front office of blame for the insurrection. In his opinion, Slapnicka and Bradley should've seen the mutiny fomenting as far back as August of 1939, and taken steps to head it off before it exploded. The obvious step would've been declining to re-hire Vitt for the 1940 season. He suggested that anyone unable (or unwilling) to read the handwriting on the wall was incapable of operating a major league franchise.

In Lewis's opinion, an effective major league manager required the confidence of his players. Vitt had failed miserably in that regard. Lewis claimed Vitt had never shed his minor league background, as he evidenced when he constantly spoke in glowing terms of his beloved 1937 Newark Bears. His Cleveland players grew weary of his praise of his Newark players and his criticism of them.

Lewis posed the entirely reasonable question of how the Indians were supposed to respond when their boss suggested with great frequency that his Newark team was superior to the team he'd been given to manage in Cleveland? The comment echoed Cobbledick's claim made earlier in the season that Vitt's apparent lack of confidence in his players was too often put on public display.

Lewis concluded his tirade with a criticism often leveled at the Tribe's ebullient manager. He talked entirely too much, usually without considering the ramifications of his comments, and the entire city of Cleveland was now a national laughingstock as a result of the situation those ill-conceived comments had created.

Vitt undoubtedly agreed with Lewis on one point. "I don't have to tell anybody I've had to deal with some touchy players," he said in his defense. "I have done the best I can. If I have hurt some feelings, I am sorry. After all, is it a crime to tell a player he's going bad when he is?"[11]

Columnist Tommy Tucker of the *News* laid the blame for the debacle at the feet of Slapnicka and Bradley, the leaders of what he labeled the bizarre conglomeration known as the Cleveland Indians. In Tucker's opinion, the mess took more than a year to make, and would require more than a year to clean up. A new occupant of the manager's office in League Park might be a step in the right direction, but the problems the Indians faced went far beyond employing 20 or so ballplayers who hated their boss. Tucker didn't blame Vitt for possessing what he called a temperament that wrecks the morale of a team. He didn't blame the players for rebelling against Vitt. He blamed Bradley and Slapnicka for hiring him, and after doing so, compounding the mistake by failing to notice Vitt and his players were oil and water. They just didn't mix. According to Tucker, management was to blame for failing to find a player-management combination that clicked, which Vitt and his players hadn't.

Tucker concluded by noting the irony in the fact that Steve O'Neill had been dismissed for being too lenient on his players. Vitt was under fire for being too hard on them. Assuming Vitt's days were numbered, what could Cleveland's baseball fans expect with the next managerial hire?

Vitt met with Bradley on June 14. Their meeting lasted more than an hour, and when it was over, Vitt was still the manager. He was encouraged when Bradley told him, "worse tangles than this in baseball have been straightened out."[12] What tangles Bradley was referring to aren't known, as there had never been such a tangle in major league baseball's 64-year history. Vitt informed his players in a terse statement, "I'm still the manager. Let's play ball."[13]

And they did, beating the Athletics behind the two-hit pitching of Allen, 5–2. The *Plain Dealer*'s game story noted that the normally vigorous Vitt sat alone in the dugout, glum and silent. How else could he have responded to the knowledge that the vast majority of his players had no respect for him, and considered him a laughingstock and an embarrassment?

Vitt was asked if he planned to speak privately with each of the players who'd marched into Bradley's office demanding his dismissal. "I haven't gotten that far yet," he answered. "I'm just laying the groundwork. You know, I'm a hard fellow to hurry."[14] With Bradley determined to conduct a thorough investigation into the players' charges, Vitt appeared to have the luxury of time. No decision on his future seemed imminent.

McAuley noted on June 14 that, should Vitt choose to resign, which he'd shown no inclination to do, it would be accepted with great reluctance by Bradley. McAuley said Bradley remained close personal friends with the three managers...Roger Peckinpaugh, Walter Johnson and O'Neill ... he'd dismissed during his tenure as club president. He also said Bradley had great personal admiration for Vitt, in spite of his frequent warnings that the manager talked too much. McAuley said Vitt was the type Bradley believed added prestige to the game; being well-groomed, well-mannered, and with a captivating personality. He added that Vitt's personality may have captivated his boss, but it had the opposite effect on his players.

Ed Bang's commentary in the *News* was similar to everyone else's, but he added a history lesson. Quoting the nation's 16th president, Abraham Lincoln, Bang noted that a house divided against itself cannot survive. The Indians, if not divided against themselves, were certainly arrayed almost as a unit against their manager. If the situation wasn't rectified, and quickly, Bang said the 1940 pennant was out of the question.

After consulting with Vitt, Bradley presided over the monthly board of directors meeting, discussing routine club business as well as the rebellion against the manager. He was mum afterward about any decisions the board made. He tried to maintain his sense of humor amid the carnage. "If you want to have fun, just buy a ball team some time," he advised.[15]

Cobbledick wrote in his column of June 15 that the players had not only placed themselves and Vitt in precarious positions, to say nothing of Bradley, they'd also created an uncomfortable situation for coach Luke Sewell. They told Bradley they liked and respected Sewell and preferred to play for him rather than Vitt. They assured Bradley they could win for Sewell. As a coach, Sewell's loyalty was to the manager. How was he supposed to respond to the players' request that he be promoted to manager? How was Vitt supposed to deal with the reality that his players wanted him replaced by one of his coaches?

Lee (Buck) Ross, who'd beaten the Indians on a two-hitter the last time he'd faced them, beat them again on June 15, getting the best of Harder, who struggled through six innings before being tagged for four runs in the seventh. That was the difference in a 7–4 Philadelphia victory, which dropped the Tribe into third place. Vitt was reported to have shown slightly more animation as he watched the game from a seat in the dugout, even smiling a couple of times, when his players did something worth smiling about, which wasn't often enough. The Indians were without the services of Hank Helf, who was hospitalized with a minor intestinal problem. They expected to be without the services of Weatherly for the next two weeks, after he sustained a severe strain of the abdominal wall. Weatherly wasn't shelved nearly that long.

On June 15, when baseball's trading deadline and possible deals Cy Slapnicka could make to shore up Cleveland's pitching staff and add some punch at the plate should've been the main topic of discussion, the mutiny was still on the front burner and boiling furiously.

"All I can say is that I want further time to deliberate the justice involved in this case," said Bradley. "I will probably talk to the players again … before I arrive at a decision." The team president denied reports that Vitt had offered his resignation the day before.

"There was no talk of resigning or firing," he insisted. "I want to get to the bottom of the case. I don't believe in snap judgment in a matter as complex and serious as this."[16]

In his column of June 16, Cobbledick reminded his readers of Bradley's inability as team president to find a suitable manager for the Indians. Bradley's first hire, Roger Peckinpaugh, was fired in

June of 1933 after 5½ mediocre or worse seasons. Peckinpaugh's replacement, former Washington star pitcher and manager Walter Johnson, had been, in Cobbledick's words, "a disaster." Johnson "resigned" in early August of 1935, although he'd actually been fired in late July. Coach Steve O'Neill was elevated to succeed Johnson, and while he was popular with the players, he was thought to lack the toughness needed to demand full effort from those players. O'Neill was fired after the 1937 season. Vitt had been hired to do what O'Neill couldn't: get a bunch of talented, but underachieving, players to perform up to their capabilities ... or what Bradley, and Tribe fans, thought were their capabilities. As the 1940 season neared its half-way point, Vitt was hanging on by a thread.

When Bradley re-assured Vitt that worse catastrophes than the player rebellion he faced had been overcome in the past, he may have been referring to a similar situation five years earlier, when Johnson managed the Indians and was convinced catcher Glenn Myatt and third baseman Willie Kamm were plotting against him, and were poisoning the minds of their teammates, particularly the young ones, with their anti–Johnson rhetoric. Both players denied Johnson's charge, but both were given their releases, which infuriated Tribe fans even further against Johnson, whom they decided they didn't like the day he arrived to replace Peckinpaugh, a native Clevelander. Bradley dispatched club secretary Walter McNichols to Detroit, where the Indians were playing, to get each player's signature, for reasons that weren't divulged to the players. A few days later, those 21 signatures were beneath a full page letter in each of Cleveland's daily newspapers in which "the undersigned" denied all reports of dissension on the team, and declared their total loyalty to, and admiration for, Johnson. The players claimed to never have seen the document until they read it in the newspapers. Nobody bought the ruse, and Johnson was out two months later.

Bradley tried the same ploy days after the players had demanded Vitt's ouster. He gathered the players in the League Park clubhouse before the June 16 doubleheader against the Athletics, and asked them to sign a simple document stating that "we, the undersigned, publicly declare to withdraw all statements referring to the resignation of Oscar Vitt. We feel this action is for the betterment of the Cleveland baseball club." Bradley had learned his lesson from his past mistake. The letter supporting Johnson had done the beleaguered manager more harm than good, and turned the players and fans against him even more than they'd already been. There was no such pablum in the letter 21 of the 25 players signed on that June morning. There was no mention of being "happy players" or being "loyal to our manager, the Cleveland ball club, and our fans," as the statement allegedly supporting Johnson had included. Just a straightforward withdrawal of the accusations against Vitt "for the good of the ball club." Heath and Helf were both in a hospital and not present at the clubhouse meeting. Both said they'd have signed the document had they been present. Weatherly, who was unable to play due to an injury but not hospitalized, left the meeting without signing. He hadn't been part of the plot to unseat the manager. Whether or not Vitt knew Weatherly had supported him isn't known. How Weatherly's teammates felt about his bailing out on them also isn't known.

One unidentified player wanted to make sure the fans understood he and his teammates hadn't been coerced into signing the document. "He didn't threaten us into signing it," the player said. "Don't make that mistake. We just reached a new understanding."[17] As the season progressed, it became obvious the "new understanding" consisted of the players ignoring their manager to the fullest extent possible.

"It has been the toughest experience of my life," said Vitt of the player insurrection. "I hope I never have this kind of trouble again. I'll do all I can in the interest of good spirit, but that doesn't mean I won't criticize where I feel it is needed."[18]

"I am glad the boys decided to call it off," said Bradley. Whether or not the boys had decided to call it off, or had been strongly advised to do so, was probably a debatable question. "But I am still considering the truth of a number of things. No, I am not ready to say we can forget the matter entirely."[19]

Cobbledick expressed the opinion that the letter ended the rebellion, which he termed one of the strangest episodes in the history of a ballclub "that has won nationwide fame for its remarkable behavior, sometimes on the field, sometimes off." And Bradley agreed. A club spokesman said the team believed the wisest course of action was to smooth the matter over, wipe the slate clean, and start all over with everybody as friends. The only thing missing was Pollyanna herself. But the saga of the "Cleveland Crybabies," as the team had quickly become known from coast to coast, was far from over. The hatchet couldn't be buried so easily.

In his *Plain Dealer* column "The Sport Trail," which took a humorous look at sports, James E. Doyle wrote of the apparent truce between Vitt and his players, "yes, the renowned redskins, whose tepees are pitched high above Cuyahoga's waters, have extended the pipe of peace to ol' Chief Os—but he's taking a good look to make sure it isn't a lead pipe, intended for his noble dome. These braves are true Indian givers, 'twould appear … even when they hand a guy the razzberry. They're taking back what they said about the chief, but they hope it will be a lesson to him just the same." Doyle didn't seem convinced the storm had blown over.

And it hadn't, as far as sportswriters for out of town newspapers were concerned. The first to express an opinion about the "Crybabies" had been columnist Shirley Povich of the *Washington Post*, who toasted Vitt and roasted the players and Bradley. "Oscar Vitt deserves a medal for not quitting after his players boo-hooed to an owner who lacks the nerve to tell 'em off," Povich opined.[20]

The *Press* re-printed excerpts from six columns written by sportswriters from around the country. Among them was this opinion expressed by Harry Salsinger of the Detroit *News*: "it could only happen in Cleveland. One manager [O'Neill] lost his job there because he didn't get mad at his players, another may lose his job because he does." Not one of the columnists quoted expressed one iota of sympathy for the "Crybabies," as they'd be known for the rest of the season.

On the field that afternoon, the Indians sent two of their best pitchers to the mound and beat the Athletics twice. Feller won his ninth game in the opener, 4–2, and Milnar notched his ninth win in the nightcap, 4–3. In his game account, Cobbledick noted the Indians had won four of the five games they'd played since they'd told Bradley they couldn't play winning baseball for Vitt and demanded … but didn't get … his dismissal.

Vitt received a huge ovation from the crowd of 18,000 at Municipal Stadium when he participated in the pre-game line-up card exchange before the opener. Unlike 1935, when both the players and fans couldn't stand Johnson, the fans in 1940 were totally in sympathy with the Tribe's beleaguered manager. Trosky, perceived by the fans as the ringleader of the insurrection, was lustily booed. It paled in comparison to the abuse the players would take when they hit the road.

With the crisis apparently having passed, and Vitt having won the power struggle with his players, Cobbledick posed the question: would Vitt crack down, and crack down hard, on the insurrectionists, who comprised the vast majority of his players, or would he take a thoughtful approach, considering their complaints and trying to correct the faults that led to the demand for his dismissal? Would the players accept Bradley's request that they let bygones be bygones and wipe the slate clean? Or would an atmosphere of tension and mistrust … which was hardly conducive to prevailing in what was shaping up as a tight pennant race … permeate the Cleveland dugout and clubhouse for the rest of the season?

According to Lewis' book, the players decided that while they'd have to tolerate Vitt's presence for the remainder of the year, they didn't have to listen to him. They developed a number of secret signals they used to circumvent his orders, when they disagreed with them, which was frequently. Vitt, obviously, knew when his players were ignoring what he'd told them to do. But there was nothing he could do about it.

Harder thought the incident left an impression on Vitt. "He was quieter. I think it floored him. He was surprised it was handled this way."[21]

As for the pennant race, which seemed to have gotten lost in the shuffle amid the chaos of the past several days, the Indians were tied with the Tigers for second, 2½ games behind the Red Sox. The Yankees were four games back.

The Indians didn't need any additional distractions as they battled the Red Sox, Tigers and Yankees for first place, but they got one on June 18, when Frankie Pytlak, the reluctant catcher, jumped the team and returned home to Buffalo, declaring he was through with baseball. Pytlak had caught the second game of the twin bill with Philadelphia, then bolted for Buffalo, claiming to be ill. It was revealed that Pytlak had threatened to quit while the Tribe was on its eastern road swing, but had been talked out of it by Slapnicka, who'd been down that road before. Pytlak had threatened to quit during the 1939 season and been coaxed into re-considering. Slapnicka ordered Pytlak to return to Cleveland while the Indians were in Boston, and undergo a physical examination to prove his claim to being a sick man. Doctors couldn't find anything wrong with him, but he continued to insist he was ill, and asked Slapnicka to place him on the voluntarily retired list. Slapnicka refused, so Pytlak jumped the team and went home. His absence left the Tribe with only one catcher, as Helf remained hospitalized and wasn't expected to be available for two weeks.

No one was taking Pytlak's so-called retirement seriously. The *Plain Dealer* nonchalantly wrote that the Indians would be glad to welcome him back when he returned, as everyone assumed he would … although they were growing weary of his constant threats to quit.

On the field, in the club's second night game of the year, Cleveland edged Washington, 2–1, in front of a crowd of 12,500 spectators. Hemsley, at the moment the Tribe's only catcher, drove in the winning run. Al Smith allowed the Senators five hits and won his seventh decision against just one loss. The Yankees and Red Sox both lost, and the Tigers were rained out.

Slapnicka asked American League President Will Harridge to place Pytlak on the ineligible list on June 19. That meant Pytlak could be re-instated within a few days, if he decided to end his retirement. Had he been placed on the voluntarily retired list, as he'd requested, he couldn't be re-instated for 60 days.

Cleveland topped Washington, 4–1, at League Park on June 19 on Allen's four-hit pitching and Trosky's 15th home run, but fell into third place, percentage points behind Detroit, which took a doubleheader from Philadelphia.

The Indians, who insisted they couldn't play winning baseball for Vitt, moved into first place on June 20 with a resounding 12–1 thrashing of the Senators. Cleveland scored four times in the first inning and added seven in the fourth, allowing Feller to coast. Philadelphia beat Detroit and St. Louis won both ends of a doubleheader with Boston, placing the Tigers and Red Sox in a virtual second place tie. The Yankees, who had cooled off of late, were in fourth place, 6½ games back. The stage was set for another first place showdown between the Indians and Red Sox, this time in Cleveland.

Sportswriters from coast to coast had been lambasting the Indians for their rash demand that Bradley fire Vitt. Cobbledick took one "New York columnist," whom he declined to identify, to task for pontificating on a subject on which he was ill-informed. He refuted each of the columnist's charges in detail on June 21. Had Cobbledick, Gibbons, Lewis, McAuley and Bang chosen to defend the team against the venom spewed at it from coast to coast for the rest of the season, they'd scarcely have had time to write about anything else. The Indians would feel the full force of the national ridicule they'd brought upon themselves when their homestand ended, and they had to leave the friendly confines of Municipal Stadium and League Park.

Before that happened, however, they took on the Red Sox in a weekend series that started on Friday, June 21. Before a crowd of 12,000 in League Park, Cleveland won the first game, 7–4, with Milnar getting the victory despite allowing 10 hits. A disappointing Saturday afternoon crowd of 8,000 watched the second game, a 7–5 Tribe victory sparked by a four run fourth inning and a three run sixth, both at the expense of Jim Bagby Junior, the son of the 31-game winner who helped the Indians win the 1920 pennant and World Series. Harder started and was again shaky, allowing 10 hits in seven innings and giving way to Joe Dobson in the eighth.

The victories inspired Bradley to declare, "I don't see why we can't win the pennant." Reflecting on recent events, the team president added, "maybe things happen for the best. Doesn't seem to be a thing wrong with the boys now."[22]

With the Yankees again skidding, languishing in fourth place, 7½ games behind the pace-setting Tribe, the experts looked for reasons behind the defending world champion's baffling woes. The United Press simply studied the statistics for an explanation. In 1939, pitchers Lefty Gomez, Atley Donald, Steve Sundra and Oral Hildebrand combined for 46 of the Yankees' 106 victories, against just 16 losses. With one week left in June of 1940, the same four pitchers had won just three games while losing six. The rest of New York's pitchers hadn't been able to pick up the slack.

Cleveland's front office had scheduled most of the team's Sunday home games in mammoth Municipal Stadium, in the hope of drawing mammoth crowds. Such a crowd filed into the big ballpark on the lakefront on June 22. In the first game of a doubleheader, Smith out-pitched Lefty Grove, who'd started the season needing 14 victories to reach the coveted 300 mark for his Hall of Fame career. The Indians didn't cooperate and prevailed, 4–1. The Red Sox didn't cooperate in the nightcap and avoided a sweep of the twin bill, and the series, with a 2–0 victory which snapped the Tribe's eight game winning streak, and Boston's seven game losing streak. A pair of solo home runs by third baseman Jim Tabor off Dobson was all the offense the Red Sox could muster, and more than they needed.

Dobson turned in an admirable performance filling in for Allen, who told Vitt his arm was sore and he couldn't pitch. The split was witnessed by 56,659 fans.

The Red Sox left Cleveland trailing the Indians by 3½ games. The Yankees arrived trailing the Indians by eight.

Rain delayed, but didn't postpone, the season's third night game, at Municipal Stadium on Monday, June 24. The Indians waited longer than they might normally have to start the game because of the huge advance ticket sale. They didn't want to have to deal with 46,667 rainchecks later in the season. The large crowd cheered the Tribe to a 7–1 victory over the Yankees, the sixth time in nine meetings Cleveland had prevailed over New York. The Indians beat the Yankees only six times during the entire 1939 season. Feller picked up the win, and Vitt proved the traumatic events of the past several days hadn't robbed him of his feistiness. He was ejected in the fourth inning for arguing a call by home plate umpire Lou Kolls, who ruled Keltner had interfered with Yankee catcher Bill Dickey's attempt to throw out a baserunner attempting to steal. Vitt didn't think so, and expressed his opinion too vigorously for Kolls' liking.

Base hits hard been hard to come by for outfielder Ben Chapman during the first two months of the season, so much so that he'd reacted violently, pounding his bat on the dugout roof, and glaring and shouting at the press box, when a ball he'd hit hard which wasn't fielded cleanly was ruled an error rather than a hit by Cobbledick, the official scorer during a game earlier in the homestand. The petulant outburst earned Chapman a stern rebuke by Cobbledick in his column a few days later. Chapman's batting average was hovering around the .250 mark in late June when he decided to wear glasses. Though glasses were becoming slightly more common in baseball by 1940, most players still declined to wear them, considering it to be a sign of weakness. Chapman explained how he'd strained his eyes during the off-season.

> I refereed a lot of basketball games in the south last winter [something Boudreau had also done to pick up extra cash], and it seemed that every night I had to drive in rain or snow until two or three o'clock in the morning. My eyes were watering all the time, so I slipped off to a doctor in Fort Myers during spring training. He gave me some stuff to put in them and said it might help. The club found out about my eyes when all players had to be examined a few weeks ago, and the club doctor said the same thing. So, I decided to give glasses a try. They can't hurt my average any, the way I've

been hitting. I think I'll be back up there pretty soon. I always get straightened away in July, and if I don't, I'll just stop using them. [23]

Cobbledick had some fun with a letter he'd received from a reader in his June 25 column. He identified the reader by his initials, WCM, who brought to his attention a criticism of the Indians printed in a Washington, D.C., newspaper, with which the reader agreed. The criticism had nothing to do with the recent rebellion against Vitt. Instead, the article expressed the opinion that the owners of the Indians, the men known in Cleveland as the millionaires being real estate men by trade, weren't qualified to operate a baseball team. Baseball, according to the article, needed to be a team owner's primary business, a theory with which WCM agreed. The fact the Indians hadn't won a pennant, or even seriously contended for one, since the millionaires had purchased the club after the 1927 season, proved WCM's point. In WCM's opinion, Bradley and his fellow owners "don't know the score" as far as running a baseball team was concerned.

Cobbledick disagreed that being primarily real estate men disqualified the millionaires from owning and operating the Indians. He noted baseball's most successful team, the Yankees, were owned by Col. Jacob Ruppert, who made his fortune as a brewer of beer. The Cincinnati Reds, reigning National League champions and in first place at the moment Cobbledick's column was written, were owned by Powel Crosley Junior, whose primary business was manufacturing radios. And the Chicago Cubs, winners of four pennants (but no World Series) since the millionaires had taken over the Indians, were owned by Phil Wrigley, whose family ran the world's best known chewing gum company. In the meantime, the Athletics, owned by the Mack family, whose only business was baseball, and the Senators, owned by Clark Griffith, whose only business was baseball, were fighting it out for last place.

Back at League Park on June 26, rain threatened again, but didn't prevent the Indians from defeating the stumbling Yankees. Trosky hit a pair of home runs, one in the first inning off Monte Pearson, and one in the third off ex–Tribesman Hildebrand. The third inning blast put Cleveland back on top after New York had tied the game at three off Milnar. The elements put an end to the day's activity after five innings with the Indians ahead, 5–3.

"If the game had been called before 4½ innings had been

completed, I would have lost credit for two home runs, but I was far more interested in a Cleveland victory," said Trosky. "I would rather go hitless and have the Indians win than hit three homers in a lost cause. And I think the other fellows feel the same way about it."

After seemingly hitting their stride and clawing their way back into the pennant race, the Yankees had again hit the skids. The loss was their ninth in 12 games on their western trip, and dropped them 10 games behind the Indians. But Trosky wasn't counting them out. "I suppose the Tigers should be rated as the Indians' most dangerous opponents, but I still think the Yanks will make a belated bid for the pennant. Detroit has as much power at the plate as the Red Sox, and has much better pitching. I am also inclined to discount all this talk about the veteran Tiger infielders being certain to crack when the weather gets hot."[24]

The strategy of using lefthanded pitchers to stifle Cleveland's hitters was failing miserably. The Tribe had a record of 18–6 against southpaws.

Harder's best performance of the season wasn't enough to give the Tribe a sweep of the series. Joe DiMaggio's fourth inning single drove in a pair of runs, and the allegedly "washed up" Red Ruffing made them stand up in a 3–1 victory. Harder pitched eight innings and was charged with all three runs.

"If I hadn't lost my control in the fourth and put Frankie Crosetti and Red Rolfe on the bases, we might have pulled out a victory," Harder said. "Then I had to make another mistake by giving Joe DiMaggio a good pitch." Most pitchers who gave the Yankee Clipper a good pitch to hit paid for the mistake, and Harder did. Still, he was encouraged by his outing.

"My arm feels great, my control is improving, and I'm able to get more on my fastball, so I guess it's safe to predict that I'll pitch a complete game pretty soon. Just one out kept me from going the route this time."[25] Harder's catcher was Pytlak. Those who didn't take his retirement threat seriously and predicted he'd soon return to the Tribe knew whereof they spoke. They'd seen that routine before.

"I went fishing the first few days after I returned to Buffalo," said Pytlak of his brief retirement. "But the weather has been awful for more than a week. There wasn't anything I could do except stay around the house, and I got pretty tired of that. It rained every day. I went to the doctor for a physical examination the other day, and he told me that I had recovered from my illness. I had gained six pounds and felt so good I decided to return to the Indians."

Pytlak said his "illness" had been the result of trying to get into playing shape too quickly after holding out all through the spring and into the season. "You just can't get into shape to play in four days. I tried it and almost had a nervous breakdown. The same thing happened in 1935. I had to go home and get better." He said he appreciated Slapnicka's refusal to place him on baseball's voluntarily retired list, as Pytlak had requested.

"I never thought I would get my health back so quickly," he said. "But I guess a little home cooking and a rest was all that I needed. If Mr. Slapnicka hadn't put me on the ineligible list, I wouldn't have been able to come back."[26] And to start collecting his salary again.

The furor over the Indians' rebellion against Vitt having subsided somewhat, Cobbledick, in his June 26 column, looked back on previous efforts by players to get rid of their managers. Efforts Cobbledick believed to have been far less honest and above board than the Tribe's insurrection had been.

He claimed that in 1932, led by first baseman Bill Terry, the New York Giants simply stopped paying attention to their manager, the legendary John McGraw. McGraw gave the orders and his players ignored them, taking their orders from Terry instead. McGraw had managed the Giants since 1902, and won 10 pennants and three world's championships. He was also a notorious control freak, and the new breed of player in the sport by the early 1930s didn't respond well to McGraw's heavy-handed style. McGraw realized his players had tuned him out and resigned. He was replaced by Terry.

Cobbledick also mentioned an incident in 1925, when New York Yankees slugger Babe Ruth, whose contempt for his manager, Miller Huggins, was widely known, threatened to physically throw Huggins off the team's train on a road trip. Cobbledick claimed it took half a dozen powerful men to restrain Ruth. The press generally ignored Ruth's many foibles and didn't report them to the public, which adored the Bambino. So did the reporters. The Huggins incident couldn't be kept under wraps but, according to Cobbledick, was dismissed by the press as a boyish prank by the lovable Ruth, whom everyone knew was just an overgrown kid at heart. The incident, which could've been tragic, was just "Babe being Babe."

Why, Cobbledick asked, was Ruth forgiven for attempting

to physically assault his manager, while Feller was being brutally assailed in the national press, which called him a "swell-headed whelp," among other things, for his part in the rebellion against Vitt? Feller felt he had a legitimate grievance against Vitt, and took his complaint to the proper authority.... Bradley. Ruth, on the other hand, simply didn't like anyone who tried to assert any type of authority over him, which was part of Huggins' job. Following Huggins' death in 1929, Ruth didn't care much for his successor, Joe McCarthy, who also tried to rein in the home run king's legendary excesses.

"Maybe I'm crazy," wrote Cobbledick, "but it doesn't seem to make sense."

The Indians weren't scheduled to play an American League game on Thursday, June 27. They spent the day in Milwaukee, losing an exhibition to their American Association affiliate, 6–3. They weren't scheduled at all on June 28. They opened a three-game series in Comiskey Park against the sixth place White Sox on June 29. It would be their first game away from Cleveland since the rebellion of June 13. White Sox manager Jimmy Dykes had promised the Indians a "brutal riding" in their series against his club.

Feller easily tamed the Pale Hose in the first game, 7–3, for his 12th win of the season. If the Indians were on the receiving end of a brutal riding either from the Chicago fans, or the White Sox bench jockeys, especially Dykes, no mention was made of it in the *Plain Dealer*, the *Press*, or the *News*. The Tribe and White Sox split the Sunday doubleheader. Cleveland's offense was enough to overcome a shaky outing by Smith, who allowed four runs in six innings of the first game. The Tribe won, 7–5. Milnar held the White Sox scoreless in seven of the eight innings he pitched in the nightcap, but a three-run outburst in the fourth propelled Chicago to a 3–1 victory. Again, if the players or the paying customers gave the Cleveland Crybabies a brutal riding, nothing was written about it in the *Plain Dealer*, the *Press*, or the *News*. There was a reason.

"The anticipated barrage of abuse from the White Sox and their fans didn't materialize," reported the *Press*. "Reason was the Sox were behind most of the way. A few fans yelled 'Lollipop Kids' and 'Crybabies,' but that was about all."

The American League All-Star team's roster was announced on June 30, and the Indians would be well-represented in the contest to be played in Sportsman's Park in St. Louis on July 9. The All-Stars were selected by a vote of the managers in their respective leagues, and the American League's skippers bestowed the exalted status on Feller, Milnar, Boudreau, Mack and Hemsley.

Rookies, and thus first time All-Stars, Boudreau and Mack were surprised when informed of their selections.

"You're kidding," said Mack. No, they weren't.

"Yeah, and I've been elected president, too," said Boudreau sarcastically.

Milnar and Mack were hometown products, having gotten the Tribe's attention while performing on Cleveland's sandlots. Cobbledick had expressed the opinion that, with the Yankees scuffling, the All-Star game wouldn't amount to the Yankees versus the National League All-Stars, as it had in the past. But he was mistaken. Seven Yankees were chosen for the All-Star team.

At the conclusion of the day's activities on June 30, the American League standings looked like this:

INDIANS	42–25	.627	---
Detroit	38–25	.603	2
Boston	36–26	.581	3½
New York	32–32	.500	8½
St. Louis	31–37	.456	11½
Chicago	28–34	.452	11½
Washington	27–41	.397	15½
Philadelphia	24–38	.387	15½

Since the rebellion on June 13, the Indians had won 14 games and lost four.

Not bad for a ball club that couldn't play winning baseball for its current manager.

Bottles, Buggies and Bonnets

July opened with a short homestand.

In the fourth night game of the season at Municipal Stadium, there were 17,000 paying customers in the seats, and it felt, to the Indians, as if they'd left that many runners on base. Cleveland left 14 runners stranded in a frustrating 2–1 loss to the Browns, which cut its first place lead over Detroit to one game. With Johnny Allen again shelved by arm problems, Joe Dobson took the mound and held the visitors to seven hits. The Browns broke a scoreless tie in the sixth inning on a 330 foot home run by Harlond Clift that barely landed in the leftfield seats. Home runs which departed the playing field in cavernous Municipal Stadium could only be deposited in one of two places: directly down the leftfield or rightfield lines, where the foul lines met the stands. Clift's blast landed in the first row of the leftfield seats, inches beyond the outstretched glove of Ben Chapman. The Browns added an insurance run in the eighth, and it was necessary. The Indians scored once off Eldon Auker in the bottom of the ninth. Fittingly, they left the bases loaded.

Dobson had chances to win his own game. He struck out with the bases loaded in the second inning, struck out again with a runner on second in the fourth, and grounded out with a runner on second in the sixth. As the *Plain Dealer*'s game story pointed out, Dobson was paid to pitch, not to hit.

Some offensive help for the Tribe was on the way. Jeff Heath worked out before the game following his release after spending two weeks in a hospital.

Third baseman Ken Keltner was selected as a reserve on the American League All-Star team on July 2. In a column questioning the criteria for choosing All-Stars, Gordon Cobbledick noted that Keltner was batting .236. He'd been snubbed the year before, while batting .350 in mid-season.

The Indians left 12 more men on base in League Park in the second game of the series, allowing the Browns to break a 3–3 tie in the ninth inning on a two-run home run by pitcher Vern Kennedy off Nate Andrews. Kennedy was able to do what Dobson couldn't do the day before: he won his own game. Kennedy allowed the Indians 13 hits but went the route for the victory. Mel Harder, Allen, and Andrews allowed 10 hits to the Browns. The loss dropped the Tribe out of first place. But not for long.

Cleveland returned to the top spot on July 3, when Bob Feller polished off the feisty Browns, 5–2. Ray Mack and Hal Trosky supplied the muscle. Mack homered and Trosky slammed three doubles. Feller gave up seven hits and struck out 11. The White Sox defeated the Tigers, putting the Indians back in first place by one game. They hoped to improve on that the next day, when they'd make a quick day trip to Detroit for an Independence Day doubleheader. A few hundred Tribe fans would be in attendance, but they'd no doubt have their cheers drowned out by 56,000 Tiger rooters. Briggs Stadium was sold out.

The crowd of 57,633 was the largest in Detroit baseball history. The Tiger rooters showed their disdain for the "Crybabies" by placing baby bottles on top of the Cleveland dugout, hanging diapers around the ballpark, and wildly applauding Vitt at every opportunity. It was just the tip of the iceberg. Interestingly, the *Plain Dealer*, the *Press* and the *News* mentioned none of it in their game accounts and feature stories. The throng watched the Indians and Tigers divide their twin bill. Detroit took the opener, 5–3, taking an early four run lead against Al Smith and withstanding a late Tribe rally against Tommy Bridges. The Indians needed 11 innings to win the nightcap, 2–1. Allen got the win with an inning and third of scoreless and hitless relief after bailing Al Milnar out of a 10th inning jam. The winning run was unearned as a result of an error by Tigers second baseman Charlie Gehringer. The split kept the Indians in first place by one game.

The Indians returned to Cleveland immediately after the second game and spent a scheduled off day on July 5 at home. They'd stay at home for a brief, two-game visit from the White Sox before embarking on an eastern road trip. White Sox manager Jimmy Dykes held court with reporters as soon as the club arrived in Cleveland, and continued to dismiss the Indians as legitimate pennant contenders.

"Cleveland—bah! You can't convince me that the Indians are pennant contenders. The Yankees are dangerous, but they're going to have a hell of a time making it five in a row. The Red Sox have the power, but I have to laugh every time I think of their pitching staff. The Detroit Tigers are the team to watch. They have long range hitters, good pitching, and a fair defense. All clubs had better keep an eye on those Tigers."[1] He was right about the Tigers, Red Sox and Yankees, but wrong about the Indians. Dykes had managed the White Sox since 1934, and stayed in Chicago's dugout until 1946. He'd eventually manage both the Tigers (1959 and '60) and the Tribe (1960 and '61). It seemed like Dykes managed every major league team at some point. He managed six different teams and never won a pennant.

A Saturday afternoon crowd of 15,000 in League Park enjoyed a vintage performance by Harder on July 6. Harder kept the White Sox off the scoreboard until tiring in the ninth inning, by which time his teammates had given him a seven run lead. They also assisted him by turning four double plays behind him. Allen retired the last two White Sox batters. The Indians scored six of their runs in the fifth inning off Chicago starter Bill Dietrich and reliever Clint Brown. Dykes was tossed for too vigorously protesting one of home plate umpire Lou Kolls' decisions during Cleveland's fifth inning uprising. A *Plain Dealer* photographer caught Dykes lighting what it termed his "inevitable post-game cigar" after yet another White Sox defeat. Dykes managed the White Sox to a lot of defeats in his 12 years at the helm.

Not, however, on Sunday, July 7. A crowd of 18,813 at Municipal Stadium groaned as Ted Lyons out-pitched Feller, 3–1. Keltner's 460 foot fly ball to centerfield, which would've broken a tie and given the Indians the lead, wound up being just a long out. The White Sox executed a perfect relay and cut Keltner down at home plate, ending his bid for an inside-the-park homer.

The defeat plunged the Indians into second place at the All-Star break. Their record of 45–29 trailed Detroit by a half game, and led third place Boston by three games.

Individually, the Tribe's top batsman was Roy Weatherly, with a .322 average, three home runs and 22 runs batted in. Mack was next at .318 with seven homers and 39 runs batted in, followed by Trosky with a .302 average, 17 homers, and 49 RBI. As far as the pitching was concerned, and newspaper statistics ranked pitchers by winning percentage but didn't include earned run averages, Smith was Cleveland's top winner with an .818 percentage on nine wins and two losses. Milnar was next at 11–3 (.786) and Feller third at 13–5 (.722). The Tribe's "big three" had a combined record of 33–10. The question entering the season's second half was whether Smith and Milnar, who'd essentially emerged from out of nowhere, could continue to anchor the staff along with Feller?

A short break of two days awaited most of the Tribesmen. Mack, Lou Boudreau, Keltner, Rollie Hemsley, Feller and Milnar boarded a plane bound for St. Louis after the loss to the White Sox to join the American League's All-Star team. The Indians would re-assemble in Wilkes-Barre, Pennsylvania, for an exhibition game against their farm club on July 10, then open an eastern road trip in nearby Philadelphia on the 11th.

Five of Cleveland's six All-Stars participated in the game. None made much of an impact. Feller pitched two innings, allowing a hit and a run. Hemsley caught two innings, committing the game's only error, and fouling out in his one plate appearance. Feller, Mack and Keltner batted once, and each struck out. Boudreau played in the field but didn't come to the plate. The National League won, 4–0.

On July 8, the day before the All-Star Game, Frank Gibbons reported that Alva Bradley's investigation of the complaints against Vitt included meetings with coaches Luke Sewell, Johnny Bassler and Oscar Melillo, to discuss general conditions. He also met with Feller, Hemsley and Trosky, each of whom assured the team president that, in spite of their grievances against their manager, the players had no intention of letting down.

Gibbons wrote that Bradley had concluded his investigation of his players complaints, and there was no reason to believe any action would be taken. There was also no reason to believe there would be any further difficulties. He was correct about the former, but way off base about the latter.

Less than 24 hours after playing in the All-Star game, the six Tribesman found themselves involved in an exhibition game in Wilkes-Barre. Mack's failure to turn a double play in the 11th ... yes, an exhibition game against a minor league team went into extra innings, and Cleveland's All-Star second baseman was still in the contest ... led to a 6–5 Tribe defeat. The Indians played their regulars the entire game, except for Boudreau, who was excused after batting twice. The Indians were 0–2 against their minor league affiliates, having lost to Milwaukee earlier.

The Indians opened their eastern trip with an 8–5 victory over the Athletics in Shibe Park on July 11. Milnar, the only Indian who didn't play in the All-Star game, handled the pitching, along with Dobson. Detroit lost to Washington, giving Cleveland possession of first place by a half game.

Trosky was named team captain when the club arrived in Philadelphia. He was the first Indian to be appointed captain since 1927.

On an unseasonably cool mid–July day (the crowd was described as wearing top coats and huddled under blankets), Feller cooled off the Athletics, coming close to his second no-hitter of the year. Dick Siebert's eighth inning single was the only safety Feller allowed, and he needed to be on top of his game, because Philadelphia's Johnny Babich gave the Indians only one run. It was all they needed.

Feller showed Hemsley a blister that had formed on his right hand after the seventh inning, and the injury ... which didn't force him out of the game and wasn't considered a potential problem ... may have cost him the no-hitter. Hemsley signaled for a first pitch fastball to Siebert, figuring fastballs put less pressure on Feller's sore finger. "If I hadn't known about the blister, I never would have called for a fastball on the first pitch. Siebert always has a cut at the first ball if it's in there, and I'd have given him a breaking ball to hit."[2] Siebert shot the fastball through the right side of the infield, past Mack.

Rain washed out all the other American League contests, so the Indians picked up a half game on the Tigers.

The Indians finished a series sweep with a 6–4 victory. In doing so, they defeated Lee (Buck) Ross, who'd beaten them twice. Ross and his replacement, George Caster, weren't helped by their defense, which committed five errors. Harder and Allen pitched for the Tribe. Harder permitted just six hits, but one was a three-run home run by catcher Frank Hayes in the third inning, which put the Athletics up, 3–2. The Indians scored two in the fifth, only to have the Athletics reach Harder for another tally in the seventh. Cleveland sewed it up with one in the eighth and another in the ninth. The victory was Harder's fifth.

In his column of July 13, Cobbledick, who had written the day after the rebellion a month earlier that Vitt wasn't the right manager for the Indians since the players had no confidence in him, reversed his field and praised Bradley for not making a change under duress. The columnist said the players had every right to complain to the team president, but noted that the Indians had played well since airing their grievances, and getting their gripes off their chests.

Also on July 13, the Indians announced that five games originally scheduled for League Park would be played in Municipal Stadium instead, in anticipation of large crowds.

The Indians opened a series in Washington on July 14 with a 6–5 loss in 11 innings. Cleveland took a 5–3 lead into the ninth inning, but Smith and Dobson coughed it up, and Dobson surrendered a run in the 11th to suffer his fifth loss of the season. He had yet to win a game. The Tribe muffed a golden opportunity to put some distance between itself and the Tigers, who were swept in a doubleheader by the Athletics.

Milnar put the Indians in an early 6–0 hole in the second game of the series, giving way to Nate Andrews after just three innings. The Tribe rallied, but came up short, 8–6. Detroit topped Philadelphia and tied Cleveland for first place.

Desperate for someone to start the final game of the series against the Senators, Vitt sent Harry Eisenstat to the mound. Eisenstat was forgotten man of the pitching staff, having not worked since May 27. He didn't work long against the Senators, being sent to the showers after allowing two runs in two innings. The Indians had battered Washington starter Joe Krakauskas and reliever Alex Carrasquel for seven runs, and, entering the sixth inning, Dobson, who took over in the third, appeared to be cruising to his first victory of the season. But Washington scored seven in the sixth and added two more in the seventh. Dobson, Allen, and Bill Zuber couldn't stop the onslaught, and the Senators won, 11–8. Zuber hadn't pitched in almost as long as Eisenstat. The last time he'd been summoned to the mound by Vitt was June 4. He gave up a hit in an inning and a third. The three-game whipping in Griffith Stadium didn't hurt the Tribe in the standings, as Detroit lost again to Philadelphia. The two front-runners remained tied. Boston was 3½ games behind, and New York was 5½ back. Yankee Stadium was the next stop on the Tribe's journey through the East. So far, the rebel Indians had won three of the five games they'd played in "the house that Ruth built."

The tight pennant race got even tighter on July 17. The Indians lost a heart-breaker to the Yankees in 13 innings, 4–3, but moved back into first place when Boston beat Detroit twice. New York was breathing down the necks of the top three teams. Cleveland suffered its fourth straight defeat when, with Red Rolfe on second base, Bill Dickey cracked a line drive to centerfield. Weatherly fell down before breaking on the ball, and by the time he'd recovered, the ball had dropped, and Rolfe had scored. Both starting pitchers, Feller and New York's Monte Pearson, were still on the mound in the 13th inning. The Indians had just six hits. The Yankees had seven.

Vitt benched All-Star third baseman Keltner and replaced him with Sammy Hale. Keltner's suddenly erratic defense had contributed to the Tribe's three losses in Washington, and his bat hadn't contributed much to the offense all season. Hale was no improvement, at least defensively, making a pair of errors. He did have two of the Tribe's six hits. It was speculated that Mack might soon join Keltner on the bench. Mack's batting average had plunged 47 points in just three weeks. But Vitt didn't want to sacrifice his defense.

The losing streak was extended to five the next day. Milnar surrendered a grand slam to Buddy Rosar in the first inning, and two more runs in the second. Another error by Hale, his third in two games, didn't aid Milnar's cause in the second inning. It was followed by a home run off the bat of Rolfe. Eisenstat and Andrews, two of the lesser members of the pitching staff, took over, indicating Vitt had already determined the game was lost. It was, 9–6. The Indians fell into second place. The wheels appeared to be coming off. Was the first half of the season being exposed as merely a mirage?

While in New York, a heckler shouted "crybabies!" at some of the Cleveland players in a subway. Trosky chased the heckler, who turned and fled into the crowd.

One of the spectators in Yankee Stadium was Bradley. He hadn't come to fire Vitt, or to try to rally his suddenly inept team. "I came to New York on other business, and came to the game as a fan," Bradley said. "Naturally, I hate to see this losing streak, but I haven't any intention of talking to the players. So far as I'm concerned, we're set for the rest of the season. What will be done then, if anything, will be decided at that time."[3]

As far as bolstering the roster was concerned, the trading deadline had passed more than a month earlier. All Slapnicka had done in response to Vitt's request for more pitching had been to acquire

Andrews, a minor leaguer, for cash. The only substantive move Bradley could've made would've been to dismiss Vitt ... or, as he'd done the season before, sign him to a new contract for the coming season, to show the players who was boss. His statement indicated he wasn't going to follow either path.

Slapnicka wasn't worried about the losing streak. "I think that our top three pitchers, Bob Feller, Al Milnar and Al Smith, are insurance against a prolonged slump, and I look for a tight race with the leading teams bunched until the end of the season. Neither New York nor Boston has shown me any consistent power, that would indicate one could outdistance the field. In fact, I think a western team has the best chance for the pennant. The schedule is all in its favor. We're at home most of September. Of the 25 games in the final month of the season, I believe 17 of them are in Cleveland."

The Indians were returning to Cleveland after a two-day visit to Boston, and Slapnicka hoped they'd draw a big crowd for the first game of the homestand. "It would be a real tonic and inspiration for the players to know that the fans are with them," he said.[4]

In his July 19 column, Cobbledick wrote that the loss of star pitcher Buck Newsom to a broken thumb on his pitching hand signaled the end of the Tigers as contenders. He likened the loss of Newsom to Detroit for an extended period (speculated to be at least three weeks) to the loss to the Indians of Feller for an extended period. Cobbledick didn't think the Tigers could withstand the loss of their best pitcher. The columnist also confessed he didn't think much of any of the American League's four top clubs. He said there clearly wasn't a first class team in the American League. If there had been, the Indians wouldn't have been able to return to first place while in the midst of a four-game losing streak.

Sensing his players were downcast, Vitt called a team meeting before the final game in Yankee Stadium to deliver a pep talk. It didn't work.

The presence of Milnar and Smith hadn't prevented the Indians from being pummeled by the Yankees. Just as Milnar had done the previous day, Smith on July 20 put his teammates in a hole too deep for them to climb out of in the first inning. Smith retired only one batter ... oddly enough, it was Joe DiMaggio ... as the Yankees scored seven times, and added three more in the second, on their way to a 15–6 victory and a sweep of the three game series. So much for pep talks by beleaguered managers. The losing streak had reached six. Cleveland was in second place, 1½ games behind Detroit, and just a half game ahead of Boston. The Red Sox were eagerly anticipating the reeling Tribe's arrival in Fenway Park the next day.

The Indians took an early lead in the first game in Boston, scoring four times in the second after the Red Sox had touched Harder for a run in the first. The lead vanished as Boston scored single runs in the fourth, fifth and sixth. Cleveland scored three times in the seventh and twice in the ninth for a 9–6 win. Harder bobbed and weaved through 7⅓ innings, allowing 11 hits but earning his sixth victory. Allen pitched the final inning and two-thirds.

Pitching dominated the Sunday doubleheader that wrapped up the series in Boston, and the Tribe's eastern trip. Feller won his 15th game in the opener, when the Indians scored one in the eighth and one in the ninth for a 3–2 victory. Bob allowed five hits and struck out nine. In the second game, Dobson again didn't get much run support, but he didn't need it. He shut out the Red Sox, 2–0, on a yield of seven hits through eight innings. Rain prevented the game from being completed, and Dobson had his first victory. The Indians split their 12 game eastern swing and headed for home in second place, a game and a half behind Detroit, 3½ games ahead of Boston, and 5½ games in front of New York.

The homestand opened on July 23 with the season's fifth night game. Each team was permitted to schedule seven contests under the lights. As Slapnicka had hoped, a big crowd of 24,482 sweated out a tense 1–0 Cleveland victory. Milnar, who'd been hammered by the Yankees in his previous start, limited the Athletics to six hits, and snuffed out a ninth inning rally during which Philadelphia brought the potential winning run to the plate with two out by retiring pinch-hitter Earl Brucker on a pop foul to Hemsley. Brucker was batting for Johnny Babich, who suffered his second 1–0 loss to the Tribe in July. Babich was the victim of Feller's one-hitter on Cleveland's eastern trip. Detroit, Boston and New York all lost, enabling the Indians to gain a game on each.

The Indians received a scare before the next day's game at League Park, when Feller was hit in the face by a batted ball. "I didn't see the ball until the last second. I turned my head sharply, and the ball hit me on the neck, right under the left ear. I thought that several of my teeth had been knocked out, but with the exception of two that are chipped, I guess they're all right," he said.[5] Feller was the third Tribesman to be hit by a batted ball in 1940. Promising rookie outfielder Paul O'Dea was hit in the eye in spring training, an injury from which he never fully recovered. And Oscar Grimes was still on the mend after being struck in the face in Griffith Stadium in May. Grimes had sustained 36 separate fractures of bones in his face.

The Tribe also got a scare during the game, when the Athletics rallied from an early 7–1 deficit and chased Smith with a five-run sixth. Andrews relieved and allowed hits to the two batters he faced. Vitt summoned Eisenstat, who kept Philadelphia off the scoreboard on two hits in 3⅔ innings. The Tribe hung on, 7–6. Despite Feller's close call, Vitt said he was tempted to call on him in the ninth inning, with Eisenstat nursing a one run lead.

"I was going to send Feller to the mound if the A's got one man on," he said. "We almost blew a big lead, and I wasn't going to take any chances."[6] But Eisenstat retired the side in order.

Detroit won, maintaining its half-game lead on the Tribe. Boston and New York both lost.

The Athletics turned the tables on the Indians in the final game of the series with a 7–6 win of their own. Harder started and was ineffective, allowing seven hits and six runs in 4⅓ innings. Allen relieved and, uncharacteristically, walked the first three batters he faced. He found his control after that and held the Athletics scoreless the rest of the way, but the horse was out of the barn. Detroit won, increasing its lead to a game and a half.

Feller would have one of his chipped teeth extracted. As a result of his star pitcher's mishap, which could have derailed the Indians season, Vitt declared that infield drills, which Feller was participating in when he was struck, would no longer be held during batting practice.

Frankie Pytlak may have wished he'd stayed home in Buffalo. After going hitless in three at-bats in the loss to the Athletics, his batting average had dropped to .111, on eight hits in 72 trips to the plate. He had driven in eight runs with those eight hits. The performances of Harder, who wasn't pitching up to his usual standard, and Pytlak, who wasn't hitting his weight, proved the value of spring training ... which both players had missed, Harder due to an injury, and Pytlak due to a contract dispute. Harder could've been expected to have rounded into form by late July, but hadn't, based on his performance against Philadelphia.

July 26 was a historic day for Feller. Pitching a complete game against the Senators at League Park, he didn't issue a walk for the first time in his five-year major league career. He fanned only four and barely broke a sweat as his teammates backed his effort with 13 runs on 20 hits. Washington scored twice on eight hits.

Detroit lost to the Athletics, moving the Indians to within a half game of first place. The White Sox had managed to slip a game over the .500 mark at 43–42, meaning five of the American League's eight clubs had won more games than they'd lost as July drew to a close. The three bottom-feeders, St. Louis, Philadelphia and Washington, were a combined 50 games below the break-even mark.

In his July 27 column, Cobbledick expressed his dissatisfaction with the support Cleveland was giving its pennant-contending Indians. The Tribe wasn't enticing nearly as many patrons to League Park and Municipal Stadium as the columnist thought they should be, and many of those who paid their way in to the ballpark did so to ridicule the home team. That didn't sit well with Cobbledick, either, particularly their rough treatment of Trosky. "Year in and year out, Trosky has been just about the most valuable player on the team, no one can question his winning spirit, and his contributions to such success as the Tribe has enjoyed can't be laughed off. I'd like to see the Indians win, but not for the fans who have been booing Trosky. They don't deserve a winner."

Trosky became Cleveland's starting first baseman at age 21 in 1934, and was the club's first true power hitter of the lively ball era. A lefthanded batter, he took advantage of the short rightfield wall in League Park (290 feet away, 40 feet high) to hammer 35 homers in 1934, and set a club record of 42 in 1936. He also set the team record for runs batted in with 162 in 1936. The home run record stood until Al Rosen slammed 43 in 1953, and the RBI record stood until Manny Ramirez drove in 165 runs in 2000. In six full seasons with the Indians, Trosky had clouted 180 home runs and driven in 767 runs. He was plagued through his career with migraines that eventually forced him to retire after the 1941 season, at the age of 28. He returned during the manpower shortage created by World War II to play for the White Sox in 1944 and 1946. He didn't approach the kind of numbers he compiled with the Indians in either season.

Cobbledick didn't speculate as to whether Trosky's perceived role as one of the instigators of the June rebellion against Vitt prompted the rough reception he was getting from the paying customers. Or, for that matter, whether lingering resentment against Trosky and his teammates accounted for the lackluster attendance.

Ten thousand fans at League Park watched the Senators clobber the Tribe, 7–1, in the second game of the series. Washington's Ken Chase picked up his third win of the season against Cleveland, despite allowing the Indians seven hits in six innings. Dobson, who'd pitched an abbreviated shutout in his previous start, was disposed of quickly by the Senators, who scored four in the first inning and cruised the rest of the way. Washington had 13 hits off Dobson, Eisenstat, and Andrews. The Tribe fell two games behind the Tigers, who swept a doubleheader from the Athletics.

For the first time since becoming Cleveland's manager in 1938, Vitt wasn't able to slap groundballs at his infielders in practice before the loss to Washington. He'd somehow managed to injure his back when sneezing, and was taped up and unable to participate in fielding practice.

The Indians split their Sunday doubleheader with the Senators at Municipal Stadium, winning the opener behind a complete game from Milnar, 6–3, and losing the second as Smith continued to lack the form he'd shown consistently before the All-Star break. Washington scored three off Smith in the first inning, and the game could've ended there. Rookie Sid Hudson baffled the Tribe, while his teammates continued to pour on the offense against Harder, Dobson, Johnny Humphries and Zuber for a 9–1 victory. Detroit lost an 11 inning decision to Philadelphia, so the Indians picked up a half game in the race for first place.

Anticipating large crowds with two pennant contenders coming to town, the Indians had switched all three upcoming games against Boston, and three games against New York, to Municipal Stadium.

The Indians were idle on Monday, July 29. The Tigers weren't. They lost to the Athletics, 9–7, shaving their lead over Cleveland to a single game.

Gibbons' account of the doubleheader split with the Senators was below a headline reading INDIANS ARE RATED MOST UNPOPULAR TEAM. By whom? By Gibbons, who attempted to prove his point by writing that the crowd of 19,489 at the previous day's doubleheader against Washington at Municipal Stadium attended for the sole purpose of jeering the home team. Gibbons said it wasn't surprising the Indians got the raspberry on the road, especially in the wake of the events of mid-June, but Clevelanders seemed to delight in dumping on their team, with or without provocation from the events on the diamond. The Indians were heckled just as loudly during the first game, which they won, as the second game, which they lost. Gibbons blamed the fans discontent on the lingering residue of the rebellion against Vitt, and numerous disappointments during the 1930s from teams that promised far more than they delivered, and the fear the 1940 Indians would continue that dubious tradition.

Gibbons predicted the Tribe would draw around 750,000 fans in 1940: "that isn't potatoes, but in a pennant-winning year, it also isn't peaches."

Joe Cronin's Red Sox were on the fringe of contention when they arrived in Cleveland for a three game set. He reluctantly acknowledged what the experts had been warning of since spring training: Boston lacked the pitching to hang in the race the full season. "Failure of Mickey Harris and Wilburn Butland to make the grade was a hard blow, but both are young and will probably click the next time we bring them up," Cronin said. Old-timer Lefty Grove hadn't pitched well for much of the season as he pursued his 300th career victory, but Cronin wasn't writing him off yet. "Lefty looked good against the Browns Sunday, but I had to relieve him after the fifth inning because of the heat. If it hadn't been so hot, Grove could have gone the route and won. He had plenty of stuff."

Cronin sized up the four contenders as July neared its end. "You can't concede the flag to the Tigers, nor can you count the Yankees out of the fight. The Indians lack power at the plate. The Red Sox need pitching strength. The Yankees have pitching and power, but don't get both on the same days, while the Tigers are beginning to feel the wear and tear of battle. This race may not be decided until the last two weeks of the season. My guess is that the first team that develops a hot streak and piles up a string of victories will pull away from the field and triumph."[7]

The largest night game crowd of the year in major league baseball (of course, Cleveland had the largest stadium in major league baseball) of 49,238 watched Feller pitch the Indians to a 2–1 victory over the Red Sox in the first game. So much for Cobbledick's claim, backed up by Gibbons, Clevelanders were indifferent toward their baseball team. The much-maligned Trosky was given a rousing ovation by the assemblage. The Tribe scored single runs in the second and sixth, and Feller, who struck out eight, made them stand up. Detroit suffered its third straight loss, and the Indians were tied for first place.

"Give me one fellow.... Jeff Heath, Ken Keltner or Hal Trosky ... who will hit that ball hard and regularly, and we will walk into the pennant," Vitt pleaded after the victory.[8] If the Tribe's offense was to improve, it would have to come from within, as the trading deadline had passed six weeks earlier.

The last time Dobson faced the Red Sox, he'd shut them out for eight innings in a contest abbreviated by rain. Boston may have learned something about Dobson that day, because it routed him on the lakefront on the last day of July. The Red Sox scored four first inning runs and added two more in the third before Dobson was dismissed and replaced by Eisenstat, who gave up a run in the fourth. Unfazed by the 7–0 deficit, the Indians scored five in the fourth off Denny Galehouse. The Red Sox expanded their lead to 10–5 with three sixth inning runs, sending Eisenstat to the showers. He was replaced by Humphries, who surrendered a seventh inning run. Trailing 11–5, the Indians rallied for three in the seventh and four in the eighth. Zuber blanked the Red Sox in the eighth, and Smith pitched a scoreless ninth.

A soft single by pinch-hitter Russ Peters drove in the tying and winning runs. A rarely used reserve infielder, Peters modestly accepted congratulations from his teammates after the game, but insisted "it wasn't much of a hit."[9] His manager begged to differ.

"What do you mean? I never saw such a drive. Why, it knocked the gloves off three Red Sox fielders," said Vitt.[10] He was jokingly referring to the fact that shortstop Cronin, third baseman Jim Tabor, and leftfielder Ted Williams all heaved their gloves into the air in disgust after Peters' ball landed where no one was able to reach it.

The comeback kept the Indians tied for first place, as Detroit beat the Yankees in 11 innings.

The August issue of *Look* magazine featured an article titled CLEVELAND, GRAVEYARD OF MANAGERS. It included pictures of Keltner, Hemsley and Feller wearing baby bonnets. Gibbons wasn't impressed.

"Its message is a trifle old and not too sharp," he wrote. His boss wrote a column, too, joining Gibbons and Cobbledick in criticizing Cleveland's baseball fans for not beating down the doors to League Park and Municipal Stadium to cheer for the Indians. Whitey Lewis warned the lack of support for the Tribe could cost it the pennant.

At the end of the day on July 31, the American League standings looked like this:

INDIANS	57–38	.600	--
Detroit	57–38	.600	--
Boston	50–44	.532	6½
New York	48–44	.522	7½
Chicago	46–44	.511	8½
Washington	42–55	.433	16
Philadelphia	38–56	.404	18½
St. Louis	39–58	.402	19

The Red Sox were fading. The Yankees couldn't sustain any kind of winning momentum. No one considered the White Sox to be a legitimate dark horse contender with two months remaining in the season.

It appeared to be a two-team race between Cleveland and Detroit.

Taking Charge ... Briefly

Joe Cronin thought the team that put together a sizable winning streak and created some distance between itself and the other contenders was likely to win the American League pennant. Since neither the Indians, Tigers, Red Sox or Yankees had fashioned such a streak as of the beginning of August, the question became: were any of those clubs capable of running off a string of victories?

The Indians opened August by losing the final game of their series with Boston, 5–2, in front of 14,000 spectators in Municipal Stadium. Three seventh inning errors allowed the Red Sox to score three times and hand Mel Harder a defeat.

Harder made things difficult for himself by committing one of the errors.

"That was a hard one to take," Harder admitted. "I was faster than at any other time this season, and had plenty of confidence. My control was pretty fair, and I wasn't giving them any fat pitches even when I was in a hole. The ball that Foxx hit for a country mile was a fast pitch on the inside. It caught Jimmie flat-footed in the second inning, and he missed it by plenty in the eighth, but he certainly plastered that ball in the sixth. It only goes to prove that anything can happen in baseball. When you pitch the ball where they're swinging, you're bound to get into trouble."[1] Harder pitched the ball where Jimmie Foxx swung in the sixth inning, and the home run wiped out the Tribe's 1–0 lead.

Boston's young slugger, Ted Williams, who spent as much time studying pitchers as anyone who ever played baseball, was certain he'd been thrown an illegal pitch by Johnny Allen in the ninth inning. And he didn't like it.

"Don't try to throw another spitter," the brash second-year outfielder shouted to the cagey old veteran. "I'm watching you!"[2]

"Watch this one!" Allen responded.[3] Williams struck out on a curveball breaking down and away.

Detroit beat the Yankees and dropped Cleveland into second place, one game behind.

Righthander Mike Naymick had a major league fastball, but nothing else. And even Bob Feller wasn't talented enough to win throwing one pitch. The Indians finally farmed Naymick out to Wilkes-Barre on August 1, replacing him with Cal Dorsett, who'd compiled an impressive 8–2 record with Wilkes-Barre. Dorsett, a righthander, would pitch one inning for Cleveland in 1940.

The Yankees had feasted on Tribe pitching during their three-game sweep in late July, and the smorgasbord continued in Municipal Stadium on August 2. New York made quick work of Al Milnar, scoring two in the second and three in the third. Joe Dobson replaced Milnar, and Nate Andrews replaced Dobson, and Johnny Humphries replaced Andrews. Only Humphries escaped unscathed in his inning of work. New York banged out 13 hits and took advantage of five Cleveland errors in a 10–2 laugher. The game was hardly a defensive gem as the Yankees committed four errors themselves.

The fine art of bench jockeying was on display for the patrons. Yankee third base coach Art Fletcher tried to get under Tribe catcher Rollie Hemsley's skin by calling him a "crybaby" and a "whiskey head." Hemsley was understandably sensitive to comments about his alcoholism, from which he was recovering. Oscar Vitt, fearful that Hemsley might lose his temper and wanting to keep him in the game, asked umpire Cal Hubbard, a former professional football player (and Hall of Famer) with the Green Bay Packers, to warn Fletcher to lay off. Hubbard did, and Fletcher did.

The Red Sox out-slugged the Tigers in Detroit, keeping the Indians one game out of the league lead.

The Indians finally got a quality pitching performance against New York in the second game of the series. It was the first strong game Al Smith had pitched since before the All-Star break, and the Tribe beat the Yankees, 5–1, allowing six hits. A Ladies Day crowd of better than 15,000 watched. After the game, Smith chided those who claimed he couldn't handle the summer heat.

"I'm sorry to disappoint those writers who predicted I'd fold up in the heat, but it happens that I'm a hot weather pitcher. In the past, I've always done my best pitching in the middle of the summer, and

I see no reason to change my habits this summer," Smith said with a grin.

"Those first inning knockouts by the Yankees and Nats probably made the sportswriters think I was ready to fold up," he added. "It's a funny thing, but I never felt better in my life than when I faced the Nats last Sunday. I had everything while warming up and went into the game with all the confidence in the world. A pitcher feels like that only about once a season, and usually turns in a low-hit victory. But I couldn't get anybody out and didn't last one inning. Several other times this year I went out with misgivings and went the route without much trouble."[4] The Indians needed Smith to re-capture his early season form if they were going to stay in the pennant race.

Despite the victory, Cleveland lost ground to Detroit, which won two games from Boston.

The Indians won the final game of the series and the homestand, 3–1, on August 4 as 42,407 looked on. Feller out-pitched Red Ruffing to notch his 18th victory of the season and fourth against the defending world champions. In Gordon Cobbledick's opinion, the defeat represented the last nail in the Yankees' coffin. He declared New York's pennant chance officially dead. He was wrong.

Before departing Cleveland, Fletcher received a telegram from American League president Will Harridge, who'd been informed of the incident with Hemsley. Harridge knew as well as anyone that bench jockeying had always been a part of baseball, and some players had literally been driven from the sport by their inability to handle heckling (among them Cleveland's 1920 World Series hero "Duster" Mails), but the telegram warned Fletcher that "offensive personalities," such as Fletcher calling Hemsley a "whiskey head," crossed the line and wouldn't be tolerated.

Detroit lost to Boston, so the Tribe left for a road trip beginning the next day in Comiskey Park trailing the Tigers by a half game. The White Sox had moved ahead of the Yankees into fourth place, 8½ games out of first. It would be a rigorous trip west, thanks to postponements early in the season. Cleveland would play four games in Chicago, and six in St. Louis, in seven days, a challenging stretch for any pitching staff.

The Indians cruised to a 10–1 victory on August 5 in Chicago. Harder went the route and held the White Sox to five hits. The victory vaulted the Tribe past Detroit and into first place, as the Tigers dropped a pair to the Browns in Sportsman's Park.

Jack Doyle was a New York oddsmaker who, according to the *Plain Dealer*, had been quoting odds since Abner Doubleday threw out the first pitch at Cooperstown." Baseball had celebrated the 100th anniversary of Doubleday throwing out the first pitch the previous summer. That Doubleday wasn't anywhere near Cooperstown in the summer of 1839 ... or at any point in his life ... was conveniently ignored. Doyle had established Detroit and Cleveland as co-favorites to win the pennant, both at 6–5. However, Doyle personally believed the Tribe would win, and explained why.

Doyle called the Tribe's keystone combination of Boudreau and Mack a couple of classy kids, the important word being kids. Doyle felt Detroit's second baseman, Charlie Gehringer, and shortstop Dick Bartell, were too old to withstand the rigors of the long season. Doyle also liked Cleveland's three starting pitchers, Feller, Milnar and Smith. Boudreau, Mack, Hemsley and Weatherly gave the Indians the strength up the middle teams yearned for. Doyle didn't think the Tigers had that strength. For the record, Bartell, a refugee from the National League, was 32. Gehringer was 37, and 1940 would be the last productive season of his Hall of Fame career. Doyle set the odds on the Yankees winning the pennant at 4–1. The Cincinnati Reds, whose lead in the National League was six games over the Brooklyn Dodgers and 11 over the New York Giants, were 1–3 favorites to repeat as the senior circuit's champion.

As Doyle pointed out, Weatherly's glove in centerfield, and his performance at the plate, were crucial to the Tribe's pennant chances. It was imperative that he stay in the line-up. The man called "Stormy" had already been fined and suspended once for confrontations with umpires, and he'd been tossed out of one of the games of the doubleheader against Boston during the recently concluded homestand. That ejection prompted a telegram from Harridge, warning Weatherly's next misstep would result in an "indefinite suspension." As an inducement to be on his best behavior, even when he felt he, or his team, had been done an injustice by an umpire, Bradley offered Weatherly $500 to keep his opinions to himself. Weatherly agreed, but it remained to be seen if he could live up to that commitment during the heat of a pennant race.

Watching the Indians and Tigers trade places in the standings could've easily given a baseball fan motion sickness. On August 6, Detroit returned to the top spot with a victory over St. Louis, while the Indians split a doubleheader with the White Sox, winning the nightcap, 3–2, behind Allen's pitching, after Feller had been handed a 5–1 defeat in the opener. The first game of the twin bill marked the return to action of utility infielder Oscar Grimes, who pinch-hit and struck out. Grimes hadn't played since his near-tragic accident during infield practice in Griffith Stadium in early May.

Cleveland's sportswriters enjoyed quoting the loquacious manager of the White Sox, Jimmy Dykes, who had opinions on just about everything, and wasn't reticent about expressing them. Particularly on the subject of the clubs ahead of his in the standings. He wasn't impressed with any of them.

Before the doubleheader, as the players warmed up on the field, Dykes was overheard telling Tribe coach Luke Sewell, "the trouble with this pennant race is that it is going to be won by a lousy club."[5]

Sewell was quick to respond. "You've got a lot of nerve, calling us lousy after the going over we gave you yesterday," referring to Cleveland's 10–1 trouncing of Dykes' team.[6]

"I wasn't talking about you," Dykes assured Sewell. "I was talking about the Tigers. But if you should happen to get lucky and win, it goes double. It's a shame this league has to send a club like that into the World Series."

Dykes then spied Hal Trosky emerging from the clubhouse. "Ah, there, comrade," he said, mockingly. "How goes the revolution?"[7] The "crybabies" incident wasn't going away, just as Bradley had warned the players it wouldn't.

The Indians concluded a pleasant visit to Chicago by pounding the White Sox, 9–3, in the final game of the series. Smith picked up the victory, with relief help from Harry Eisenstat. Boudreau paced Cleveland's offense with six runs batted in. A four run Tribe outburst in the ninth inning turned a close contest into a laugher. The Tribe's pitchers helped their own cause. Smith had two hits and Eisenstat one. Detroit topped St. Louis to maintain its half-game lead. St. Louis was the second and last stop on Cleveland's western trip. A grueling six game series in four days awaited.

Though Boston had fallen 8½ games off the pace, in third place, Sewell still considered the Red Sox contenders. "If they had just one pitcher who could win three out of five starts from here in, and win 'em without help from the bullpen, they'd still be tough." Sewell added, however, "but they haven't got one."[8]

A doubleheader sweep of the Browns on August 8 would've put the Indians back in first place. Feller did his part, winning the first game, 7–4. Johnny Humphries, making his first start since 1938, pitched better than Feller, but absorbed a hard-luck 2–1 loss in the nightcap. He was bested by side-arming righthander Elden Auker who, according to Cobbledick, whose frustration at the defeat was evident in his game account, had hung around the American League the past three seasons "mainly due to his ability to beat the Indians, to whom he has been a constant puzzle throughout his career." Auker's side-arm style had puzzled every team in the league since 1933. He'd anchored Detroit's pennant winning 1934 pitching staff, and its 1935 World Series winning staff, claiming 15 and 18 victories, respectively. He won 16 games for the Browns in 1940, so he puzzled a lot of clubs besides Cleveland. In defeating Humphries, who held the Browns to four hits, Auker gave up eight safeties, including three doubles. But he was stingy with runners on base.

Detroit was idle, so the Indians trailed the Tigers by a half game. Cobbledick wrote in his August 9 column that most of the American League expected the Tribe to fold down the stretch. He didn't agree, and quoted one unidentified Tiger who also didn't believe the general consensus that Cleveland would again prove to be good, but not good enough.

"If there was any fold-up in your guys, they'd have folded long ago," said the Tiger. "We're not kidding ourselves. We look for the Cleveland club to be tough all the way. And we wish we were in as good a shape as they are for what's coming."[9]

It appeared none of the contenders was capable of achieving the lengthy winning streak Cronin felt would separate one of them from the pack. The Indians lost the third game of their series in St. Louis, 4–3, when Harder weakened after pitching six shutout innings. Walt Judnich's two-run homer tied the game in the eighth, and Bob Swift's single off Eisenstat, who'd relieved Harder in the ninth, provided the winning run. Detroit lost to the White Sox, 3–2, so the Indians lost no ground. But they didn't gain any, either, against one of the league's perennial doormats.

In his column of August 9, James E. Doyle in the *Plain Dealer* tried to make sense of the confusion that had reigned in Cleveland since the June 13 meeting in Alva Bradley's office. He noted the irony that if the Indians won the pennant, Bradley would have no choice but to re-hire Vitt. So, the players who had demanded he be dismissed were actually fighting to help him keep his job, in spite of their contempt for him. Only in Cleveland could such a convoluted situation exist. Who, Doyle asked his readers, cared to bet against the Tribe saving Vitt's job by winning the pennant?

For the first time in two months, the Indians were rained out on Saturday, August 10, when they were scheduled to play a doubleheader, one game of which was to make up a previously rained out contest. After a cool and wet spring, the Indians hadn't had a game washed out since June 10. That necessitated a twin bill the next day, and a re-scheduling of the sixth and final game of the marathon series for the Browns next visit to Cleveland. The Tribe was making its last appearance for 1940 in St. Louis, and, with the age of jet airline transportation still well in the future, the league wouldn't require the Indians to board a train on an off-day to make a one-day trip to make up one game. The make-up game would be played in Cleveland. The Indians would add two more home games to their schedule in the same manner later on.

Rain fell on Comiskey Park as well, shortening Detroit's victory in the first game of a scheduled doubleheader to five innings. The second game was postponed. The Tigers increased their lead over Cleveland to a full game.

The first game of the August 11 doubleheader featured a reunion, as Willis Hudlin, pitching for his fourth team of the season, got the start for the Browns against the team he'd spent his entire career with, until the Tribe released him in May. Since then, Hudlin had been released after brief stints with the Senators and Giants, and was being given a look-see by the Browns. It didn't last long, and neither did Hudlin against his former teammates. He retired just four batters, and allowed five runs on six hits. Milnar cruised to a 12–4 victory. The Browns won the nightcap, 7–6. What could have been a golden opportunity to gain some valuable ground in an airtight pennant race against a bottom feeder, instead proved to be a frustrating weekend filled with missed opportunities. The Indians could easily have won all three of the games they lost. Each defeat was by one run. Cleveland did manage to tie Detroit for first place, as the Tigers were swept in their doubleheader by the White Sox.

It was a pennant race nobody seemed to want to take charge of, possibly because nobody was capable of doing so. Maybe Dykes' caustic assessment of the race had been accurate. The American League pennant would be won by a lousy team, at least as far as pennant winning standards went.

A sell-out crowd of 23,720 jammed League Park (and undoubtedly left Bradley and Cy Slapnicka cursing themselves for not transferring the game to Municipal Stadium) to watch the first game of a brief two-game first place showdown between the Indians and Tigers on August 12. Cleveland made quick work of Detroit's 19-year-old southpaw sensation Hal Newhouser, while Feller was workmanlike but not spectacular. The Tribe won, 8–5, to take sole possession of the league's top spot. It was Feller's 20th victory of the season. With at least 10 starts remaining, barring injury, Feller had an outside chance at the 30 victories he'd told John Lardner he coveted during spring training.

Feller explained Detroit's three run seventh inning, during which an 8–2 game became an 8–5 game. "I knew that I was going to have trouble as soon as I started warming up," he said. "I caught a cold in my back on the train coming from St. Louis, and my neck and right shoulder were stiff. I had some heat treatments before the game, but they didn't help very much. In the first inning, I discovered that I couldn't follow through with my pitches. I thought that the shoulder would loosen up about the middle of the game, but it didn't. When I lost my control completely in the seventh, I slowed up in an effort to get the ball over the plate, and McCosky really belted one. I gave Greenberg and York everything I had, and was lucky enough to get off with only three runs scored. It's a darn good thing the boys went on a hitting spree. If they hadn't, I'd still be going after that 20th victory."[10]

The Indians took advantage of Detroit's shaky infield defense to sweep the series with a 6–5, come from behind victory in the second game, as 16,128 cheered in League Park. Eisenstat, Cleveland's fifth pitcher of the afternoon, needed just two pitches to earn the victory in relief. Ray Mack scored the game winning run on an error by Tigers rookie second baseman Dutch Meyer. Detroit wasn't able to hold a 4–1 seventh inning lead.

"I pitched only two balls and received credit for my first victory of the season. It was a long time coming, but now that I've got it, I guess I'll have to bag a few more to keep this one from becoming lonesome," Eisenstat said.[11] He also beat out an infield hit when Vitt, surprisingly, sent him to the plate in the ninth inning with Mack on first, representing the winning run. Eisenstat's single advanced Mack to second. Ben Chapman followed with the hot grounder that went through Meyer's legs and won the game for the Tribe.

Detroit manager Del Baker, smarting from two straight losses, hoped his club could stay close to the leader until reinforcements arrived. "It's just a matter of hanging on now until our cripples get back," he said. "Gehringer? I figure it'll be 10 days or two weeks before he is back. Birdie Tebbetts has a bad finger. Buck Newsom can't grip a ball right. But if we can hang around until those men are ready again, we'll be in this thing up to our necks right up to the last day."[12] They could, and they were.

Vitt, who had begged for his sluggers to start slugging two weeks earlier, was impressed with what his club did offensively. "They looked as if they really meant it out there. Heath today? Well, maybe. From the way he hit Sunday in St. Louis, he ought to be all right. Bell or Heath, off their last games, it's a toss-up which to use. Brother, did we turn on the power."[13] Vitt's pre-occupation with power, which his team lacked, bothered his players, who eventually decided to do something about it.

The Tigers left Cleveland trailing by two games. The Red Sox and Yankees, quickly becoming afterthoughts, were 7½ and nine games behind, respectively. The White Sox were between the Red Sox and Yankees, trailing by 8½ lengths.

The White Sox provided the opposition for the season's next night game at Municipal Stadium, and a throng of 59,086 watched Smith twirl a one-hitter as the Tribe maintained its two-game lead over Detroit with a 4−0 victory. Skeeter Webb's third inning bloop single was Chicago's only safety.

"Chalk it up to control," Smith said of his masterpiece. "I hit the corners repeatedly and never gave them a good ball to hit."[14]

A story in a Detroit newspaper, printed the day after the Tigers departed Cleveland, claimed Vitt would resign at the end of the season. That came as news to the Tribe's manager.

"Who wrote that story?" he asked. "What paper was it in? I don't know the paper or the reporter. I wouldn't know him if he walked up to me now. I didn't even talk to, or see, any Detroit reporters when the Tigers were here Monday and Tuesday. So, if there's a story around that I've made any plans for this fall, it's a lot of baloney. I'm trying to give everything that I have to this ball club. The boys are all hustling, as you'll notice every time we play. They want to win the pennant. They think they're good enough to win. We've got what it takes to beat the Tigers and anyone else. What I'll do this fall, or any fall, is too far away to even consider."[15]

Whitey Lewis, whose byline accompanied the story about the Detroit newspaper article, added "observers close to the Indians have failed to detect any signs of internal rumblings since that notorious Black Friday [actually a Thursday] when a dozen players asked Bradley to replace Vitt. Whether relations between Vitt and his players could ever be restored to a basis of permanent peace remains to be determined." Those "close observers" weren't observing closely enough.

In his August 15 column, Cobbledick claimed Sewell and Bradley had a recent conversation during which Sewell said he wouldn't be interested in managing the club in the future, no matter how lucrative the contract offer might be. Sewell said he didn't want to possibly be tainted by the stigma of the rebellion against Vitt, when the players asked that he replace the embattled manager. The players preference for Sewell didn't appear to have caused any friction or ill feelings between the two men. Sewell would be plucked from the Tribe's coaching staff to manage the Browns early in the 1941 season.

Before the second game of the brief two-game series, Dykes was asked how many victories would be required to win the pennant. "It'll take 93 victories, but it's hard to believe punk clubs like the Indians or Tigers could win that many." He also dismissed Boston, New York, and his own club as contenders. "It's strictly a two club fight from now on. We got started too late, the Red Sox are staggering around, and the Yankees might as well go home and pray they'll get contracts next season."[16] Dykes was right about the Indians and Tigers being unable to reach 93 victories. Neither club did.

The Indians finished a sweep of the White Sox with a 5–4 victory in League Park. Allen relieved Milnar with the score tied in the seventh, and picked up the victory when the Tribe broke the tie in the eighth. Detroit beat St. Louis to stay two games behind, and the Yankees lost to Boston to fall 10 games back. The Indians were still looking over their shoulders at the defending world's champions. And with good reason.

The pesky Browns followed the White Sox into Cleveland and

continued to pester the Indians in a weekend series that began on August 16. Auker's side-arm deliveries posed no problem for the Tribe in front of a Ladies Day crowd of 12,000 in League Park. He allowed six runs in seven innings, and Cleveland added two more against the St. Louis bullpen in the eighth. Feller allowed single runs in the first two innings but posted an 8–3 win, his 21st of the year. It was also the Tribe's 21st victory in its last 30 games. Playing .700 ball for a month had given Cleveland a three-game lead in the standings, as Detroit lost to the White Sox.

Feller explained his early problem with the Browns. "I've had trouble with my curve in my last three starts," he said. "It either breaks outside, or seems to hang in the air. I seemed to have more stuff in the late innings."[17] The hanging curveball is the bane of every pitcher's existence.

Harder was the hard luck loser in the second game. The veteran righthander held the visitors to a pair of runs, but his teammates couldn't figure out Johnny Niggeling's knuckleball and lost, 2–1. No ground was lost in the standings, as the White Sox handled the Tigers for the second straight day.

As of August 16, the Indians had received 3,000 applications for World Series tickets. So much for fan apathy.

A Sunday doubleheader crowd of 44,686 in Municipal Stadium didn't get its money's worth. The first game was tied, 2–2, after nine innings. The Browns hit the Tribe with a four spot in the top of the 10th, but rain descended on downtown Cleveland and didn't let up. The game was called before the Tribe could bat in the 10th, thus reverting to the score at the end of regulation, and the second game was postponed. The Browns would have to return to Cleveland on what had been open dates on both club's schedules in early September to make up the washed out twin bill. The fans were out of luck. Their rain checks wouldn't be honored because a legal, five inning game had been played. The second game was inconsequential.

Smith carried a 2–1 lead into the top of the ninth, but faltered. "We should have won in nine innings," he moaned. "The Browns wouldn't have won if I hadn't passed [third baseman Harlond] Clift. That was one spot in which I needed good control and didn't have it."[18]

The Indians gained a half game on the Tigers, who lost again to Chicago. They headed for Boston to open the last eastern swing of the year with a 3½ game lead.

The last time Joe Dobson pitched in Fenway Park, he'd picked up his first victory of the season, shutting out the Red Sox in a contest shortened to eight innings by rain. The results were different when Dobson took the mound on Monday, August 19, with a 1–0 lead. Boston pounded Dobson for six runs in 2⅓ innings and kept on pounding his replacement, Humphries, for nine more runs in 4⅔ innings. The Red Sox put the game out of reach early, and Vitt saw no reason to waste the rest of his bullpen in a lost cause. In the eighth inning, trailing 15–7, Vitt sent rookie Cal Dorsett to the mound to mop up. Dorsett allowed a home run to Red Sox second baseman Bobby Doerr, then retired the next three batters. In spite of a gaudy minor league record compiled at Wilkes-Barre, it was Dorsett's only appearance of the season.

The *Plain Dealer* reported Bradley watched the game from a box seat. The newspaper said it was the team president's was first trip ever to watch his team play. Bradley had been team president since 1928. He reportedly managed to smile throughout the entire game, despite the pounding his team was absorbing.

The humbling loss cost Cleveland a half game in the standings, as the Tigers and Yankees were idled by rain.

The Indians appeared headed for another drubbing in the second game of the series, and it looked as if Feller would lose again to his "jinx pitcher," Boston's Jack Wilson. An otherwise non-descript righthander with a record of 68–72 for his nine year career, Wilson had a knack for beating Feller. He'd won his last three decisions against Cleveland's ace, and was well on his way to making it four, leading 5–1 after six innings. The Indians scored once in the seventh, then drove Wilson from the mound with a seven run flurry in the eighth that included a grand slam home run from Ken Keltner. Cleveland added two more runs in the ninth for an 11–6 victory. Feller notched his 22nd win, despite allowing 10 hits and five runs in seven innings. He credited the victory to Keltner's bat.

Said the Tribe third baseman of his slam, "at first I thought the ball wouldn't be high enough to clear the fence, but I knew that it was a base hit. Gee, I was tickled when I saw it disappear. You can't build up too big a lead against these Red Sox."[19]

Keltner's jubilant teammates got a little carried away in the post-game celebration of his blast.

"That drive won the pennant!" declared one unidentified Tribesman.[20]

"No other club has had this big a lead since the season opened," said another.[21]

"They can't catch us now!" said a third.[22]

The come from behind victory, coupled with Detroit's loss to New York, extended the Tribe's lead to 4½ games. It was the largest lead any team had enjoyed so far in 1940. But Keltner's drive didn't win the pennant. They … as in the Tigers … could, and would, catch the Tribe. And pass it.

The *Plain Dealer* revealed that Vitt had been thrilled by the large crowds at League Park and Municipal Stadium during the last homestand. Vitt had an attendance clause in his contract, and he received a tiny percentage from each ticket sold once a specific number had been reached. The number had been reached, and exceeded, so Vitt would make money every time the Indians played at home for the rest of the season. The newspaper said Vitt's salary for 1940 was thought to be $15,000.

The Indians experienced a "miraculous" victory in Fenway Park to close out the series with the Red Sox. That was the term used by Harder, who won a 4–2 decision despite being in trouble throughout.

"Just one anxious moment after another," he said, describing the nerve-wracking game. "When a team gets 14 hits off you in Fenway Park, you're lucky to win. And when you hold a team to two runs, it's a miracle. With six Red Sox hitters aiming at that short leftfield wall, you have to have plenty on each ball. One bad pitch with a couple of runners on the bases, and there goes your ballgame. Boudreau and Mack pulled me out of two tough holes, one in the fifth inning, and again in the ninth. If it hadn't been for those sweet plays, I probably wouldn't have been around for the finish."[23]

Harder's manager wasn't around for the finish. Sewell had told Bradley he would never manage the Indians, but he was forced to when Vitt was chased by home plate umpire George Moriarty for arguing balls and strikes in the fifth inning. "You haven't done anything right all year," the umpire reportedly told Vitt while administering the old heave-ho.[24] Sewell ran the Indians for the final four innings.

In New York, the next stop on Cleveland's trip, the Yankees finished a three-game sweep of the Tigers, increasing the Tribe's lead to 5½ games. The lead would get no bigger. The season had reached its high point.

The *Plain Dealer* deemed the Tribe's eastern trip so important, it sent feature writer Eugene J. Whitney along with Cobbledick to report on it. Following the series in Boston, Whitney crunched the numbers to determine how many games the other contenders would have to win to wrest the pennant from the Indians, if they only played .500 ball the rest of the way. Whitney's assumption was the Tribe would do better than that. Cleveland had 37 games remaining, and if it only won 19 and lost 18, it would wind up with a mark of 90–64. To top that, Detroit would have to win 25 of its 36 remaining games. Boston would have to win 28 of its remaining 38 games, and the Yankees, who had a whopping 43 games to play, would have to win a whopping 33 of them. No mention was made of the White Sox, who had 41 games on the schedule and would have to win 32 to reach 91 victories.

The 1940 American League pennant was Cleveland's to lose.

When last the Indians invaded Yankee Stadium, their hosts romped to three resounding victories. The Yankees made it four routs in a row over the Tribe on August 22, scoring eight unearned runs in the second inning and pouring it on for a 15–2 triumph. A double play that Milnar failed to turn led to the eight unearned second inning runs. Not wanting to waste his bullpen in a game beyond salvaging, Vitt turned to little-used Bill Zuber, who pitched six innings. He blanked New York in five of those innings. The Yankees scored four times in the other. Zuber tried to maintain a sense of humor about the thrashing.

"Gee, did you ever see a guy have such a batting slump?" he inquired. "My average went down 667 points today. I've been leading the team all season with 1.000 per cent, and now look at my average."[25] Zuber had been a perfect one for one at the plate. He batted twice against New York's Marius Russo and didn't get a hit.

There was nothing funny about a second inning incident that led to both benches emptying. Former Yankee player Earle Combs, then a coach, had been on Milnar's case all season. His verbal abuse went too far, and Milnar appeared to be ready to retaliate physically. Both benches emptied, and Sewell grabbed Milnar to prevent him from punching Combs.

"Milnar had been taking a rough riding from Combs and was boiling mad," explained the Tribe coach. "I had a hard time holding Al. I think he would have pushed me aside if I hadn't reminded him that he would draw a long suspension and be lost to the team if he threw a punch."[26]

Milnar admitted he'd been pushed to the limit by a season's worth of ribbing from Combs. "I can take a riding from coaches, but there are certain things a guy can't take. Combs has been riding me all season, but I let him get away with it because he didn't get personal. But, he can't call me dirty names and expect to get away with it."[27] According to Tribe players, Combs called Milnar a yellow belly with no guts. That was more than Milnar could stand.

The Yankees, players and coaches alike, were a frustrated bunch. They weren't accustomed to being in fifth place in late August, which was where they'd been just days before the Tribe arrived. They'd moved past the White Sox and Red Sox, and shaved two games off their first place deficit, following their victory over Cleveland. The loss reduced the Tribe's lead over Detroit to 4½ games.

> "All we need is one victory in this series to cool off the Yankees," said Vitt. That would put them eight behind us when we leave here, and they would have to step plenty fast to catch us. But don't get the idea we'll be satisfied with one victory in three games. Al Smith has had an extra day of rest, and should give them a sweet battle tomorrow. Then we'll have Bob Feller going for us on Saturday.
>
> This was the third time in our last three games here that the Yankees have knocked us out of a ballgame before we could get started. Our last trip here, they piled up a lot of runs in the early innings of two straight games. That can't go on forever, and I expect it to end tomorrow if Smitty has good control.[28]

Bradley, after watching the Indians get steamrolled by the Red Sox in the first game of the trip, had been summoned back to Cleveland by a death in the family. He re-joined the team in New York, and watched it get steamrolled by the Yankees. The two beatings he'd witnessed personally probably hadn't done much for his health, or his disposition.

Just as the *Plain Dealer* had deemed the Indians' eastern trip important enough to send a second reporter to assist Cobbledick, so did the *Press* send a second reporter to help Frank Gibbons. That second reporter was Whitey Lewis, the paper's sports editor, whose column from New York carried the headline VITT AND PLAYERS FEUD STILL SMOULDERS on August 23.

Lewis opened his column by recalling the day in late June that the players signed a document withdrawing all their grievances against their manager "for the good of the ball club." He declared that document not to be worth the paper it was written on. Despite the Tribe's rise to first place, Lewis claimed relations between Vitt and his players hadn't changed. He said Cleveland's players were convinced they could win the pennant in spite of their contentious relationship with their manager. Those players, wrote Lewis, believed the fans had supported Vitt because they didn't truly grasp the full significance of their resentment of the manager. Lewis anointed the Indians the most amazing, interesting and intriguing team in baseball history.

For a change, the Indians weren't blown out of Yankee Stadium early, but Smith wasn't at his best, and the Tribe fell, 5–3. Detroit was rained out, so the Tribe lost only a half game of its lead.

The Indians and Yankees continued "trash talking" during pre-game warm-ups. Art Fletcher announced, loud enough for most of the Tribesman on the field to hear, "attention! The great choke up ballclub is ready to take its annual dive. You better plan on spending second or third place money, because you haven't a chance to win the flag."[29]

Veteran shortstop Frank Crosetti took a potshot at Feller. Noting that the Tribe ace hadn't been sharp in his previous starts but was bailed out by the bats, Crosetti verbally jabbed, "what a lucky stiff you are. You get your ears pinned back and still get victories. But wait until tomorrow. That's one defeat you won't be able to duck."[30]

The New York press reported friction between volatile outfielder Heath and Vitt had resulted in Heath's suspension. In an incident that wasn't reported in Cleveland's newspapers the previous week, Heath, who'd had his problems with Vitt in the past, engaged in a shouting match with his manager after striking out as a pinch-hitter. Vitt warned Heath his temper wouldn't be excused any longer. According to the *Plain Dealer* on August 24, Slapnicka, who wasn't Vitt's biggest booster and may have relished the chance to show up the manager, stepped in and restored peace. All parties involved denied the story in New York's papers, insisting Heath hadn't been suspended. He was ordered to apologize for the temper tantrum and did so. The matter was considered closed. Heath clouted a two-run homer in the loss.

The Indians had to be satisfied with no victories over the Yankees, their second consecutive sweep in Yankee Stadium. Feller held the Yanks hitless for 7⅓ innings, but the Tribe had scored only twice, and New York rallied for a 3–2 victory. The Tigers split a doubleheader, and Cleveland's lead was reduced to three.

Part of the problem in Yankee Stadium, other than the home team was suddenly on a roll, was that the Indians may have been way too full of themselves. According to the *Plain Dealer*, the players had partied hard on the train from Boston to New York, "portable radios blared, as the Tribesmen sang, danced, gave strikingly funny imitations of rival players at bat and in the field, and told humorous stories of their days in the minors." Apparently, the players truly believed, as one unidentified player had declared, "they can't catch us now!"

The atmosphere on the train from New York to Washington was much different. The players, while remaining outwardly confident, passed the time playing cards, sleeping, or meditating over the three-game tail-kicking they'd just received. Vitt said the three-game nosedive in New York hadn't done much damage, and reminded everyone of the club's last eastern trip. "After taking three in a row from the A's, we ran into a string of six straight setbacks in Washington and New York, and we still had to play the dangerous Red Sox. We took the Sox to camp and wound up with six triumphs and six setbacks for a .500 average. On this trip, we took on the tough teams first and still have five games left with second division clubs in which to make up some of the ground we lost."[31]

Said Allen of Cleveland's pratfall the last time it played in Griffith Stadium, "if we repeat that performance, we don't deserve to be in first place."[32]

And maybe they didn't. The lowly Senators handed the Indians their fourth straight loss on August 25, and, ironically, Allen was largely responsible for it. Washington scored four times off the Tribe's veteran righthander in the first inning and made them stand up for a 5–4 victory. He explained his first inning difficulties.

"[Centerfielder George] Case whacked a slider for a double, and [right fielder Buddy] Lewis was hit with a curve that broke too late. I couldn't get the ball over to [third baseman Cecil] Travis and walked him. Then I got in a hole on [second baseman Buddy] Myer and made a pitch a little too good. Another pass and a single finished a great day for me."[33] Eisenstat and Zuber relieved and held the Senators to a run in 7⅓ frames.

Amid the losing streak, Vitt was confronted while dining in a

Washington restaurant with questions regarding the latest report of his imminent resignation. "They'll have to fire me," he responded. "My conscience is as clear as a baby's. All this is the result of a misunderstanding, and the wrong kind of advice for players easily misled. Other places and people could be investigated, too."

Possibly alluding to Lewis' column, Vitt added that "I still don't believe there is the hate on this team certain people would like to make out. A few of the players have got the wrong viewpoint. I hope we can win. But even if we don't, I won't quit."[34]

Bradley, who had accompanied the Tribe on a portion of its trip through the east, was asked about reports Vitt wouldn't last the season. "This is the first time I've heard of the rumors," he said. "I can't understand how they originated. There will be no changes made until after the World Series, and I don't know what will happen then."

Continued the team president, "yes, I still have plenty of confidence in the entire team. It's going to be a great race right down to the finish. The fans have been asking for a tight battle for several years, and they're going to get one."[35]

Washington manager Bucky Harris felt the Indians and Tigers should be favored for the pennant, but counseled against dismissing the Yankees. "Five and a half games are a lot to make up in five weeks, but the Yankees will be dangerous right to the end, unless they blow up on their last western trip. The Tigers appear to be out of their slump, while any team with the Indians' pitching staff always is hard to beat. It'll be a great finish, with the pennant probably going to the team that wins most of the games in those last two Indians-Tigers series."[36] Five and a half games may have been a lot to make up in five weeks, but the Tigers had made up three games in just four days. Detroit beat Philadelphia to move within 2½ games of Cleveland. The Yankees, given up for dead not long before, were suddenly only 5½ games out. That was the deficit Harris referred to.

The Indians snapped their losing streak the next day with a 4–3 victory. Feller came out of the bullpen to save the win for Harder. The Senators loaded the bases in the bottom of the ninth, but couldn't push a run across. Feller figured to do a significant amount of relief pitching during the last month of the season.

"Pitching put us on top, and I guess it's up to the pitchers to keep us there," said Vitt. "We haven't been making many runs, so we have to get good pitching to win games. Harder admitted that he was getting tired as early as the fourth inning, and I told Milnar to get ready. When Mel pulled through the sixth, Feller told me he felt strong enough to go three innings even though he had only one day of rest. We had some anxious moments in the ninth, but Bob pulled us through. He said he was willing to work out of turn for the balance of the season, and so did the other boys."

"The Indians want to win that pennant," Vitt continued, "and believe our chances will be enhanced if our regular pitchers also work in relief roles. Feller, Smith, Milnar, Allen and Harder have all agreed to pitch as often as necessary, so we will be in a position to roll down the stretch with the best pitching in the league."[37] Whether overworked starters would be as effective in relief as rested relievers remained to be seen.

New York and Detroit were idle, so the Indians gained a half game on each. They led the Tigers by three and the Yankees by six.

Connie Mack weighed in on the Tribe's chance of winning the pennant, in spite of its recent travails. Mack said the probability of a Cleveland pennant was "a little better than 100% right now. Of course, the Indians haven't cinched the title yet, but they have quite a lead, and it looks pretty good for them. They would have to go into an awful slump to lose at this stage. The Indians pitching is strong, and should hold them up there. Add to that, they have an all-round good club."[38]

In his column of August 27, Cobbledick read the Tigers their last rites as pennant contenders. "The Tigers? Well, maybe I'm wrong, but I believe you can forget about them." He was wrong.

Cleveland and Detroit were idle on August 28. The Indians weren't scheduled. The Tigers were supposed to play two in Philadelphia, but the weatherman had other ideas. The Yankees beat the White Sox to pick up a half game on the Tribe. The Indians opened their final eastern series of the season in Shibe Park the next day. It rained in Philadelphia on August 29, wiping out the game and requiring a doubleheader the next day. The Tigers and Yankees were idle.

The Indians announced on August 29 that the twin bill versus St. Louis, washed out during the previous homestand, would be made up on off days in the season's final week. The Browns would visit Cleveland between series against Detroit. Due to a strange bit of scheduling, the Indians had four days off between those series.

Games against the Browns would now fill two of those dates, for which Vitt was grateful.

"Those last two series with Detroit may decide the pennant, and it doesn't do a team any good to sit around four days," said the manager. "There's too much danger of a letdown that late in the season, and the layoff wouldn't do the players batting eyes any good. Those two games with the Browns will keep us on edge for the Detroit series."[39]

With September around the corner, rosters would expand, and the Indians would summon eight minor leaguers to Cleveland as soon as their seasons ended. They were Mike Naymick, who'd spent much of the season with the Tribe before being farmed out; Don Pulford, who'd impressed in spring training and posted a record of 7–12 at Wilkes-Barre; Millard Howell, a righthanded pitcher who won 12 and lost 10 for Wilkes-Barre; Pete Center, a righthanded pitcher considered an excellent prospect by the front office for 1941 despite an 8–11 record for Wilkes-Barre; Ken Jungels, who, like Naymick, spent much of the season with the Tribe before being demoted to Milwaukee, where he won five and lost eight; Paul Calvert, who posted a 5–3 record with Cedar Rapids of the Three-I League; shortstop Lou Rongino, who batted .250 for St. Paul, and Jim Hegan, the young catcher whose defensive skills were ready for the majors, but whose bat wasn't. Hegan had been sent to Oklahoma City to be taught how to hit by the great Rogers Hornsby. Hegan batted .275. Only Naymick and Howell would see any action in September. Trying to win a pennant was a job for seasoned veterans.

While rain fell on Shibe Park, Athletics manager Mack offered his current assessment of the American League pennant race, of which his club had ceased to be a part long ago. "Cleveland ought to be a great ballclub, and probably would be if the players worked together. But under the existing conditions, I suppose there isn't that harmony you usually find in a winner." Though the Indians were in first place, the black cloud of dissension that had hung over the club since mid–June hadn't lifted, and wouldn't. Mack was impressed with Detroit.

"You must admire and respect a team that refuses to quit. The Tigers have never given up. For that reason, I now feel Detroit has a good chance to lick Cleveland."[40] Mack's opinion of the Indians had changed drastically in a matter of days.

The rain licked both teams in Philadelphia. The entire three-game series was washed out. Some of the players ventured to Shibe Park to work out, only to find large puddles in the infield and outfield and flooded dugouts. Joked Pytlak, "If it hadn't been so chilly, I would have gone for a swim in the lagoon on the third base line."[41] The games would be made up in Cleveland when the Athletics visited in September. Meanwhile, the Tigers swept a doubleheader from Washington, and the Yankees took a pair from the Browns. Detroit was three games behind, and New York trailed by 4½.

Thanks to the weather, the Indians would play 81 games at home rather than 77. The September schedule called for 23 home games and just seven on the road. Between League Park and Municipal Stadium, the Indians had won 38 and lost 20. Away from Cleveland, the Tribe was 34–30.

The Indians hadn't experienced much trouble with the White Sox, and that trend continued when they opened a series against Chicago in Comiskey Park on August 30. A night game crowd of 44,877 watched Feller pitch the Tribe to a 4–2 victory. Heath's three-run home run off lefthander Thornton Lee paced the offense.

"About the only hits I'm getting are home runs, but I guess that one was worth five hits with the bases empty. And a home run against a southpaw is worth two against a righthander, especially where I'm concerned. That Lee has always been tough for me, and I was tickled to death to get a homer off him," Heath said.[42]

The Tigers were idle. Rain continued along the east coast, and the Yankees were rained out.

The Indians brought the curtain down on the month of August with a 12 inning, 5–4 victory in the second game of the series. Pytlak's hit produced what proved to be the winning run in the top of the 12th, and his defensive play in the bottom of the frame saved the game. With one out and Mike Kreevich on third base, Moose Solters hit a fly ball to medium deep centerfield. Weatherly's throw arrived at the plate on one hop, and was slightly up the third base line. Pytlak grabbed it and held on to the ball while making the tag on the sliding Kreevich to complete the game-ending double play.

"I wasn't going to drop that ball no matter how hard he hit me," said Pytlak. "I thought Kreevich would try to kick the ball out of my hand, so I let my glove slip off and gripped the ball with both hands. He really hit me, but I was prepared for him. Weatherly made a swell throw, or I never could have caught him. The throw had to be good, and it was."[43]

Allen got the win, his eighth, but declined to accept any congratulations. "Don't get excited about me, boys. All I did was throw balls over the plate. Give the credit to Roy and Frankie. That Pytlak not only won the game, he saved it."[44]

Pytlak's game-winning hit was only his 11th of the season, in 94 at-bats, for an average of .117. His 11 hits had driven in 10 runs, however.

The Tigers wrapped up August with a victory over St. Louis, and the Yankees polished off Washington. It was New York's 18th victory in its last 21 games, and no one was asking what was wrong with the Yankees anymore. But had they been too far behind when they began their late-season pennant push?

On the morning of the first day of the last month of the season, the American League standings showed:

INDIANS	74–50	.597	--
Detroit	72–53	.576	2½
New York	68–54	.557	5
Boston	69–58	.543	6½
Chicago	63–60	.512	10½
Washington	52–71	.423	21½
St. Louis	51–76	.402	24½
Philadelphia	46–73	.387	25½

With the exception of two three-game trips to Detroit, the Indians would spend the entire month of September at home. They'd play the team they had to beat, the Tigers, nine times, providing plenty of opportunity to eliminate their chief rival. The path to the second pennant in club history seemed to be clear.

Floyd Who?

The Indians opened September by completing a sweep of the White Sox. Al Milnar was kayoed early, exiting in the third inning on the short end of a 4–1 score. Joe Dobson relieved and held the White Sox scoreless while his teammates chipped away at Chicago's 39-year-old veteran, Ted Lyons. Cleveland scored twice in the fourth, a single run in the eighth, and three in the ninth for a 7–4 victory, which Dobson got credit for. As he'd promised to do, Oscar Vitt summoned Bob Feller to pitch the ninth. Vitt said he wouldn't hesitate to use his starters in relief if necessary, and he meant it.

With just one day gone in the last month of the campaign, the Indians had only six road games remaining. All were in Detroit.

The Yankees swept a doubleheader from Washington, and the Tigers were pounded by the Browns in St. Louis. Cleveland's lead was 3½ games. After beating up the Tigers, the Browns boarded a train for a one-day visit to Cleveland. They'd provide the opposition for the Tribe's Labor Day doubleheader.

A Municipal Stadium crowd of 52,419 looked forward to enjoying a doubleheader sweep. And a doubleheader sweep was what they got. Not, however, by the home team. The "world's worst pitching staff," in the opinion of Gordon Cobbledick, handed the Indians a double defeat, taking the opener, 2–1, and the nightcap, 3–0. Vern Kennedy pitched the Browns to victory in the first game, at the expense of Mel Harder, who suffered the defeat due to a rare error by shortstop Lou Boudreau. In the second game, Cleveland's old nemesis, Eldon Auker, twirled a complete game shutout. He was matched pitch for pitch by Johnny Allen until the ninth inning, when St. Louis pushed across three runs to finish the sweep.

Despite dropping two games in one day, the Indians lost no ground to the Tigers. After dropping three straight to the Tribe, the

White Sox took a pair from Detroit, limiting the Tigers to a single run in 18 innings. But the Indians did lose ground to the Yankees, who split their doubleheader with Washington. Every club played doubleheaders on holidays in that era. New York had moved into second place by percentage points. The Tigers and Yankees were 3½ games back of the Indians.

The Indians and Yankees were idle on September 3. The Tigers lost again to the White Sox, pushing them four games back. The Tribe opened a first-place showdown in Briggs Stadium the next day.

While in Chicago, Cobbledick had encountered Clint Brown, who'd pitched for the Indians from 1928 to 1935, and was then in the employ of the White Sox. Cobbledick asked Brown for his assessment of the pennant race. Brown said the Tribe needn't be concerned about the Yankees.

"If you've got to worry about somebody, worry about the Tigers. You've got nine games to play with them. If they should happen to beat you six or seven times, they'd be tough. But not the Yankees. They've only got two games left with you. If you split the two, you beat 'em out. Even if they win both, you probably beat 'em out, because they're going to have trouble all through the west, while you're playing at home."[1] Brown thought five victories in Cleveland's nine encounters with Detroit would secure the pennant. The Indians didn't get any victories in their visit to Briggs Stadium early in September.

After scoring just three runs while being swept in three games by the White Sox, the Tigers pounded Feller for 11 hits and seven runs in seven innings of the series opener. The Indians couldn't handle Hal Newhouser, and Detroit had cut its deficit to three games with a 7–2 victory. Making matters worse, Hal Trosky pulled a muscle running the bases in the fourth inning. He stayed in the game briefly, but was eventually replaced by Oscar Grimes.

"It's a swell time to be out of the line-up," said Trosky. "I always hit pretty well in this ballpark, and got off to a good start today, and then had to pull up lame. But, perhaps I will be able to get back in there in a day or two."[2]

Vitt thought his star first baseman was being overly optimistic. "All I can say now is that Trosky will be out for an indefinite period. You don't get over an injury of that kind in a day."[3]

Trosky's absence was felt immediately. In the seventh inning, when the Tigers put the game out of reach, Grimes dropped Boudreau's throw from second base on what would've been an inning-ending double play. Charlie Gehringer followed with a three-run homer.

Feller had pitched in three of Cleveland's past six games. Realizing he may have overworked his ace, Vitt announced Feller wouldn't pitch again until the Yankees came to town the following week.

The Yankees opened a road trip with a loss to the Senators, allowing Detroit to move back into second place. New York was third, 3½ games behind.

Detroit's suddenly invigorated offense was on full display in the second game of the series. The Indians led, 3–2, through five innings. Detroit wiped out that deficit with three sixth inning runs, and three seventh inning runs, off Al Smith. Dobson took over in the eighth and coughed up three more runs. The Tigers won, 11–3. The post-game jubilation in the Detroit clubhouse was similar to the jubilation in Cleveland's clubhouse after the Indians had wiped out the Red Sox and stretched their lead to 5½ games on August 21.

"We blasted their pennant hopes today," said one unidentified Tiger in what was described by the *Plain Dealer* as "a hilarious clubhouse scene."

The player added, "tomorrow, we'll make them glad to finish third."[4]

The Indians hadn't looked like pennant winners at any point during their previous four games, all defeats. With the Yankees taking a doubleheader from Washington, Cleveland's lead over New York and Detroit had been reduced to two games. The players sensed the season slipping away from them, and they knew who to blame for it. Again.

After the drubbing in Briggs Stadium, the players met to discuss what they were going to do about the manager they had no confidence in. They gathered in the team hotel, with the session attended by "all but two or three players," according to initial reports. That number would be revised to closer to 15. Vitt wasn't invited to, or aware of, the meeting, for an obvious reason. The previous strategy employed by the players ... demanding team president and co-owner Alva Bradley fire Vitt ... hadn't worked. A new approach was needed. The players, over the final weeks of a promising season that was rapidly spiraling out of control, would take matters into their own hands. If they didn't like Vitt's strategy ... and they often didn't ... they'd simply ignore it, and call the shots themselves. The purpose of the not-so-secret meeting (details of which were in the next day's newspapers) was to determine how.

"If we have to do it, we'll give the orders to ourselves," said one unidentified player.

> We're out to do only one thing, and that's win the pennant. We think we can do it, but not with the kind of ball we've been playing. At our best, we're not a power hitting ballclub, and with Hal Trosky out of commission for a while, this is all the more true. Being the kind of club we are, we're just beating ourselves when we try to play the old army game of slugging.
>
> We've decided we must go for one or two runs at a time, and this means that we can't overlook any chances to advance baserunners. That's what we talked about tonight. Ways and means of getting one or two runs across the plate without leaving so many men on the bases. We're going home tomorrow to play the rest of our games in the stadium, and in that park we simply have to reconcile ourselves to the fact we aren't going to score runs in bunches. [5]

Said one unidentified player of the brazen plot to defy its beleaguered manager, "we'll follow our plan whether he likes it or not."[6] The contempt in which most of Cleveland's players held their manager was put on display for everyone to see.

Despite such comments from his (unidentified) teammates, Trosky insisted the Indians weren't playing the role of Fletcher Christian versus Vitt's Captain Bligh. "I got there late, but I was at the meeting," he said. "There were about a dozen of us, and at no time did I hear any discussion of a mutiny against Vitt, or of disregarding his signals." Trosky was asked if he'd abided by all the signals he received from his manager, and would continue to do so.

"I certainly would," he answered. "I've never done anything else, no matter who was manager of the ball club."[7] Trosky had played for Peckinpaugh, Johnson, and O'Neill in addition to Vitt. If Trosky was being truthful about obeying all orders from his manager, there was plenty of evidence to indicate he was in the minority.

In his account of the meeting, McAuley wrote, "the action of the players involved [and McAuley went out of his way to indicate Feller wasn't among them] came as a complete surprise, even to the closest observers of the nationally notorious 'Vitt situation.' It is known that few, if any, of the insurrectionists had changed their attitude toward Vitt since the first outbreak, but it was believed they had resigned themselves to let matters stand until the end of the season."

In an opinion column the same day, McAuley unloaded on Bradley with both barrels. He said the players meeting was the direct result of Bradley's pathetic attempt at compromise and made him a tragic figure among baseball's club owners. It left him with a clubhouse full of malcontents, and a manager reduced to spending the rest of the season walking on eggshells.

In McAuley's opinion, Bradley had two options following the meeting in his office on June 13. He could've fired Vitt, or backed him to the hilt. Instead, he chose a middle ground, trying to please everybody, which ultimately satisfied no one and led directly to the meeting in Detroit, which he termed the sorriest mess baseball had encountered since the notorious "Black Sox" scandal of 1919. McAuley said the players were correct when they claimed to have had no leadership since the middle of June. McAuley wrote that following the rebellion, Vitt tried to save his job by cozying up to the players who hated him. They saw right through the charade, and their contempt for their embattled manager only intensified. McAuley said Vitt was terrified one of his players would run to management with a new complaint against him, and that Bradley would've lent a sympathetic ear.

McAuley said Vitt became so frightened of his players that he tolerated their often open defiance of his orders. He cited an instance of an unidentified pitcher who, when told by Vitt he was to start that day, declined because he simply didn't feel like it. Vitt didn't push the issue. McAuley also mentioned the case of Heath, who ignored the "take" sign Vitt had flashed to coach Luke Sewell on a three-and-oh pitch and popped out. He intimated it wasn't the first sign Vitt's players had ignored since the middle of June. He said it was merely a continuation of a policy the players had adopted weeks before, secure in the knowledge, based on comments from Bradley in meetings between the rebels and the club president, that Vitt wouldn't return in 1941. Since their manager's fate had already been decided, the rebels saw no reason not to undermine his authority, and assert their own, for the rest of the campaign.

McAuley wrapped up his scathing column by wondering if Bradley wished he could turn the clock back to that fateful Thursday morning in June and handle the matter differently.

According to the *Plain Dealer*, the incident that inspired the players to hold another anti–Vitt session occurred in the eighth inning of the second game of the Labor Day doubleheader against the Browns. Neither club had scored. With Frankie Pytlak on third, Vitt ordered Ben Chapman to bunt. But Vitt ordered the safety squeeze, in which the runner holds third base until he's certain the ball is on the ground. The players felt Vitt should've called for a suicide squeeze, with the runner breaking for home plate as the pitch is delivered. They felt the extra steps gained with a suicide squeeze would've made the difference between Pytlak scoring, which he didn't, and being thrown out, which he was. Vitt wasn't a proponent of the suicide squeeze. His players were.

In a nutshell, the players believed Vitt was managing the pop-gun Tribe as if it was the power-packed Yankees. Aside from Trosky and Ken Keltner, the Indians had no consistent power threats. And hitting home runs in spacious Municipal Stadium was nearly impossible. Vitt's strategy wasn't working.

Bradley, undoubtedly tiring of the whole mess, declined comment after being informed that his ball club was once again conspiring against its manager. Or, perhaps more accurately, continuing to conspire against its manager. But only briefly. The press, and the public, demanded a reaction from the team president, and it got one. After a quick investigation of the meeting in Detroit, Bradley issued a short statement claiming, "as best [Bradley] could find out, the meeting held by the players was a pep meeting, and that the players, manager Vitt, and I have but one thing in mind, and that is to win the pennant for Cleveland."[8]

Vitt pretended to be undisturbed by the latest incursion into his authority. "Let them have as many meetings as they want as long as we win some ball games," he said.[9]

Cobbledick chose to downplay the latest uprising in his column of September 6. He called team harmony one of sport's over-rated commodities, and said timely hitting and clutch pitching were more important than players getting along with each other ... or with their manager. He then mentioned the notorious Chicago "Black Sox" of 1919. But there was a difference between the Indians and the other clubs torn by disharmony. The White Sox had no quarrel with their manager, Kid Gleason. Their beef was with their penurious owner, Charles Comiskey, and it led to eight players selling out to gamblers in the World Series. The Indians weren't fighting among themselves. They were nearly unanimous in their dislike for, and their lack of confidence in, their manager. They believed in June that they could win the pennant, but not for Vitt. They still believed it in September. Bradley hadn't removed Vitt, so the players would, to the fullest extent possible.

Frank Gibbons, whose inclination had been to be sympathetic toward the players throughout the whole affair, changed his tune after the meeting in Detroit. Calling the players treatment of Vitt shabby and unfair, he wrote, "if Vitt is a rotten manager, the vague efforts of 15 or so leaderless players aren't going to improve the situation."

Gibbons noted that the Detroit meeting was the fourth such gathering held by the players without Vitt, either with Bradley or among themselves. Gibbons expressed the opinion that the proper way of handling the delicate situation would have been to invite Vitt to attend the meeting with Bradley on June 13, to allow him the opportunity to address the grievances against him directly, in the presence of the team president. Having spoken with Trosky about the meeting before it took place, Gibbons said he assumed inviting Vitt was an option he the players had simply never considered. He criticized the players for failing to inform Vitt of the meeting in Detroit and asking him to attend, an invitation the columnist said he was sure Vitt would've accepted, considering he'd been bending over backwards since mid-June to accommodate his players in any way possible. Gibbons said Vitt deserved the chance to answer the charges against him ... a chance his players declined to give him. Instead, the players met to plan the tactics they'd use for the rest of the season to run the team as they saw fit, ignoring the manager when necessary.

Gibbons characterized Vitt's insistence on hanging on to the bitter end as grim, hopeless, and pathetic. Why he didn't resign was, and still is, a mystery. Gibbons took the players to task for what he saw as their vindictiveness. He considered conducting the "secret" meeting in Detroit, then brazenly bringing it to Vitt's attention, as nothing more than an effort to get even with the manager for past indignities. He believed the knowledge Vitt wouldn't return in 1941 should've been sufficient balm for the players' hurt feelings. Gibbons said an unidentified player confided to him that his teammates needed to "purge themselves of the Vitt hate."[10] The player admitted he didn't know if, or how, they could.

Vitt, probably numb after almost three months of constant turmoil, claimed that "I think I have this thing licked now. We're still in first place, and we're going to win in spite of everything."[11]

Detroit completed its three-game demolition of the American League's first place team with a 10–5 victory on September 6. The Tribe took a 3–1 lead against Buck Newsom after three innings. The Tigers wiped that out with three fourth inning runs and four fifth inning tallies, pinning the loss on Allen. Cleveland's pitching had allowed 28 runs in the sweep, to a team that had scored three runs in its previous three games. Washington beat New York. The Yankees were two games behind, the Tigers just one.

When the Indians returned to Cleveland following the debacle in Briggs Stadium, Bradley tried to calm the waters by issuing a statement declaring his unconditional support for Vitt. "I have assured Oscar Vitt that he has my full cooperation as manager of the club, and any action he takes will have my full support," the statement read.[12] It also said Bradley believed the Indians could win the pennant.

Vitt surprised many by not resigning in June. He stuck to his guns again after the latest uprising. "I'm working for Mr. Bradley. I'll continue to work for him until he tells me he doesn't want me."[13]

One action Vitt considered taking, but didn't, as pointed out by McAuley, was a fine for Heath, when Heath took a hack at a 3-and-0 pitch after being given a "take" sign in the 11–3 loss to the Tigers. He said he would've fined the outfielder $250 for disregarding an order had the circumstances been different. It was presumed Vitt meant he would've levied a fine had the game been close. McAuley's column assigned an entirely different meaning to Vitt's decision not to dock Heath for insubordination.

In his September 7 column, Cobbledick described the suddenly floundering Indians as a ship missing a rudder, a plane minus a pilot, an army in need of a commander. He said the Tribe needed a leader, and needed one desperately, but none was to be found. He dismissed Bradley's statement that his embattled, beleaguered manager had his full support. Vitt was the Indians manager in name only. The players were calling most, if not all, of the shots. Who knew how long that had been going on? Cobbledick didn't think Vitt had the backbone to assume command of the clubhouse once again, with or without Bradley's full support, if such a thing could possibly be accomplished.

He was also astonished by how brazen the mutineers were. They did at least try to keep their June meeting with Bradley a secret ... although Trosky had discussed the plan with Gibbons ahead of time. The revolt, at that point, was still in the planning stages. They didn't meet with the press afterward to provide details of what was talked about in Bradley's office. The unidentified player who spilled the beans to Cobbledick about the players only meeting in a Detroit hotel room surely knew Cobbledick would print the information, and Vitt would read it in the next day's newspaper. From all indications, that was precisely what the players wanted. Cobbledick admitted as much. He said he'd stopped at Vitt's table in the hotel dining room to chat when he was told by a waitress that a gentleman wanted to see him. The gentlemen was a Cleveland player,

> who invited me to sit down and there unfolded for me, in full view of the manager's table, the story of the meeting, which had disbanded just a few minutes earlier.
>
> He knew the information would be printed, and he knew Vitt would know, almost to a certainty, the identity of my informant. And he didn't care.

In the meantime, there were on-field developments. Allen had suffered a strain to his right arm making a throw to first base in the loss to the Tigers. "The injury isn't serious, but I didn't want to take any chances. So, I removed Johnny at the close of the inning. We're going to need him the next three weeks," said Vitt.

The Indians were also going to need Trosky, but weren't likely to have him available anytime soon. "I don't think there's a chance of Hal getting back in the line-up for at least five days," Vitt said. "Heat treatments have failed to help much."[14]

The losing streak reached six on September 7. Cleveland's favorite patsies, the White Sox, won for only the fifth time in 20 match-ups with the Indians, 5–4. Chicago knocked out Mel Harder with four runs in the fourth inning. Former Indian Clint Brown pitched 2⅓ scoreless innings to preserve the victory. The Tribe's lead of 5½ games had been wiped out in less than three weeks. The Tigers and Yankees both won, so Cleveland and Detroit were tied for first place. Technically, the Indians led by a percentage point. New York, the club Brown had counseled his former team not to be concerned about, was one game behind.

The Indians suffered another blow when Weatherly pulled a

muscle. "Weatherly definitely won't play for the next two days and may be out for an even longer period," said Vitt. "It's a tough break, but there's nothing we can do about it."[15] Trosky would be out at least two more days, so the Indians would finish the series with Chicago minus two of their .300 hitters. Trosky was batting .314, and Weatherly .308. Boudreau was the other .300 hitter at .302 ... unless pitchers are counted. Bill Zuber, Harry Eisenstat and Al Smith were all hitting better than .300 in limited at-bats.

White Sox manager Jimmy Dykes didn't miss a chance to gloat over a rare victory over the Tribe. "We were overdue to take the Indians," he said. "The law of averages should give us a sweep of the series. Cleveland hasn't any right to beat us 15 times in 20 starts."

As for the pennant race, Dykes said, "our club and the Red Sox are a little too far behind. But the Tigers, Indians and New York should stage a merry battle right down to the wire. If the Indians and Tigers grab a wonderful opportunity, they can derail the Yankees and then fight it out themselves."[16] The Yankees would visit Detroit and Cleveland during their last western trip of the season. They'd be in Cleveland for two games after the White Sox left. For the moment, however, the Indians just needed to beat somebody. Anybody. And they did the next day.

The Indians beat the White Sox, 5–4, in 10 innings to break the losing streak at a half dozen games. Despite his promise not to use Feller until the series against the Yankees, Vitt summoned him to relieve Al Milnar, who allowed four runs in eight innings. Feller pitched two scoreless frames, and won his 24th game when the Tribe pushed across a run in the 10th. The heavy workload was beginning to take a toll on Bob.

"If my arm stiffens up, I may ask for an extra day's rest," he said. "If it doesn't, I expect to open the series."[17]

Milnar failed again to win his 16th game, and he was becoming frustrated. "One bad pitch to Moose Solters upset the cart," he moaned. "That relief job in Detroit and a long warm up the next day got my arm in good shape and improved my control, but I still couldn't go the route."[18] Milnar hadn't won since beating the Browns in Sportsman's Park on August 11.

Cleveland's winning streak was brief. The White Sox squeezed out a 2–1 victory in the rubber game of the series and the final match-up between the two clubs for the season. The loss, the Tribe's seventh in eight games and 10th in 15 contests, dropped it into second place behind the Tigers, and only a half game ahead of the Yankees, who were on deck.

The Indians won the season series from the White Sox, 16–6.

The Tribe and Yankees were rained out on September 11. The Tigers lost a 13 inning decision to the Red Sox, 6–5. The Tribe was back in first place by one percentage point, with New York half a game behind.

Weatherly pronounced himself fit and ready for combat against the Yankees. "I took a light workout at the park, and my leg wasn't a bit stiff," he reported. "The bruise on my hip hasn't healed, but that doesn't bother me. I may not be quite as fast as usual, but I expect to play both games."[19] Hope that Trosky would be ready to return to first base by the time the Yankees came to town had faded, but he would be able to pinch-hit.

"With Weatherly back in centerfield and Trosky available for pinch-hitting duties, we will be in pretty fair shape for the Yankees," proclaimed Vitt. "We need as much power as we can crowd into the line-up."[20]

The Indians and Yankees split a damp doubleheader, with New York winning the first game at Feller's expense, 3–1, and Cleveland taking the nightcap, 5–3, in a contest delayed by rain and ultimately called due to darkness ... a seemingly odd decision since Municipal Stadium was equipped with lights. Smith got the win in the second game. Some of the 33,471 in attendance treated the visitors to some atypical Cleveland hospitality in the first game, showering the Yankees with apples, oranges, lemons, tomatoes and eggs. New York manager Joe McCarthy pulled his club off the field and demanded the umpires ask the ushers to find, and eject, the miscreants. The umpires refused. What inspired the barrage wasn't explained.

"The way the fans acted was disgraceful," spluttered an understandably agitated McCarthy. "The police should have confiscated the vegetables and evicted the throwers."[21] When it was suggested by a local sportswriter the behavior was caused by the bench-jockeying the Yankees had been directing toward the Indians all season, and that McCarthy's irritation indicated his team could dish it out but couldn't take it, he had the clubhouse cleared of reporters.

Detroit beat Boston and re-claimed first place by a half game. New York was one game behind. Much had been made of the Indians' favorable September schedule. The Tigers' schedule was equally favorable. As of September 12, the Indians had 16 home games remaining and only three on the road. The Tigers had 15 games at home and only five on the road. The Yankees, conversely, had but five remaining home games and 15 on the road. The Indians and Yankees were finished for the year. New York won 12 of the 22 games. Despite dropping the season series, it was Cleveland's best showing against the Yankees in nine years.

Harder was a mystery throughout the 1940 season. On occasion, he looked like the dean of Cleveland's pitching staff, and the guy who'd won at least 15 games per season since 1932. More often, however, he looked like an old pitcher (although he was only 30) whose right arm had logged 2,390⅓ innings since 1928, and was showing the wear and tear of being the staff workhorse for better than a decade. Fortunately for the Indians, the Harder of his prime was on the job on September 12, pitching Cleveland to an easy 8–1 victory over the Red Sox in Municipal Stadium. He kept Boston off the scoreboard until the ninth and allowed just three hits. Cobbledick called it Harder's best game in two seasons.

"I wasn't as fast as I was in the Labor Day game against the St. Louis Browns," Harder explained. "But I had good control, and my curve was dipping over the corners. In many of my starts this year, my curve seemed to hang in the air over the plate, and it wasn't difficult for the batters to wait for it to break and then sock it. During the seasons when I won 20 games, I pulled out of jams with a sharp-breaking hook. But this season, except in a few instances, I just didn't have it."[22] Harder was a 20-game winner in 1934, and won 22 games in 1935.

No one was more encouraged by Harder's performance than Cy Slapnicka. "With Harder to add to the pitching we know we can get from Bob Feller, Al Milnar and Al Smith, and with the team coming to life at bat, we may have easy sailing to the pennant," he enthused. "It wasn't only the fact that Harder allowed the Red Sox only three hits. It was the way he handled the batters. He was the master of the hitters all the way."

Slapnicka was excited about more than the thought of Harder returning to form in the season's final weeks. "I'm happy about the way they snapped out if it in the second game of the Yankee doubleheader, and yesterday. This club won't crack. The Yanks might, as they indicated in Detroit yesterday, but not the Indians. I wouldn't be surprised if the Yanks weren't out of the race when they leave St. Louis, their last western opponent." Slapnicka then took a shot at the resurgent defending world's champions. "The Yankees said they didn't like our tactics Wednesday. Well, we just gave them a little bit of their own stuff. We showed them that if they wanted to play baseball that way, we could, too. The pennant might be decided in our last six games with Detroit, and then again, it might not. I'm happy enough tonight to believe that we might have a lead by that time to give us plenty of insurance for that series."[23]

The Indians plated eight runs against the Red Sox without Trosky or Rollie Hemsley in the line-up. "Trosky's injured leg has almost healed," said Vitt. "There's always a risk of sending Trosky back too soon and having him hurt his leg again, especially with the field in its present soggy condition. Hemsley has been spiked and battered all season and deserved a rest. With the team fighting hard for every run and not getting many of them, I was anxious to get Trosky back in condition to play. That five run outburst against the Yankees, and the seven run inning against Boston, changed everything. I didn't want to break up a winning combination."[24]

Managers never do.

Slapnicka's suggestion that the Yankees might crack referred to Detroit's come from behind victory in the first game of a three-game series in Briggs Stadium. The Tigers win kept the Indians a half game behind them. The Yanks slipped two games back.

Informed that Detroit had scored four times in the eighth inning to pull out the victory, Ben Chapman said, "I hope the Tigers take three straight," even though three Detroit wins would make Cleveland's task of overtaking them that much more difficult. The Indians knew the Yankees were just as much a threat to their pennant hopes as the Tigers. And, as Weatherly pointed out, the Indians were done with New York. They weren't done with Detroit.

"If the Tigers knock off the Yanks, we will get a chance to pull them down in the six games we will play with them," the Tribe's centerfielder said. Then he added words that proved to be prophetic. "If Detroit's in front and we can't beat them, we don't deserve to win the flag."[25]

The Indians achieved a victory over the Red Sox the next day in a game that was as difficult as the previous day's had been easy. For the second consecutive game, a Tribe pitcher limited the powerful Bosox to three hits. Milnar pitched a shutout, and he had to in order to win. Boston's Jim Bagby Junior, the son of one of Cleveland's many 1920 World Series champions heroes, held the Tribe to just two hits. Both came in the fourth inning. The game's only run scored on a double play ball off the bat of Boudreau.

Milnar took care of the heart of Boston's batting order in the ninth inning, including Ted Williams and Jimmie Foxx. "A home run by either Foxx or Williams would have beaten me," he admitted. "I suppose some of the boys were worried, but I had plenty of confidence. I can't remember when I had better control. I was so sure of myself that I threw curves with the count 3-and-2 on the batter. I not only hooked them when I was in a hole, but I broke curves over the plate. Williams was caught flat-footed by a hook in the fourth, and Foxx took one for a strike in the seventh."[26]

Bradley spent two days in Chicago, meeting with Commissioner Kenesaw Mountain Landis and representatives of the Yankees, Tigers, Red Sox, White Sox, Cincinnati Reds, and Brooklyn Dodgers, to make preparations for the upcoming World Series. If the Indians won the pennant, the World Series would open in the National League pennant winner's ballpark. The first game in Cleveland would be played on October 4. There was little doubt as to who'd win the National League pennant. The Reds held an 8½ game lead on the Dodgers with 19 games to play. Brooklyn had only 16 games remaining. Surprisingly, there wasn't much talk of an all–Ohio World Series in Cleveland's newspapers, as there had been in 1920, when such a possibility existed until the Reds faded down the stretch.

The Red Sox won the final game of the series, and the final game of the season between the two clubs, 6–1. Allen blanked Boston through five innings, then was driven from the mound by a six-run sixth inning barrage. The Indians couldn't figure out Earl Johnson, a 21-year-old lefthander who'd been a senior pitching for St. Mary's College in Moraga, California, in 1939. Johnson held the Tribe to four hits. Cleveland coughed up a golden opportunity to re-claim first place, as the Tigers were blasted by the Yankees, 16–7. The Indians stayed a half game behind, and the Yankees were two games in arrears.

"I certainly gave a great exhibition of how baseball shouldn't be pitched," groaned Allen.[27] His performance was symbolic of the

Tribe's pitching woes throughout the season. Milnar, Smith, even Feller were brilliant in one outing and miserable in the next. Sometimes, as in this case, brilliant for several innings, then running into a brick wall.

Vitt lamented the lack of consistent offense. Cleveland had scored all of its runs in the 5–3 win over New York in one inning, and seven of its eight runs in the 8–1 trouncing of Boston in one inning. To shake things up, Vitt decided to temporarily bench Chapman for the upcoming series with Philadelphia, and replace him with Heath. "We've only made six hits in our last two games, and we have to get some punch. I've decided to give Chappie a few days rest, and Heath will play both games, even if Connie Mack sends a pair of southpaws at us."

Then, the manager did some quick math. "The Indians made four hits, which was twice as many as they got on Friday, so perhaps we'll get eight in the opener, and 16 in the second game. I'll gladly settle for eight a game, provided we get them in the right spots."

Vitt expected the cellar dwelling Athletics to arrive in a sour mood. "Those A's are going to be in a battling mood after dropping five straight, but we should take them if our pitchers get a little batting support. If we are going to jump ahead of the Tigers and increase our margin over the Yankees, we will have to do it during the series with the Mackmen."[28]

The Indians said farewell to the Red Sox having won 14 of the 22 games played between the clubs. Had they fared that well against some of the weaker clubs ... such as the Athletics ... they'd have cruised to the pennant.

Cleveland took care of business in front of 26,039 spectators in Municipal Stadium on Sunday, September 15, sweeping the stumbling Athletics, 5–0 and 8–5. Feller toyed with the visitors in the first game, giving up just two hits. The Tribe had to come from behind to win the second game. Smith didn't have a strong outing, allowing four runs and seven hits in five innings. Dobson got the victory despite allowing the Athletics to take a 5–4 lead in the seventh inning because his teammates responded with a three-run rally, then added an insurance tally in the eighth. Vitt again called on one of his starters to save the contest, and Milnar kept the visitors off the board in the eighth and ninth.

"It would have been nice to hold them hitless, but I'm satisfied with a two-hitter," said Feller. "I've pitched four one-hit games already, so I guess I'll hang up a few two-hitters. My control was just about perfect. It was only the second game I have ever pitched without giving a base on balls. You don't have to work half as hard when you have good control, and I wasn't a bit tired after the game. It probably will be a long time before I face only 28 batters in a game again."[29]

According to Vitt, all his starting pitchers had volunteered to double as relievers down the stretch. Milnar, however, sounded as if he was tiring of being available in the bullpen every day. "I've been clamoring for plenty of work, and now I'm getting it," he said after saving Dobson's victory ... although saves didn't exist in 1940. "That 1–0 game with the Red Sox took plenty out of my arm, however, and I'll gladly pass up any more relief appearances between my next two starts."[30]

Heath said there was no clubhouse celebration following the sweep. The Indians had done what a contender is supposed to do: defeat an also-ran. The players may have learned their lesson following their party on the train from Boston to New York after increasing their lead to 5½ games on August 21. They were promptly swept in Yankee Stadium, and their seemingly commanding lead was soon gone.

"We'll save our demonstrations until after we clinch the pennant," Heath explained.[31]

It was an eventful day for the Tribe. Detroit lost to Washington and New York dropped a pair to St. Louis. The Indians were back in first place, leading the Tigers by a game and the Yankees by three. It was the largest lead the Indians would enjoy for the rest of the season.

The Tribe was also given permission by Commissioner Landis' office to print World Series tickets. Games three, four and, if necessary, five would be played in Municipal Stadium if Cleveland won the pennant. Eighty-one thousand tickets would be printed for each game. Tickets for most box seats were priced at $6.85; some boxes and all reserved seats were $5.65; general admission tickets sold for $3.45; and bleacher seats cost $1.15. Printing 243,000 tickets would prove to be a lot of work for nothing.

National sports columnist Joe Williams wrote an article in mid–September speculating the Indians would hire Rogers Hornsby as their manager for 1941. Hornsby, one of the game's greatest players, had managed the St. Louis Cardinals to the 1926 National League pennant, and a startling seven game upset of the Yankees in the World Series. He'd served as interim manager of the Boston Braves in 1928; managed the Chicago Cubs from late in 1930 until late in 1932; and the Browns from midway through the 1933 season until the middle of 1937. Williams also criticized Bradley for agreeing to meet with the mutinous players back in June. But allowing them to air their grievances was the way Bradley and his brother, Chuck, had always done business.

"I've been in business all my life," he said. "Baseball is only one of my activities. From the start, my brother and I decided to be as close to our employees as we possibly could. We decided there would never be a time when one of our employees could not come to us with a grievance."[32] The players were Bradley's employees, and his door was always open to them.

The Indians met the Athletics in another doubleheader in Municipal Stadium the next day and split. Harder was perfect through six innings in the opener, and had a shutout through eight, leading the Tribe to an 8–3 victory. Johnny Babich pitched Philadelphia to a 3–2 win in the nightcap. Babich's victory was the Athletics' first in 10 games.

Babich loved pitching in Municipal Stadium's vast expanse. "It's beautiful," he said. "If there is such a thing as a pitcher's paradise, this is it. Gee, how I would like to pitch here all season. Every time I got in a jam, I'd toss one down the middle, and let the outfielders get on their horses."

Babich was pleased to end the Athletics' losing streak, and a season's worth of personal frustration at the hands of the Indians. "It's about time I beat those guys. Before today, I held them to six runs in three games and lost every time. Bob Feller whipped me, 1–0. Al Milnar beat me by the same score, then Milnar did it again, 4–3. The Indians pitchers have been poison for the A's every time I was on the mound, and it's about time my luck changed."[33]

Harder was at a loss to explain how Philadelphia's offense suddenly came to life in the ninth inning of the first game. "I allow four hits in 17 innings, and all of a sudden, the A's rap me for five in a row. It certainly has me puzzled. I didn't get tired. The only possible explanation is that I must have unconsciously eased up. I was taking plenty of time before each pitch in the first eight innings, but I worked fast in the ninth. I wanted to get the game over in a hurry. It's a good thing that I had a big lead."[34] Harder worked so deliberately through the first eight innings that the game took an hour and 47 minutes to play.

Detroit defeated Washington, and the Browns obliterated the Yankees, 16–4. The Tigers trailed the Tribe by a half game. New York had slipped four games behind, and led the fourth-place White Sox by just a half game. Cobbledick pronounced the Yankees out of the pennant race.

An overworked Milnar allowed the Athletics nine hits and four runs in 6⅓ innings of the final game of the series, and Philadelphia won, 4–3. Milnar wasn't hit hard, but the balls the Athletics hit kept finding holes.

"It was a new experience for me," he said. "In my other starts this season, I either was pretty good or got hit hard. After they popped a few hits over the infield, I learned how Smith must feel. Al is nicked for more bloopers than any other pitcher in the league."[35]

Before boarding their train for the next stop on their western tour, several Athletics players were asked their opinion of the team from which they'd won two of five games. The consensus was that while the Indians weren't hitting, they had a strong defense and good pitching. Philadelphia coach Earle Mack, son of manager Connie, sensed something was missing.

"We're in last place, and the Tribe has an even chance to grab the pennant, but our kid infielder Larry Davis has more pepper than the whole Cleveland team," was Mack's assessment of what he'd just seen.[36]

Detroit beat Washington, and New York, a day after being obliterated by St. Louis, returned the favor, clobbering the Browns, 9–0. The Tigers led the Indians by a half game, and the Yankees by 3½. For Cleveland, winning three of five from the last-place team, which came to town on a seven-game losing streak, just wasn't good enough.

Pitching paced the Indians to a doubleheader sweep of the Senators on September 18. The wildly inconsistent Allen won the opener, 3–1, and Feller prevailed in the nightcap, 2–1, assisted by a home run and a diving, bare-handed catch in centerfield by Weatherly.

"I probably could have caught the ball in my glove, but I was afraid that it would bounce out," said Weatherly of the catch. "That has happened several times this season, and I wasn't going to take the chance. When I stuck out my hand, the little finger dug into the ground, but I had a good grip on the ball."

A sore pinky finger didn't stop Weatherly from depositing a pitch from Sid Hudson in the rightfield seats in the sixth inning. "The finger is a little painful, but it can't be more than a slight sprain," he said. "When a pitch comes down your alley, it takes more than a swollen finger to keep you from riding the ball."[37] Weatherly added a seventh inning single that should have scored Feller from second base but didn't. The exertion did, in Bob's opinion, cost him a shutout. He was working on just two days rest.

"I began to tire in the first of the seventh, and that run didn't help matters. It was the last out of the inning, and I didn't get a chance to rest. If I hadn't broken my stride by almost missing third base, I would have beaten the throw to home plate," he said.[38] He allowed a run in the eighth inning, but had enough in the tank to keep the Senators scoreless in the ninth.

The twin win moved the Indians back into first place by a half game, as the Tigers played an odd doubleheader with the Athletics. Detroit won the first game, 14–0, and carried a 6–4 lead into the ninth inning of the nightcap. Philadelphia exploded for nine runs in the ninth and won, 13–6. The Yankees split two games with the White Sox and trailed by four. Chicago trailed by five.

Despite scoring just eight runs in three games, the Indians swept the Senators with a 3–1 victory in the third and final game of the series, and the last game of the season between the two teams. Smith picked up his 15th victory. In the heat of the tightest American League pennant race since 1920, the game drew a crowd of only 5,000 to Municipal Stadium.

"I didn't have any particular number of victories in mind when the season opened," Smith said. "I figured that each one I won would be so much velvet. If you put the ball in the right spots, you win, and if you don't, you lose. You also have to have a little luck. I have been very fortunate this year."[39] Smith had earned his last victory for 1940.

While the Indians were beating Washington, Detroit pounded the Athletics twice, 13–2 and 10–1. The victory in the first game went to Floyd Giebell, a 15 game winner in the minor leagues who'd been summoned to Detroit earlier in the month. New York won to stay four games behind. The Indians would arrive in Detroit for their final three road games of the season tied with the Tigers at 85–61.

Vitt's plan for moving into first place, and hopefully eliminating Detroit from the race, was simple. The Indians had to hold Tiger sluggers Hank Greenberg and Rudy York in check. The players were certain leaving mammoth Municipal Stadium and playing in the much smaller confines of Briggs Stadium would revive the stagnant offense.

"Greenberg and York have been keeping the Tigers in the running with extra base wallops, and if we can stop them, we ought to win the series," explained Vitt. "I believe it will be smart baseball to pass them if first base is open. When a player is hot, it doesn't pay to fool around with him. Greenberg and York have been driving in a big majority of the Tigers' runs, and if you can stop them, you can spike Detroit's attack."

"Harder, Feller and Milnar are in great shape, and if they pitch as they did in their last two starts, we should gain an edge in the series," Vitt concluded.[40]

In his book *The Cleveland Indians*, published in 1949, Whitey Lewis described the reception the club got when it arrived in Detroit on September 19 for its crucial series with the Tigers. "No group was ever received with a more diversified bombardment. When the Indians walked up the ramp through the station foyer, they were hit with tomatoes, eggs, lemons and other edibles. Shouts of 'cry babies' came from everywhere. The next afternoon, bottles bearing nipples were dangled from the upper deck in Briggs Stadium, in front of the Cleveland dugout."

The Associated Press reported on September 19 that the Indians hadn't filed a formal protest with the American League office and president Will Harridge over the "unmerciful verbal scalping" they'd taken, on the road and at home, from their opponents since the "crybabies" incident more than three months earlier. Harridge, who'd stepped in once on the Tribe's behalf to silence Yankee coach Art Fletcher's personal attacks on Hemsley, noted that "bench jockeying, or riding," had always been a part of baseball, and keeping it from getting out of hand was up to the policy of the individual teams. It wasn't the purview of the league president. There was, of course, nothing Harridge or the league could do about the abuse the Indians had taken from fans in every ballpark in the league, who'd given them an earful and then some for the past three months. To have whined to the league president, and have that fact become public, could only have made the situation worse. Bradley warned the players of the abuse they were bringing on themselves, and he'd been right.

Looking to the future, the Tribe's business office announced on September 19 that arrangements had been finalized to hold spring training in Fort Myers in 1941.

A Briggs Stadium crowd of 22,508 groaned for seven innings as the Indians, behind Harder's stout pitching, took a 4–1 lead. Harder weakened in the eighth, and Feller, coming off a complete game just two days earlier, couldn't stop the rally. Detroit scored five in the eighth, and Cleveland's ninth inning rally fell short. The Tigers moved into first place with a 6–5 victory.

"I wasn't as strong as I was in the early innings, but it's only natural to lose some of your stuff as the game progresses," said Harder, who didn't fault Vitt's decision. "My curve didn't break quite enough, and I walked Barney McCosky. Then Charlie Gehringer hit an outside curve and plunked it for a single. I was prepared to continue, but was told that Vitt decided to make a change. Perhaps I could have pulled through, but that's merely guessing. Neither Greenberg nor York has had much success against Feller this season, and I thought it was a good move to bring him in."[41]

Vitt defended his decision to turn to a weary Feller on one day's rest. "It was apparent that Harder was getting tired," the manager said. "Mel had pitched beautiful ball for seven innings, but appeared to be losing his stuff. I figured that Feller would be able to step in and hold them for the last two innings. It proved a lousy guess, but I'd make the same decision in another similar situation."[42]

Feller said he possibly didn't warm up sufficiently before entering the game. "I didn't throw many balls in the bullpen, but I thought my arm was in shape to go. I just didn't have it."[43]

In his September 21 column, Cobbledick placed the blame for the defeat squarely on Vitt. "To replace a tiring pitcher, Vitt called on one who was so arm-weary that it was apparent to many in the stands as he warmed up. If the Indians fail to win the pennant, and they'll have to fight up hill to win it now, it will be because Bob Feller has been worn to a frazzle by working in and out of turn."

When the Indians arrived in their dugout before the game, they found a gift waiting for them. Some Tiger fans had placed a doll buggy in the dugout, which the Tribe players used to hold their bats. An usher confiscated a milk bottle suspended from a fishing pole by a fan in the centerfield stands. The *Plain Dealer* termed it the "usual cry-baby razzing." The Indians were booed throughout the game, but when Vitt emerged to remove Harder in the eighth inning, he got a rousing ovation.

Milnar, the next day's Tribe starter, had a warning for the Tigers and their fans. "Mel Harder proved that those guys can be stopped. I'll give it a try tomorrow. If those Tigers think they have the flag sewed up, they may be in for a surprise. We still have five more cracks at 'em."[44]

Half of the World Series match-up was set. The Reds clinched the National League pennant, their second in succession.

Milnar held the Tigers scoreless for the first four innings of the second game. Lynwood (Schoolboy) Rowe held the Indians score-less for nine innings. Detroit chased Milnar with two runs in the fifth and two more in the sixth. They added a run in the seventh against Millard Howell, as Vitt decided not to waste any of his primary relievers in a game the Indians stood little chance of winning. They simply couldn't solve Rowe, and lost, 5–0. The "usual crybaby razzing" included a fan hanging a clothesline of baby clothing on the Cleveland dugout. The police removed the clothing and escorted the fan from the ballpark.

Trailing Detroit by two games, Vitt felt he had no alternative but to send Feller, on one day's rest, to the mound to attempt to salvage the final game of the series ... and possibly the entire season. "I was pulling for a victory today so we could give Bob a little rest. If we had evened the series, I would have started Harry Eisenstat or somebody else tomorrow. Now, we will have to sink or swim with Feller."

"This is a tough park to pitch in," Vitt continued, "and it wouldn't have been good judgment to send Eisenstat to the mound. Detroit has a bunch of powerful righthanded hitters in its line-up, and they hit long flies off a curveball pitcher like Harry. If Feller has a good day, we'll go back home only one game behind and in a favorable position. If Bob doesn't have it, we won't be any worse off than if I had started somebody else."[45]

Feller declared himself ready for the challenge of keeping the Tribe alive in the race for the pennant. "I only threw a few balls yesterday and should be in good shape," he said. "I have been tired lately, but I didn't do any throwing today, and don't see any reason why I shouldn't be pretty fast."[46]

Having sewn up the National League pennant, the Reds were anxiously awaiting the identity of their opponent in the World Series. They hoped it would be the Indians, for purely financial reasons, according to their manager, "Deacon" Bill McKechnie.

"I honestly believe that we would have a better chance to beat the Tigers," said McKechnie, who'd also managed the Pittsburgh Pirates and St. Louis Cardinals to pennants. "I haven't seen much of either team, to be truthful, but any team that has a Bob Feller is certain to be tough. A Cleveland-Cincinnati would pack them in and build up a much larger players pool, and it's only natural the boys should plug for the set-up that would give them the biggest cut. I think that the Reds can triumph in the World Series, but I believe we would have an easier time with the Tigers."[47]

The third and final game of the series was one the Indians had to win, and they did, tuning out the howls of 56,771 fans in Briggs Stadium to batter Tommy Bridges and a parade of relievers for 10 runs and five home runs. An exhausted Feller contributed his second round-tripper of the season and pitched Cleveland to a 10–5 victory. The Indians scored three runs in the third and four in the fourth and held an eight run lead when Feller, by his own admission, eased up. But the deficit was too large for the Tigers to overcome, and Bob went all the way for his 27th victory. The Tribe headed for home and the final five games of the year trailing Detroit by one game. The last three games of the season would be against the Tigers in Municipal Stadium.

"I wasn't as fast as usual, and my control was spotty, but after the boys staked me to a big lead, I knew I couldn't miss. I worked hard in the first five innings, then conserved strength." Of his home run, off Detroit reliever Archie McKain, Feller said, "I figured that McKain would try to slip a fat pitch over after he got two strikes on me. It was inside, and I didn't swing hard, but I did meet the ball right on the nose."[48] Cleveland's other homers were supplied by Trosky, Weatherly, Chapman and Keltner.

The "usual crybaby razzing" included a barrage of lemons thrown at Trosky the first time he came to the plate. He responded with a line drive home run into the rightfield seats.

"It makes a fellow feel rotten when he lets his club down in a pinch," said a disconsolate Bridges in the Detroit clubhouse. "If I had done my part today, we would have practically clinched the flag."[49]

Greenberg told reporters the race would probably be decided in the ninth inning of the season's last game. "The Indians and Tigers will probably be tied going into next Sunday's game in Cleveland," said the Detroit slugger. "And the teams will probably be tied going into the ninth with the bases crammed and me at the dish." He was asked how he thought he'd fare in such a pressure-packed situation.

"Aw, hell, I would probably pop up," he joked.[50] In Cleveland's victorious clubhouse, Allen was informed of Greenberg's prediction.

"If things turned out that way, I'd ask Vitt to send me in there to pitch to Hank," responded Johnny. "I'd throw him the best spitballs that have been thrown in this league in years."[51]

Meanwhile, the Yankees beat Boston. Still mathematically alive, New York trailed by 3½ games. The Yanks would be busy during the final week of the season. Cleveland and Detroit each had five games to go. The Yankees had eight.

The Tribe's gritty performance in the "must win" game didn't surprise Bradley. "I've never doubted it for a minute. We've got a fine ball club that has always bounced back when the going was toughest. It will be tough this week—and just watch."[52]

"We'll win six straight this week!" enthused Chapman, who forgot the Tribe had only five games left on the schedule.[53] Or maybe Chapman was counting the victory over the Tigers as the first in the streak.

The St. Louis Browns may have been in sixth place when they arrived in Cleveland for a pair of make-up games on September 23, but they were on a roll, having won nine of their past 11 games. Browns manager Fred Haney had perennial Tribe nemesis Auker ready to pitch the first game, against Harder. On the injury front, Hemsley had been hurt in the second game of the Detroit series and wouldn't be available. Trosky was nursing a painful leg bruise, but hadn't been ruled out. And the Indians would need all the offense they could muster against Auker.

The closest pennant race since 1920 had the American League on a pace to establish a new attendance record. The previous mark was set in 1924 at 5,255,430. Detroit had already drawn over a million fans. Harridge said the paid attendance for 1939 would be exceeded by at least a million customers, undoubtedly the result of the Indians, Tigers, Red Sox and Yankees scratching and clawing for the pennant rather than New York cruising to a 17 game margin over second place Boston, as it had in 1939. Harridge tipped his cap to the league's schedule maker for pitting Cleveland and Detroit against each other in the season's last two weekends.

"I contend that we did a smart job of schedule making by deciding last November to have the Indians and Tigers wind up the season against one another,"[54] he said with a grin.

Harder and Auker battled each other through six innings in Municipal Stadium on September 24 with the score tied at two. Eisenstat relieved Harder in the seventh and the roof caved in. The Browns scored three off Eisenstat, then added two more off Allen in the eighth and ninth. That was more than Auker needed, and he nailed his fifth victory of the season over Cleveland, 7–2.

Auker made an interesting admission after the game. "I've been pulling for the Indians to win the pennant, and it makes a fellow feel kind of funny to keep on whipping them," he confessed. "It's my business to win all the games I can, even if the Browns aren't going anywhere. I thought all season that the Indians would finish on top, but I'm beginning to doubt it now. They had plenty of chances to break away from the field, but they failed to take advantage of them."[55]

Vitt had announced that Allen would pitch the second game of the series against St. Louis, but he hadn't meant it. "If I had been planning to start Johnny Allen in the second game, I wouldn't have used him as a relief pitcher," the manager explained. "I announced that Allen would pitch so that the Browns would save Vernon Kennedy for the second game. Kennedy is a pretty fair lefthanded hitter, and I wanted him to bat against Milnar rather than Mel Harder. Milnar has beaten the Browns four times in an equal number of starts this season, and he should be able to do it again if the Indians give him some batting support. If the White Sox take two from the Tigers, or even split even, we still have a fair chance to take the pennant."[56]

It's never easy for a club to depend on outside help in a pennant race, and the Indians needed help from the White Sox, whose game with the Tigers had been rained out, setting up a doubleheader. The Tribe trailed Detroit by 1½ games. The Yankees swept a doubleheader from Washington and were 2½ behind.

If Auker had been the Tribe's "jinx" pitcher, a term Auker dismissed as "bunk," then Milnar was the Browns' "jinx" pitcher. In another game the Indians had to win, Milnar out-pitched Kennedy, 4–2. It was Al's fifth win of the season versus the Browns. The Indians did all their scoring in the first four innings, and Milnar made the lead stand up. He permitted just six hits.

Across Lake Erie, the Tigers nipped the White Sox twice, 10–9 and 3–2. Detroit improved to 89–62. The Indians were 87–64. In order to win the pennant, they'd have to sweep the three-game series with Detroit that began on September 27 in Municipal Stadium. The Tigers needed to win only one of the three games to clinch the pennant.

In his column of September 26, Cobbledick acknowledged the less than friendly and sportsmanlike treatment the Indians had received in Detroit the previous weekend. He said he'd heard that Tribe fans planned a similar reception for the Tigers upon their arrival in Cleveland for the pennant showdown. He didn't approve.

Cobbledick wrote that he'd be in favor of giving the Tiger fans who pelted the Cleveland players with produce a taste of their own medicine, if they could be rounded up and placed with their backs to a wall. But it would be wrong of Tribe fans to retaliate against Detroit's players, who weren't responsible for the barrage.

Cobbledick undoubtedly knew his opinion would be disregarded by fans determined to give the Tigers a taste of what the Indians had endured in Briggs Stadium ... and all season, at least since the ill-advised meeting in Bradley's office on June 13.

There would be plenty of Detroit fans in Municipal Stadium for the final series of the season. Tribe business manager Frank Kohlbecker said the team had received 3,000 requests for tickets from Detroit, and assumed a lot of Tiger fans would make the trip around the western end of Lake Erie to Cleveland without ordering tickets first. Getting to Cleveland would be easy. The New York Central, Nickel Plate and Pennsylvania railroads were running special trains to transport Tiger fans from Detroit to Cleveland, and the Detroit and Cleveland Navigation Company was sponsoring an all expenses paid trip.

Most of the Indians may have held their manager in low regard, but they weren't going to cheat him out of his World Series share. Gibbons addressed what he termed a "vicious rumor" that, when the Tribesman met to divvy up the World Series loot, should they earn any, they'd decided to freeze out Vitt. Not so, said Gibbons, who reported the manager had been voted a full share by his players.

The Indians expected to face Rowe in the series opener, the same pitcher who'd shut them out in Detroit six days earlier. Tigers manager Del Baker wasn't sure who his starter would be. "I won't make up my mind about Rowe until about half hour before game time. The Schoolboy is a pitcher with a sore arm, and I'd be foolish to start him if the weather is cold or damp."

Baker was asked about possibly facing Feller twice in the three-game set. Trailing by two games and needing a sweep, Vitt had no choice but to start Feller in the opener. Bob would be pitching on full rest, and the Indians had to win the game. A defeat meant the season was over, and if Vitt and the Indians were going to lose, they were going to lose with their ace pitcher on the mound. If the Indians won the first two games, setting up a "winner take all" third contest, was Baker concerned about facing Feller again?

He said he wasn't. "Feller has worked hard lately, and he isn't as fast as he was early in the season. If he returns with one day of rest, the Tigers will pin his ears back like they did in Detroit, when he went in as a relief pitcher."[57]

But Baker was simply being cagey. He had no intention of starting Rowe, but didn't want the Indians to know it. Baker's plan was to pit rookie Floyd Giebell against Feller, and he had the backing of his players, with whom he'd discussed his strategy. Baker's thinking was sound. If Feller was on top of his game, the Tigers were likely to lose. Why waste one of the Tigers' aces, Rowe (16–3) or Newsom (21–5) against the American League's best hurler? If Feller won, Baker still had Rowe and Newsom available to pitch the second and third games, although Newsom had pitched in both games of Detroit's doubleheader sweep of the White Sox and would've been working on short rest. Cleveland would've countered with Harder and Milnar. The Indians had to lead with their ace. The Tigers didn't.

Giebell wasn't a total unknown commodity, as baseball legend, passed down through the decades (especially in Cleveland) has made him out to be. Giebell had won 15 games in the minor leagues for Buffalo (managed, ironically, by ex–Indian skipper Steve O'Neill) in 1940, and was one of Detroit's top pitching prospects. Still, he figured to be no match for Feller.

A Ladies Day crowd of 45,553 descended on Municipal Stadium on Friday, September 27, itching for a fight. The behavior of much of the gathering was anything but lady-like. The crowd came armed with vegetables and other projectiles to hurl at the visitors ... even a bag of groceries that was dropped from the upper deck onto the head of Detroit catcher Birdie Tebbetts as he sat in the Tiger bullpen. Tebbetts was not only startled, but briefly knocked unconscious. None of it intimidated Giebell or his teammates.

The only runs were provided by York, who snuck a Feller pitch into the leftfield seats with Gehringer on base in the fourth inning. It was one of only three hits Feller surrendered. The Indians put two runners on base in four separate innings, but couldn't drive any of them home. Giebell checked the Tribe on six hits and out-dueled the best pitcher in baseball, 2–0. Baker's strategy had worked to perfection. Giebell had earned immortality by pitching the game of a lifetime.

Yankees manager Joe McCarthy protests to the umpires when Cleveland fans bombard the field, and McCarthy's players, with vegetables during a game in Municipal Stadium in 1940.

Detroit Tigers catcher Birdie Tebbetts (right) and rookie pitcher Hal Newhouser munch on some of the fruit tossed on the field by Cleveland fans at Municipal Stadium on September 27, 1940. Detroit won the game and clinched the pennant.

The grounds crew clears the Cleveland Municipal Stadium field of debris, mainly fruit and vegetables, thrown from the stands by a crowd of better than 45,000 on September 27, 1940. Detroit beat the Indians, 2-0, to clinch the pennant.

Philadelphia's 6–2 victory over New York ended the Yankees slim chance of tying the Tigers and forcing a pennant play-off.

Cobbledick hailed the new American League champs as a team with more weaknesses than any other championship team in history. But they were pennant winners nonetheless, because the Indians were just as badly flawed. Probably more so. And because the four-time defending world's champion Yankees spend the season tripping over their own feet.

"We just couldn't get hits when we needed them," said an exhausted and disappointed Bradley. The lament described the loss to Detroit that clinched the pennant for the Tigers, and the season as a whole. "The boys put up a fine fight. I'm proud of them."[58]

With the pennant out of reach, the Indians faced the grim specter of tumbling to third place. They had to win their two remaining games to hold off the onrushing Yankees. It wouldn't hurt that the Tigers had nothing left to play for, although they wouldn't play that way. "We'll finish up fighting," promised Vitt. "The difference between second and third is about $500 a man. The boys certainly are entitled to that consolation."[59]

And they earned it. The Indians won the Saturday game, 2–1, behind Harder. Newsom, pitching in relief of Detroit starter Johnny Gorsica, took the loss. On Sunday, the champions and the runners-up battled through 14 innings, with Cleveland emerging a 3–2 victor. Milnar pitched all 14 innings, allowing 10 hits, for his 18th victory against 10 defeats.

It really didn't matter. Still, 18,346 attended Saturday's game, and 27,434 showed up for the season finale.

The final American League standings for 1940:

Detroit	90–64	.584	--
INDIANS	89–65	.578	1
New York	88–66	.571	2
Boston	82–72	.532	8
Chicago	82–72	.532	8
St. Louis	67–87	.435	23
Washington	64–90	.416	26
Philadelphia	54–100	.351	36

"They can't catch us now!" said a jubilant Tribesman on August 21, when the club's lead over Detroit was 5½ games. But they did.

"I'm sorry we didn't win the pennant for Cleveland," said Vitt. "Three fly balls in the right places would have done it."[60]

12

California, Here He Comes

"Final decision held in abeyance."

That was the official statement issued by the Indians pertaining to the future of manager Oscar Vitt following the conclusion of the season's final game on Sunday, September 29. Vitt met afterward in the club's executive office in Municipal Stadium with his bosses, Alva Bradley and Cy Slapnicka. No decision was reached in that meeting, or, at least, no decision was announced. There was no doubt as to what the eventual decision would be. Vitt had no future in Cleveland, and that had been obvious since June 13 ... unless the Indians won the pennant. Even then, under the unprecedented circumstances that prevailed, he may not have survived. A world's championship may have saved his job. How does a team fire a manager who's just won the World Series? Then again, this was Cleveland, where unprecedented events occur.

This was long before the era of "exit meetings," as all teams now conduct with their players at the end of a season. Vitt did speak to his players in the clubhouse after the victory over Detroit. According to the *Plain Dealer*, the "vast majority" of the players shook Vitt's hand and wished him well. A few, however, departed without speaking to him. For at least some, a season's worth (and more) of ill feelings couldn't be wiped away by the end of a disappointing campaign, and the knowledge that Vitt wouldn't be back. Letting bygones be bygones, as Bradley had urged after the rebellion against Vitt in June, wasn't an option for some of the Tribesmen.

Before heading for his home in Iowa, Hal Trosky wanted to clear the air. He'd borne the brunt of the criticism of the June insurrection, and he issued a statement he hoped would set the record straight.

"I'm not backing down from anything I said or did," said the statement. "But it seems to me I have been singled out as the leader,

177

and I didn't do more than anybody else. This all started when, after we originally went in to see Mr. Bradley, he waited for me to get back home [from his mother's funeral] before he did anything. In that first meeting, I gave my whole-hearted support to the ideas we all had about the management. But I didn't call any meetings after that, and I didn't say or do anything to hurt the organization of the team. I just want that known."[1] What isn't know is whether Trosky was among the players who shook Vitt's hand before departing, or headed for home without a word to the soon-to-be ex-manager.

Bob Feller also contemplated making a statement about his role in the mutiny, but decided against it, fearing anything he said would be misconstrued. "I did what I thought was right, and I'm sticking to it," was his only comment.[2]

"I'm leaving for my home in California with a clear conscience," Vitt told reporters. "Cleveland fans deserve a pennant, and throughout the season, I did my best to reward them for their support. I did everything possible to bring the Indians home in first place. It's true that I made mistakes, but it's only human to err."

Vitt lamented the deficiencies in his club. "Our big trouble was we couldn't hit in the pinches. If we hadn't received sensational pitching, the Indians wouldn't have remained in the fight until the closing week of the season. A team just can't leave runners on third base with one or no outs day after day and still hope to win the pennant. I think the players all tried hard to win, but we just weren't good enough."

Looking ahead, and sounding much like someone who knew he wouldn't be a part of the future he referred to, Vitt said, "the Indians have a great pitching staff, an excellent infield, and the best catching in the league, and will be a tough club to whip next year if they have a stronger attack." It was interesting how often Vitt referred to his team as "the Indians" rather than as "we" or "us."

Vitt was asked if he expected to return in 1941. "I understand that a decision will be reached at a meeting of the club's board of directors in the next few weeks."[3] With that, he and his wife headed home to the San Francisco Bay area. He needed time to rest after surviving a season like no major league manager had ever endured. His players had demanded his firing, and presented Bradley with a long list of complaints to bolster their case. Then they openly mocked and defied him by announcing they would ignore his orders, and instead develop strategy of their own, when they felt the situation required it. How could any team retain a manager's services under such unprecedented circumstances?

On October 8, as the Tigers and Reds were deciding the world's championship of professional baseball, the Associated Press reported Vitt had refused to resign as Cleveland's manager. That would've been a good trick, since, technically, he wasn't Cleveland's manager. His contract expired at the end of the regular season. The AP story quoted Vitt as saying, simply and succinctly, that he was not a quitter.

Asked for a response to the AP story, Bradley replied, "I haven't been able to get the ball club directors to meet." He didn't appear to consider Vitt's future to be an urgent matter. "I'm leaving for New York Friday, and then will go to Sea Island, near Savannah, Georgia, for a two week vacation. When I return, we will call a director's meeting and arrive at a decision."[4]

Vitt told the Associated Press the turbulence of the past summer could've been avoided had the front office supported him. "A different situation would have prevailed, and this I say in all frankness, had I been given the backing that any manager is entitled to expect. On one occasion, a player I had suspended for a flagrant violation showed up in uniform the next day. I told him he was through, temporarily. He replied, 'no, I'm not. I fixed it up with the front office. They told me to come back and apologize to you and everything would be all right.' Things got so bad that finally, some of the players would not obey my signals."[5]

Said Bradley of the incident Vitt referred to, "I don't know anything about that. It's news to me."[6] That is hard to swallow, inasmuch as the incident was splashed all over Cleveland's three daily newspapers in September. One paper even printed pictures on the first page of its sports section, one of coach Luke Sewell flashing the "take" sign to Jeff Heath, the next of Heath swinging at the pitch he'd been ordered by Vitt not to swing at, and the third of Vitt's outraged reaction. The headline read that the pictures beneath it depicted how rebellious players cost teams victories.

It wasn't news to Slapnicka, who fired back at Vitt the next day. "In answer to the statement that Vitt made to the Associated Press in regard to not receiving the support of the front office, I wish to say that it was not a true statement of fact."

Slapnicka then gave his side of the story. "His reference to a certain player whom he suspended on one occasion for a flagrant violation likewise is only partially correct. It was at manager Vitt's own suggestion and request that I talk to the player. The understanding was that if the player apologized to him, Vitt would be satisfied and consider the matter closed. I requested the player to call at my office at the stadium the next day before reporting to the clubhouse. Without any solicitation on my part, the player stated that he realized he was wrong, and agreed to make amends by apologizing to Vitt. He then went to the clubhouse and apologized. Since that was all Vitt requested, I cannot construe this incident as a failure of the front office to support the manager."[7]

The relationship between Vitt and Heath had been contentious from spring training of 1938. The "new attitude" Vitt believed Heath brought to camp in 1940 apparently didn't last long. And the relationship between Vitt and Slapnicka was also contentious by 1940. Slapnicka had lost confidence in the manager, and there's evidence to suggest he'd encouraged the rebellion of the 13th of June, either in the hope Vitt would resign or, if not, providing the general manager with the grounds to fire him.

Cleveland's fans, for the most part, took Vitt's side in the dispute with the players, and he thanked them for it. "The fans really stuck with me," he told the AP. "They acted like champions, even if we weren't."[8]

The *Plain Dealer* reported on October 18 that Bradley, even though still vacationing in South Carolina, had offered Bucky Harris a three-year contract to manage the Indians. Harris was still under contract to Washington, but Bradley had asked Senators owner Clark Griffith for permission to speak to him about the Tribe's managerial vacancy, and it had been granted. The Indians' board of directors were scheduled to meet on October 28, and the contract offer to Harris was among the items on the agenda.

At that meeting, the board confirmed what everyone had known … or at least assumed … probably as far back as June 14. Vitt would not be offered a contract to manage the Indians in 1941. Why the process of dismissing the manager was dragged out for a full month wasn't explained.

"I made plenty of money for the Indians in the last three years," Vitt told the Associated Press immediately after getting the verdict from the board of directors. The Tribe had drawn 902,576 spectators in 1940, third highest attendance in the American League, and had no doubt made a profit.

> I have no regrets. Unless I get a job that will pay me well, I presume I will retire from baseball.
>
> I am not surprised at the decision. I realized it was coming. It would have been necessary to make changes to the playing personnel at the time of the trouble. The changes were not made, so I saw the handwriting on the wall.

Although only Roy Weatherly had declined to participate in the rebellion, and Lou Boudreau and Ray Mack had been ruled out by their teammates, due to their youth and the negative impact association with the insurgents could've had on their careers, Vitt remained convinced only two or three players had orchestrated the insurrection. One of them had been Hal Trosky, the slugging first baseman. Would the front office have dared support its manager, and show the players who was in charge, by releasing a player of Trosky's stature? Bob Feller had been another insurgent. He wasn't going anywhere. Twenty-five game winners who were just 21 years old were much harder to find than managers. For that matter, so were 27-year-old first basemen who hit 42 home runs and drive in 162 runs ... although Trosky's best days were behind him, though no one knew it at the time. Vitt apparently expected management to do something drastic to cement his status as the leader of the ball club, and when it didn't, he knew he was finished. Why he hung on to his job so determinedly when management failed to give him the support he felt he'd earned is difficult to understand.

"I am just as well satisfied to sever connections with the club," he continued. "At no time were next year's plans discussed with me, so I knew long before the close of the season that I was through." But he steadfastly refused to resign, instead finishing the season as the lamest of lame ducks.

Vitt said he had no hard feelings toward Bradley or anyone, including Slapnicka, in the front office. "I gave them all I had. My conscience is clear. Whoever gets the job has my best wishes ... also my sympathy. Just let the boys back there know I don't intend to apply for unemployment compensation."[9] The last comment was a dig at third baseman Ken Keltner who, the *Plain Dealer* had revealed, did just that at end of the 1939 season, to tide him over until the 1940 season started. The newspaper didn't indicate whether Keltner's application for unemployment had been approved.

A successor to Vitt wasn't hired at the meeting. Bradley said the board left it up to him to choose the club's next manager. It was known that Harris had been sounded out as to his interest in leaving Washington and coming to Cleveland. Whether or not Sewell was offered the job isn't known, but if he was, and Sewell was considered prime managerial timber, he'd meant it when he said he didn't want to manage the Indians. He was kept as a coach. Rumor had it Gordon (Mickey) Cochrane, the former Philadelphia Athletics catcher who, as a player-manager, led the Tigers to pennants in 1934 and '35, plus the World Series title in '35, in addition to a pair of runner-up finishes, was under consideration, despite not having managed since being fired in 1938. The front-runner was thought to be Roger Peckinpaugh, who'd managed the Indians with minimal success from 1928 until June of 1933. When Bradley visited New York in early November, a wild rumor spread that he planned to interview Babe Ruth for the Cleveland managing job. Ruth's burning desire to manage was well known. Bradley scoffed at the report, and said he was in New York on business that had nothing to do with baseball.

As for the beleaguered Bradley, who was harshly criticized on some occasions (and praised on other occasions) by Gordon Cobbledick, how else could he have handled a situation without precedent in the history of American professional sports? He refused the demand that Vitt be fired immediately, but agreed to investigate the players complaints against him. How vigorously he did so isn't known. Urging the players to let bygones be bygones, forget the whole matter and be friends again was ludicrous and deserving of the ridicule it received. But what alternative did Bradley have, other than to sit tight and ride out the storm? Giving in to the players demand to fire Vitt would've set a dangerous precedent that players on other professional sports teams would surely have followed, to this day. No matter how difficult a coach or manager is to play for, the inmates can't be permitted to run the asylum ... although Cleveland's rebellious players attempted just that over the season's final weeks. At least Vitt was still the titular head of the club.

One additional question. Had the board of directors offered Vitt a contract for 1941, would he have accepted it? The roster didn't figure to change much, so he'd have been managing many of the same players he knew didn't like him, didn't respect him, had demanded his dismissal, and had undermined him at every opportunity in 1940.

In spite of his insistence that he wasn't a quitter, Vitt would have had to be a masochist to accept such an assignment.

In his October 30 column, Cobbledick revealed that the player insurrection against Vitt was supposed to have taken place late in the 1939 season. Vitt had already signed his 1940 contract. The Tribe was languishing in fourth place with a record of 72–61, 22½ games behind the Yankees. Cobbledick didn't provide a date, other than to say it was "late in September." It was, in fact, the middle of September. Cobbledick wrote that the Indians had swept a doubleheader from New York in Yankee Stadium, a feat he claimed to have been an extreme rarity for the Indians. According to the website baseball-reference.com, the Indians didn't play a doubleheader in Yankee Stadium in September of 1939. They did, however, sweep a two game series from New York, which had already clinched the pennant, on September 12 and 13, winning 4–3 (in 10 innings) and 9–4. The Tribe arrived in the Bronx having won four of its previous five games.

According to Cobbledick, the players anticipated a trouncing at the hands of the Yankees, and had decided to pay a visit to Bradley afterward, using the losses to New York as proof they couldn't win for Vitt, and asking that he be fired, his new contract notwithstanding. After defeating the American League champs twice, the players felt the time wasn't right to approach Bradley with their grievances, which were virtually identical to those put forth in June of 1940, and put their plans on hold. As it turned out, for the rest of the season, as the Indians won 13 of their remaining 19 games and moved up a notch in the standings from fourth place to third. Their grievances against Vitt remained on the back burner ... until June of 1940.

For the record, the Indians did sweep a doubleheader from the Yankees in New York during the 1939 season ... and in front of a howling mob of better than 76,000 fans, no less. It was on Sunday, August 6. Cleveland was in fourth place, 17½ games behind. The Tribe's record, following the sweep, was a modest 51–47. This would have been before Bradley signed Vitt to a contract for 1940, so a player protest might have influenced Bradley's thinking as to whether to retain his manager for another season. But the events which followed don't match the events that took place after the aborted insurrection as described in Cobbledick's column, and it isn't likely a writer of Cobbledick's caliber (his work as a baseball scribe for the *Plain Dealer* earned him a spot in the writer's wing of the Hall of Fame) would've mixed up his dates so badly, mistaking early August for mid–September. Cobbledick cited no sources for his information.

However, if Cobbledick had his dates confused, the scenario laid out in Cleveland's newspapers when Vitt was re-hired fits perfectly. As noted earlier in this book, Bradley had said he'd wait until the end of the season to decide Vitt's status. Cleveland's papers reported his sudden change of heart may have been influenced by a report in a New York newspaper that Vitt would be fired. It's possible the New York writer may have been tipped off about the planned player rebellion, which was put on hold after the doubleheader sweep, and arrived at the conclusion Vitt was on the way out, after the 1939 season if not sooner.

The Indians returned to Cleveland after the doubleheader sweep for a brief homestand, making a visit to Bradley's office the next day entirely feasible. In the middle of September, after the sweep of the series in New York, the Tribe continued a lengthy road trip. They played the Red Sox in Fenway Park the next day, making a visit to Bradley's office impossible. The Indians swept the doubleheader on August 6. Bradley re-hired Vitt on August 11. If he did so as a response to the story in the New York paper about Vitt's imminent firing, the scenario fits perfectly.

There's also the possibility Bradley may have been informed of the player's plan and decided to nip the problem in the bud by re-hiring Vitt immediately. He did say when announcing the manager's new contract that the players needed to know who was in charge, and it would continue to be Vitt.

Cobbledick also claimed in his column that, following the player rebellion, Vitt had sought advice on how to deal with his unprecedented situation from Connie Mack and baseball commissioner Kenesaw Mountain Landis. Cobbledick said Landis told Vitt if he was unable to control his players, he should resign.

The curtain finally fell on the tumultuous 1940 season when Bradley introduced ... or, more accurately, re-introduced.... Peckinpaugh as Cleveland's manager for 1941. Cobbledick noted that Peckinpaugh showed how he'd learned from his predecessor's mis-steps by saying very little when he met with the press and broadcast media on November 12. Vitt never met a microphone, or a podium, he didn't embrace. Even Bradley warned Vitt that he talked too much.

Peckinpaugh did say that his players would report to Fort Myers for spring training with a clean slate. "As for the trouble on the club last summer, I don't know anything about it, and I don't want to know anything. As far as I'm concerned, it never happened."[10]

The ringleader of the player insurrection, Trosky, gave his stamp of approval to Peckinpaugh's hiring. "I am very happy to hear of the appointment," said the Tribe first baseman from his home in Iowa. "I know Peckinpaugh very well. We'll go out and give a good account of ourselves under him."[11]

Feller, also one of the rebellious Tribesmen, was certain Peckinpaugh wouldn't make the same mistakes Vitt made. "He knows the inside of the Indian situation," said Bob, who, just days before Peckinpaugh's hiring, had finished second to Hank Greenberg in the American League Most Valuable Player balloting. "He knows what caused the internal trouble last season, and he knows what to do to keep it from cropping up again."[12]

Vitt was asked for his opinion of the man who'd replace him in the Cleveland dugout in 1941. "He is a resident of Cleveland, and he knows the ins and outs," said the now officially former manager.[13] Vitt had learned the "ins and outs" in the city known as "the graveyard of managers" the hard way.

Said Bradley of his new manager ... who was both the first and the fifth manager he'd employed since purchasing the Indians and assuming the club presidency in 1928, "I am satisfied that we have made a wise and happy choice, and I look forward to a long and pleasant association with Roger."[14]

In keeping with the idea of starting 1941 with a "clean slate," the coaches Vitt had hired, Oscar Melillo and Johnny Bassler, were fired. Sewell, who'd been forced upon Vitt by management, was retained. But he wouldn't be around long. Sewell would be hired by the St. Louis Browns, who fired manager Fred Haney 44 games into the season.

That "long and pleasant association," at least as a manager, would last one year. The club Vitt said would be tough to beat if it could add some punch at the plate started quickly under Peckinpaugh in 1941, holding first place as late as June 28, before hitting the skids and limping home in fourth place (tied, ironically, with Detroit) 26 games behind the revived Yankees. Peckinpaugh would be replaced by Boudreau, the Tribe's 24-year-old star shortstop, in 1942.

The introduction of Peckinpaugh didn't quite conclude the Vitt saga. In December, Vitt accused Bradley of reneging on a clause in his 1940 contract requiring he be paid a $2,500 bonus for every 100,000 fans the Indians drew in excess of 600,000. The Tribe's attendance was slightly more than 900,000. Under terms of the contract, Vitt would've been owed $7,500. Bradley begged to differ, and asked Vitt, who'd been named manager of the Portland Beavers of the Pacific Coast League (at a salary of $10,000) to allow commissioner Landis to arbitrate the dispute. Vitt agreed. My research failed to determine Landis' ruling.

Jimmy Dykes may have been right about the American League pennant being won by a lousy team. Detroit's 90–64 record was the worst ever for an American League champion, a half game worse than the 1908 Tigers mark of 90–63. It followed then, that Detroit's .584 winning percentage was the lowest ever for an American League champion, slightly below the 1908 club's mark of .588. Ironically, Cleveland had finished second to Detroit in the furious, three-team race of 1908 (with a record of 90–64) between the Naps, as the Indians were then known, the Tigers, and the White Sox.

The American League in 1940 boasted of five good teams (Cleveland, Detroit, New York, Boston and Chicago) and three weak ones (St. Louis, Washington, and Philadelphia). What happened to the juggernaut Yankees is hard to pinpoint. New York was in the midst of a run of seven pennants (and six world's championships) in eight years. After faltering in 1940, the Yankees would win pennants in 1941, '42 and '43, and capture the World Series in 1941 and '43. With essentially the same cast as in 1939, when they won 106 games, the Yankees bumbled and stumbled all through the 1940 season. They started slowly, got hot, and then alternated between hot and cold for the rest of the year. They were pounding on the door when the season ended. Had it been another week longer, they might have roared past the Indians and Tigers and won another flag. They rebounded in 1941 to win 101 games. What went wrong in 1940? Had hubris set in? It would be understandable that even a Hall of Fame manager such as Joe McCarthy might've had trouble keeping his team motivated after four straight world's championships.

The Tigers did extend the National League champion Reds, who won 100 games, to the full seven games before losing the World Series. Cincinnati overcame a three games to two deficit by winning the sixth and seventh games on its home field.

Pitching, as Vitt suggested, may have kept the Indians in the race until the season's final weekend. But the second half performance of the Tribe's "big three" starters, Feller, Al Milnar and Al Smith, couldn't match the first half. Before the All-Star break, the "big three" had combined for a record of 33–10. After the break, their record was 27–18. Smith, in particular, couldn't maintain the pace he'd set in the first half. Johnny Allen was consistently inconsistent. Mel Harder didn't round into form until late in the year. Vitt's plea to Slapnicka to bolster the staff produced only Nate Andrews, who pitched 12 innings in six appearances. That wasn't nearly enough. Vitt couldn't count on his bullpen, featuring Joe Dobson's ERA of 4.95 and Johnny Humphries' horrendous 8.29, forcing him to use his starters in relief in August and September. The wear and tear on Feller and Milnar was obvious down the stretch run.

How much the ill feelings between Vitt and his players affected the Indians can't be calculated. The fact the players not only staged a second mutiny in September, but took steps to make sure Vitt was aware of it, is a clear indication Bradley's request that everyone become friends again had been tossed in the trash. Did the players frequently overrule the manager and employ their own strategy in the final three weeks of the season? Occasionally? Always? Never? There's no way of knowing, just as there's no way of determining how Vitt's knowledge that most of his players disrespected, and even hated him, affected his performance. Did the lack of harmony in the clubhouse cost the Indians the pennant? It would seem unlikely, given the fact they surged to a 5½ game lead (71–46) on August 21. The players weren't bickering among themselves. They were allied, almost unanimously, as a unit against their manager. They were united in their determination to prove they could win the pennant in spite of Vitt. Had they played just .500 ball the rest of the way (actually 19–18), they would've won 90 games and the pennant. But they went 18–19 the rest of the way, and the Tigers caught them and passed them.

One other reason the Indians came up short in 1940 was their inability to handle Eldon Auker and the St. Louis Browns. Although the Browns were the American League's most improved team in 1940, adding 24 victories to their pathetic 1939 total of 43, they were still a sixth place team. They still finished 20 games below .500. Yet the Indians could do no better than a split of the 22 game season series with the Browns, including five losses to Auker. Two more victories (such as the Labor Day doubleheader at Municipal Stadium the

Indians lost to St. Louis, in which they scored just one run) would've won the pennant.

Vitt was hired to motivate a group of players management was convinced had underachieved throughout the 1930s. In 1940, he brought them much closer to a pennant than they'd been under Peckinpaugh, Walter Johnson, or Steve O'Neill. Ultimately, however, Vitt may have hit the nail on the head when he said he was certain the players had tried hard, but just weren't good enough. Feller enjoyed a spectacular season, leading the American League in nearly every pitching category. Milnar was steady, but Smith, a reclamation project, faded in the second half. Had Harder recovered sooner from his arm problem, he may have provided the pitching needed to put the Tribe over the top. Only two more victories was all it would have taken.

Offensively, Boudreau and Trosky were Cleveland's best run producers. Trosky was the only consistent power threat, but his 25 homers and 93 runs batted in paled in comparison to the numbers he'd compiled in previous seasons. Weatherly was the Tribe's only .300 hitter. Heath didn't come close to duplicating his sensational 1938 season, or even his not as sensational 1939 season, which Vitt had been counting on. Heath's batting average was just .219, with 14 homers and 50 RBI. Mack's strong first half at the plate proved to be something of a mirage in the second half, as his average declined from .347 to .283. He contributed 12 homers and drove in 69 runs. Keltner's batting average rose from .236 at the All-Star break to a final mark of .254, with 15 home runs and 77 RBI. Cleveland's offense produced a .265 team batting average, with 101 homers and 710 runs scored, an average of 4.6 per game. The Indians had very little speed, stealing just 53 bases. Ben Chapman led the club with a mere 13 steals.

In contrast, the champion Tigers plated 888 runs (5.8 per game) with 134 homers and a .286 average. The third place Yankees scored 817 runs (5.3 per game) and slugged 155 homers. New York's team batting average was .259.

Detroit's team earned run average was 4.01; New York's was 3.89. The Tribe's pitchers compiled an earned run average of 3.63. As Vitt noted, it was pitching, not hitting, that kept the Indians in the pennant race through 152 games of a 154 game season.

Like the Cleveland teams that came before them in the decade of the thirties, the 1940 Indians were a good team. Maybe a very good team. But not quite good enough.

Chapter Notes

Chapter 1

1. *Cleveland Plain Dealer*, June 4, 1935.
2. *Cleveland Press*, June 6, 1935.

Chapter 2

1. *Cleveland Plain Dealer*, October 21, 1937.
2. *Ibid.*
3. *Ibid.*
4. *Cleveland Plain Dealer*, October 20, 1937.
5. *Ibid.*
6. *Ibid.*
7. *Ibid.*
8. Oscar Vitt biography, Society for American Baseball Research.
9. Oscar Vitt biography, Society for American Baseball Research.
10. *Ibid.*

Chapter 3

1. *Cleveland Plain Dealer*, August 12, 1939.
2. *Ibid.*
3. *Ibid.*
4. *Ibid.*

Chapter 4

1. *Cleveland Plain Dealer*, February 24, 1940.
2. *Cleveland Plain Dealer*, February 26, 1940.
3. *Cleveland Plain Dealer*, February 27, 1940.
4. *Cleveland Plain Dealer*, March 2, 1940.
5. *Cleveland Plain Dealer*, March 9, 1940.
6. *Cleveland Plain Dealer*, March 7, 1940.
7. *Cleveland Plain Dealer*, March 5, 1940.
8. *Cleveland Press*, March 6, 1940.
9. *Cleveland Plain Dealer*, March 12, 1940.
10. *Ibid.*
11. *Cleveland Plain Dealer*, March 14, 1940.
12. *Cleveland Plain Dealer*, March 11, 1940.
13. *Cleveland Plain Dealer*, March 17, 1940.
14. *Saturday Evening Post*, March 16, 1940.
15. *Cleveland Plain Dealer*, March 21, 1940.
16. *Cleveland Plain Dealer*, March 26, 1940.
17. *Cleveland Plain Dealer*, March 27, 1940.
18. *Ibid.*
19. *Cleveland Plain Dealer*, March 30, 1940.
20. *Cleveland Plain Dealer*, April 2, 1940.
21. *Cleveland Plain Dealer*, April 3, 1940.
22. *Cleveland Press*, April 8, 1940.
23. *Cleveland News*, April 8, 1940.
24. *Cleveland Press*, April 5, 1940.
25. *Cleveland News*, April 3, 1940.
26. *Cleveland Plain Dealer*, April 5, 1940.
27. *Cleveland Press*, April 5, 1940.
28. *Cleveland Plain Dealer*, April 8, 1940.

29. *Cleveland Plain Dealer*, April 9, 1940.

30. *Cleveland News*, April 11, 1940.
31. *Cleveland Press*, April 11, 1940.
32. *Cleveland Press*, April 16, 1940.
33. *Ibid.*

Chapter 5

1. *Cleveland News*, April 17, 1940.
2. *Cleveland Press*, April 17, 1940.
3. *Cleveland Plain Dealer*, April 19, 1940.
4. *Ibid.*
5. *Ibid.*
6. *Cleveland Plain Dealer*, April 20, 1940.
7. *Ibid.*
8. *Ibid.*
9. *Ibid.*
10. *Cleveland Press*, April 22, 1940.
11. *Cleveland Press*, April 24, 1940.
12. *Cleveland Plain Dealer*, April 30, 1940.

Chapter 6

1. *Cleveland Plain Dealer*, May 6, 1940.
2. *Cleveland Plain Dealer*, May 8, 1940.
3. *Cleveland Press*, May 14, 1940.
4. *Cleveland Plain Dealer*, May 16, 1940.
5. *Ibid.*
6. *Cleveland Press*, May 16, 1940.
7. *Cleveland Plain Dealer*, May 19, 1940.
8. *Cleveland Plain Dealer*, May 21, 1940.
9. *Cleveland Plain Dealer*, May 22, 1940.
10. *Cleveland Plain Dealer*, May 23, 1940.
11. *Cleveland Plain Dealer*, May 25, 1940.
12. *Cleveland Plain Dealer*, May 28, 1940.
13. *Cleveland Plain Dealer*, May 31, 1940.

Chapter 7

1. *Cleveland Plain Dealer*, June 4, 1940.

2. *Indians Baseball: 100 Years of Memories*, p. 67.
3. *Cleveland Plain Dealer*, June 13, 1940.

Chapter 8

1. *Cleveland Plain Dealer*, June 14, 1940.
2. *Ibid.*
3. *Cleveland Press*, June 14, 1940.
4. *Ibid.*
5. *Ibid.*
6. *Ibid.*
7. *Ibid.*
8. *Ibid.*
9. *Ibid.*
10. *Cleveland News*, June 14, 1940.
11. *Cleveland Press*, June 14, 1940.
12. *Cleveland Plain Dealer*, June 15, 1940.
13. *Ibid.*
14. *Ibid.*
15. *Cleveland News*, June 14, 1940.
16. *Cleveland Press*, June 15, 1940.
17. *Ibid.*
18. *Ibid.*
19. *Ibid.*
20. *Indians Baseball: 100 Years of Memories*, p. 68.
21. *Ibid.*
22. *Cleveland Press*, June 22, 1940.
23. *Cleveland Plain Dealer*, June 25, 1940.
24. *Cleveland Plain Dealer*, June 26, 1940.
25. *Cleveland Plain Dealer*, June 27, 1940.
26. *Ibid.*

Chapter 9

1. *Cleveland Plain Dealer*, July 5, 1940.
2. *Cleveland Plain Dealer*, July 12, 1940.
3. *Cleveland Plain Dealer*, July 19, 1940.
4. *Cleveland Plain Dealer*, July 25, 1940.
5. *Ibid.*
6. *Ibid.*
7. *Cleveland Plain Dealer*, July 30, 1940.

8. *Cleveland Press*, July 31, 1940.
9. *Cleveland Plain Dealer*, August 1, 1940.
10. *Ibid.*

Chapter 10

1. *Cleveland Plain Dealer*, August 2, 1940.
2. *Ibid.*
3. *Ibid.*
4. *Cleveland Plain Dealer*, August 4, 1940.
5. *Cleveland Plain Dealer*, August 7, 1940.
6. *Ibid.*
7. *Ibid.*
8. *Cleveland Plain Dealer*, August 8, 1940.
9. *Cleveland Plain Dealer*, August 9, 1940.
10. *Cleveland Plain Dealer*, August 13, 1940.
11. *Cleveland Plain Dealer*, August 14, 1940.
12. *Cleveland Press*, August 13, 1940.
13. *Ibid.*
14. *Cleveland Plain Dealer*, August 15, 1940.
15. *Cleveland Press*, August 15, 1940.
16. *Cleveland Plain Dealer*, August 16, 1940.
17. *Cleveland Plain Dealer*, August 17, 1940.
18. *Cleveland Plain Dealer*, August 19, 1940.
19. *Cleveland Plain Dealer*, August 21, 1940.
20. *Ibid.*
21. *Ibid.*
22. *Ibid.*
23. *Cleveland Plain Dealer*, August 22, 1940.
24. *Ibid.*
25. *Cleveland Plain Dealer*, August 23, 1940.
26. *Ibid.*
27. *Ibid.*
28. *Ibid.*
29. *Cleveland Plain Dealer*, August 24, 1940.
30. *Ibid.*
31. *Cleveland Plain Dealer*, August 25, 1940.
32. *Ibid.*
33. *Cleveland Plain Dealer*, August 26, 1940.
34. *Cleveland Press*, August 26, 1940.
35. *Ibid.*
36. *Cleveland Plain Dealer*, August 26, 1940.
37. *Cleveland Plain Dealer*, August 27, 1940.
38. *Cleveland Press*, August 24, 1940.
39. *Cleveland Plain Dealer*, August 29, 1940.
40. *Ibid.*
41. *Cleveland Plain Dealer*, August 30, 1940.
42. *Cleveland Plain Dealer*, August 31, 1940.
43. *Cleveland Plain Dealer*, September 1, 1940.
44. *Ibid.*

Chapter 11

1. *Cleveland Plain Dealer*, September 4, 1940.
2. *Cleveland Plain Dealer*, September 5, 1940.
3. *Ibid.*
4. *Cleveland Plain Dealer*, September 6, 1940.
5. *Ibid.*
6. *Cleveland Press*, September 6, 1940.
7. *Cleveland News*, September 6, 1940.
8. *Cleveland Press*, September 6, 1940.
9. *Ibid.*
10. *Cleveland Press*, September 7, 1940.
11. *Ibid.*
12. *Cleveland Plain Dealer*, September 7, 1940.
13. *Ibid.*
14. *Ibid.*
15. *Cleveland Plain Dealer*, September 8, 1940.
16. *Ibid.*
17. *Cleveland Plain Dealer*, September 9, 1940.
18. *Ibid.*
19. *Cleveland Plain Dealer*, September 11, 1940.
20. *Ibid.*
21. *Cleveland Plain Dealer*, September 12, 1940.

22. *Cleveland Plain Dealer*, September 13, 1940.

23. *Ibid.*

24. *Ibid.*

25. *Ibid.*

26. *Cleveland Plain Dealer*, September 14, 1940.

27. *Cleveland Plain Dealer*, September 15, 1940.

28. *Ibid.*

29. *Cleveland Plain Dealer*, September 16, 1940.

30. *Ibid.*

31. *Ibid.*

32. *Cleveland Press*, September 12, 1940.

33. *Cleveland Plain Dealer*, September 17, 1940.

34. *Ibid.*

35. *Cleveland Plain Dealer*, September 18, 1940.

36. *Ibid.*

37. *Cleveland Plain Dealer*, September 19, 1940.

38. *Ibid.*

39. *Cleveland Plain Dealer*, September 20, 1940.

40. *Ibid.*

41. *Cleveland Plain Dealer*, September 21, 1940.

42. *Ibid.*

43. *Ibid.*

44. *Ibid.*

45. *Cleveland Plain Dealer*, September 22, 1940.

46. *Ibid.*

47. *Ibid.*

48. *Cleveland Plain Dealer*, September 23, 1940.

49. *Ibid.*

50. *Ibid.*

51. *Ibid.*

52. *Cleveland News*, September 23, 1940.

53. *Ibid.*

54. *Cleveland Plain Dealer*, September 24, 1940.

55. *Cleveland Plain Dealer*, September 25, 1940.

56. *Ibid.*

57. *Cleveland Plain Dealer*, September 27, 1940.

58. *Cleveland News*, September 28, 1940.

59. *Ibid.*

60. *Cleveland Press*, September 30, 1940.

Chapter 12

1. *Cleveland Press*, September 30, 1940.

2. *Ibid.*

3. *Cleveland Plain Dealer*, September 30, 1940.

4. *Cleveland Plain Dealer*, October 8, 1940.

5. Associated Press, October 8, 1940.

6. *Cleveland Plain Dealer*, October 8, 1940.

7. *Ibid.*

8. Associated Press, October 8, 1940.

9. Associated Press, October 29, 1940.

10. *Cleveland Plain Dealer*, November 13, 1940.

11. *Ibid.*

12. *Ibid.*

13. *Ibid.*

14. *Ibid.*

Bibliography

Books

DeVries, Jack. *Indians Baseball: 100 Years of Memories.* Cleveland: Cleveland Indians Baseball Co., 2000.
Lewis, Franklin. *The Cleveland Indians.* New York: G.P. Putnam's Sons, 1949.
Schneider, Russell. *The Cleveland Indians Encyclopedia.* Norwalk, CT: Easton Press, 2001.

Newspapers

Cleveland News, June 1935; October 1937; August 1939; February–December 1940.
Cleveland Plain Dealer, June 1935; October 1937; August 1939; February–December 1940.
Cleveland Press, June 1935; October 1937; August 1939; February–December 1940.

Internet

baseball-reference.com
Society for American Baseball Research
Wikipedia

Index

Allen, Johnny 27, 31, 32, 37, 40, 55, 56,
  58, 62, 65, 66, 69, 71, 73, 76, 79, 81, 83,
  84, 95, 101, 103, 109–111, 114, 117, 124,
  125, 133, 140, 142, 145, 146, 153, 154,
  159, 163, 169, 170
American Association (major league) 5
American Association (minor league)
  15, 36
American League 1, 5, 7, 25, 31, 35, 41,
  61, 64–66, 75, 76, 81, 107, 109, 112, 113,
  116, 119, 124, 129, 131, 137, 143, 153,
  164, 170, 175, 176, 183
Andrews, Nate 84, 85, 110, 115, 116, 118,
  120, 125, 187
Appling, Luke 52
Armour, Bill 6, 7
Atlanta Crackers 38
Auker, Eldon 129, 134, 146, 169, 170, 171,
  187
Averill, Earl 55, 79, 85

Babich, Johnny 117, 162
Bagby, Jim 159
Bagby, Jim, Jr. 102, 159
Baker, Del 24, 55, 132, 172
Baltimore Orioles (1901) 6
Bang, Ed 45, 95, 101
Bartell, Dick 127
Bassler, Johnny 31, 40, 51, 112, 185
Beckman, Bill 61
Bell, Beau 27, 37, 77, 81, 85, 132
Benton, Al 60
Berg, Moe 64
Besse, Herman 61
Bildilli, Emil 69
Birmingham, Joe 7, 8
Black Sox 150, 151
Boston Bees (Braves) 77, 162
Boston Red Sox 1, 7, 8, 12, 14, 21, 25, 26,
  35–37, 39, 40, 44–46, 53, 64, 65, 67,
  70–72, 74, 75, 76, 78, 82–85, 100–103,

111, 114, 115, 117, 118, 121, 123, 124,
  126, 132, 133, 135, 137, 138, 140, 156,
  157, 159, 160, 161, 169, 170, 184, 186
Boudreau, Lou 2, 26, 27, 29, 35, 36, 38,
  43, 44, 51, 59, 77, 90, 108, 112, 113, 127,
  128, 136, 146, 148, 155, 159, 181, 185
Bradley, Alva 8, 10–17, 21–24, 32, 33,
  37, 40, 41, 54, 57, 62, 70, 87–100, 102,
  104, 107, 112, 114–116, 127, 130, 131,
  133, 135, 136, 138, 141, 148, 150–152,
  154, 162, 166, 169, 171, 175, 177–180,
  182–185
Bradley, Chuck 162
Braves Field 52
Bridges, Tommy 110, 168, 169
Briggs, Walter 24, 57
Briggs Stadium 51, 110, 147, 148, 153,
  158, 165, 166, 171
Broaca, Johnny 33, 37, 48
Brooklyn Dodgers 52, 69, 127, 159
Brown, Clint 111, 147, 154
Brucker, Earl 117
Buffalo (IL) 15, 44, 74
Burton, Harold 54
Butland, Wilburn 121

Calvert, Paul 143
Campbell, Bruce 27, 55, 85
Campbell, Clarence 27, 37, 38, 85
Carrasquel, Alex 114
Case, George 140
Caster, George 113
Castle, M.H. 73
Center, Earl 33, 36, 59
Center, Pete 143
Chandler, Spud 29
Chapman, Ben 26, 27, 31, 38, 55, 60, 81,
  103, 109, 132, 151, 158, 160, 168, 169,
  188
Chapman, Ray 63
Chase, Ken 120

Chicago Cubs 77, 83, 104, 162
Chicago White Sox 6, 8, 11, 44–47, 51, 52, 58, 66, 68, 74, 79, 80, 107, 110, 119, 123, 126, 128, 132, 133, 137, 138, 142, 144, 146, 147, 154–156, 159, 164, 170, 171, 186
Cincinnati Reds 1, 25, 39, 46, 104, 127, 159, 167, 168, 179, 186
Cleveland Bronchos 6
Cleveland Naps 6
Cleveland News 45, 107
Cleveland Plain Dealer 11, 15, 17, 22, 29, 35, 44, 53, 55, 63, 69, 81, 88, 99, 107, 137–140, 148, 150, 167, 177
Cleveland Press 1, 10, 12, 17, 19, 41, 42, 45, 48, 85, 107, 138
Cleveland Spiders 7
Clift, Harlond 57, 109, 134
Cobb, Ty 7
Cobbledick, Gordon 15–17, 18, 20, 22, 23, 30–33, 35–38, 44, 51, 54, 57, 62, 64, 66–68, 76, 77, 79, 81, 88, 92–94, 96–98, 100, 101, 103, 104, 106–108, 113, 119, 121, 123, 126, 129, 133, 142, 146, 147, 153, 154, 157, 163, 166, 171, 175, 183, 184
Cochrane, Mickey 182
Columbus Red Birds 15, 38, 84
Combs, Earl 137, 138
Comiskey, Charles 151
Comiskey Park 38, 47, 51, 52, 107, 126, 130, 144
Cronin, Joe 26, 36, 39, 44, 64, 65, 75, 121, 122, 124, 129
Crosetti, Frank 26, 39, 67, 105, 139
Crosley, Powel 104

Dahlgren, Babe 39, 67
Daniel, Dan 89
Davis, Harry 7
Davis, Larry 163
Dean, Chubby 59
Dean, Dizzy 35, 83
Detroit *News* 99
Detroit Tigers 2, 10, 11, 14, 15, 25, 39, 44–46, 51–54, 56, 57, 59, 60, 62, 68–70, 74, 76, 79, 82–87, 100, 101, 105, 109–111, 113–120, 122–128, 130, 131, 133, 134, 136–138, 141, 142–144, 146–148, 153, 154, 156–159, 161, 163–173, 175, 179, 182, 186, 188
Dickey, Bill 29, 35, 39, 45, 115
Dickman, Emerson 65, 66
Dietrich, Bill 111

DiMaggio, Joe 39, 67, 105, 116
Dobson, Joe 37, 58, 71, 75, 82, 102, 103, 109, 110, 113, 114, 117, 120, 122, 125, 135, 146, 160, 161, 187
Doerr, Bobby 135
Donald, Atley 39, 40, 102
Dorsett, Cal 33, 59, 125, 135
Doubleday, Abner 127
Doyle, Jack 127
Doyle, James 17, 99, 129
Dunn, Jim 8
Dykes, Jimmy 47, 51, 66, 107, 110, 111, 128, 131, 133, 186

Eisenstat, Harry 32–36, 42, 56, 68, 75, 85, 89, 114, 115, 118, 120, 122, 128, 129, 131, 132, 140, 155, 167, 170
Evans, Billy 8, 11

Fallon, Jack 15
Feller, Bob 30, 33, 35–38, 41, 45, 47, 49, 50–54, 56, 58, 60, 64, 66, 67, 71, 73, 76–78, 82, 84, 85, 87–91, 99, 103, 107, 108, 110–113, 115–119, 121, 122, 125–129, 131, 134, 135, 139, 141, 142, 144, 146, 147, 155, 157, 160, 162, 165–167, 172, 173, 178, 181, 185, 187, 188
Fenway Park 64, 84, 86, 89, 117, 135, 136, 184
Fletcher, Art 125, 126, 139, 165
Fohl, Lee 8
Fort Myers 25, 29–36, 38, 41, 166, 185
Foxx, Jimmie 75, 124, 159
Franks, Herman 69

Galehouse, Denny 122
Gehrig, Lou 39, 67
Gehringer, Charlie 110, 127, 132, 148, 166, 173
Gibbons, Frank 41, 45, 46, 86, 89, 91, 101, 112, 120–123, 138, 152, 154, 171, 172
Giebell, Floyd 164, 172
Gleason, Kid 151
Glenn, Joe 32
Gomez, Lefty 39, 68, 102
Gordon, Joe 39
Gorsica, Johnny 176
Green Bay Packers 125
Greenberg, Hank 55, 59, 131, 165, 166, 169, 185
Griffith, Clark 104, 180
Griffith Stadium 53, 114, 118, 128, 140
Grimes, Oscar 26, 38, 62, 63, 71, 88, 91, 118, 128, 147, 148

Grove, Lefty 53, 65, 66, 102, 121
Gumbert, Harry 43

Hadley, Bump 39, 40
Hale, Sammy 38, 43, 62, 88, 91, 115
Haney, Fred 68, 169, 185
Harder, Mel 27, 31, 33, 37, 38, 41, 43, 64,
  66, 67, 69, 70, 75, 78, 82, 83, 87–90,
  92, 100, 102, 105, 110, 111, 113, 117, 118,
  120, 124, 126, 129, 136, 141, 142, 146,
  154, 157, 162, 163, 165, 166, 167, 169,
  170, 172, 176, 188
Harridge, Will 65, 68, 101, 126, 127, 165,
  169, 170, 172
Harris, Bucky 72, 141, 180, 182
Harris, Mickey 64, 66, 121
Hayes, Frank 27, 113
Heath, Jeff 23, 26, 27, 29, 34, 38, 45, 48,
  55–58, 77, 81, 88, 98, 122, 132, 139, 150,
  153, 160, 161
Hegan, Jim 32, 37, 38, 78, 143
Helf, Hank 37, 38, 57, 59, 64, 98, 101
Hemsley, Rollie 32, 37, 38, 45, 48, 49,
  57–59, 64, 69, 88, 101, 108, 112, 113,
  122, 125, 127, 158, 165, 169
Higgins, Pinky 55
Hildebrand, Oral 39, 40, 102, 104
Hollywood Stars (PCL) 16, 69
Hornsby, Rogers 77, 78, 143, 161
Howell, Millard 143, 167
Hubbard, Cal 125
Hubbell, Carl 44
Hudlin, Willis 31, 33, 35, 37, 43, 56, 57,
  59, 61, 65, 69, 71, 73, 130
Hudson, Sid 73, 120, 164
Huggins, Miller 106
Humphries, Johnny 34–37, 56, 59, 65,
  82, 120, 122, 125, 129, 135, 187

Indianapolis (AA) 36
International League 34

Jennings, Hughie 15
Jersey City (IL) 48
Johnson, Ban 5, 6
Johnson, Earl 159
Johnson, Walter 9–12, 22, 23, 48, 95, 97,
  99, 149, 188
Jones, Del 32
Judnich, Walt 129
Jungels, Ken 37, 51, 72

Kamm, Willie 10, 97
Keller, Charlie 39, 67

Keltner, Ken 38, 61, 103, 109–111, 115,
  122, 135, 136, 151, 168, 181, 188
Kennedy, Vern 68, 110, 170, 171
Kieran, John 66, 67
Kirksey, George 46, 65
Kohlbecker, Frank 171
Kolls, Lou 103, 111
Krakauskas, Joe 114
Kreevich, Mike 52, 144
Kuhel, Joe 52

Lajoie, Napoleon 6
Landis, Kenesaw Mountain 159, 184, 186
Lardner, John 35, 36, 131
League Park 11, 12, 14, 15, 22, 42, 47, 51,
  58, 69, 71, 72, 74, 75, 79, 86, 87, 101,
  102, 104, 110, 111, 114, 117, 119, 120, 131,
  133, 134, 136, 144
Lee, Thornton 58, 79
Lewis, Buddy 140
Lewis, Whitey 1, 17, 38, 42, 45, 48, 49,
  85, 87, 93, 94, 100, 101, 123, 132, 138,
  139, 141, 165
Lyons, Ted 111, 146

Mack, Connie 7, 8, 25, 71, 72, 82, 104,
  142, 143
Mack, Earle 163
Mack, Ray 2, 26, 27, 29, 32, 36, 38, 44,
  45, 52, 53, 62, 76–78, 81, 83, 90, 107,
  110, 112, 115, 127, 131, 132, 136, 181, 188
Mails, Duster 126
Masterson, Walt 83
McAleer, Jimmy 6
McAllister, Jack 8
McAuley, Ed 45, 95, 101, 149, 150
McCarthy, Joe 18, 25, 67, 78, 107, 156,
  186
McCosky, Barney 131, 166
McGraw, John 106
McGuire, Jim 7
McKain, Archie 168
McKechnie, Bill 168
McNally, Dave 70
McNichols, Walter 11, 97
Melillo, Oscar 31, 51, 112, 185
Meloy, W.E. 62
Messersmith, Andy 70
Meyer, Dutch 131, 132
Mills, Howard 57, 68
Milnar, Al 34, 35, 37, 41, 43, 58–60, 65,
  66, 68, 73, 74, 78–80, 82–85, 99, 102,
  104, 108, 110, 112, 113, 115–117, 125,
  127, 130, 133, 137, 142, 146, 155, 157,

159–163, 165, 167, 170, 171, 172, 176, 187, 188
Milwaukee (AA) 59, 72, 107
Milwaukee Brewers (1901) 6
Moriarty, George 83, 136
Municipal Stadium 14, 24, 42, 55, 58, 69, 74, 79, 99, 102, 103, 109, 111, 114, 119, 123–125, 131, 132, 136, 144, 146, 156, 157, 160, 161, 162, 164, 165, 171, 173, 177, 187
Murphy, Johnny 39, 40
Myatt, Glenn 10, 97
Myer, Buddy 140

National League 1, 5, 7, 25, 39, 46, 87, 104, 107, 127, 159, 167, 168, 186
Navin Field 11
Naymick, Mike 33, 35, 37, 59, 65, 72, 79, 82, 125, 143
New York Giants 10, 35, 36, 38, 41–44, 46, 47, 71, 74, 106, 127, 130
New York Highlanders 6
New York Yankees 1, 2, 6, 8, 11, 14–16, 18, 19, 21, 25–27, 29, 33, 35, 39, 41, 44–46, 59, 62, 64–75, 78, 82, 83, 100–106, 108, 111, 114, 117, 118, 121, 123–126, 132, 133, 136–142, 144–148, 153–158, 160–163, 169, 170, 175, 183, 186, 188
Newark Bears 15–17, 19, 34, 48, 89, 93
Newhouser, Hal 59, 131, 147
Newsom, Buck (Bobo) 79, 116, 132, 172, 176
Niggeling, Johnny 134

O'Dea, Paul 118
Oklahoma City 143
O'Neill, Steve 12, 14, 15, 17–19, 21, 22, 74, 95, 97, 99, 149, 172, 188
Otis, Sam 69

Pacific Coast League 15, 69, 186
Pearson, Monte 39, 40, 68, 104, 115
Peckinpaugh, Roger 8, 9, 12, 22, 24, 95–97, 149, 184–186, 188
Peters, Russ 37, 122
Philadelphia Athletics 6, 25, 27, 44–46, 59, 61, 62, 71–73, 81, 82, 95, 96, 99, 100, 101, 113, 114, 117–120, 141, 144, 160, 162, 175, 182, 186
Philadelphia Phillies 12, 15, 35, 36, 46, 74
Pippen, Henry 55, 56, 60
Pittsburgh Pirates 168

Polo Grounds 8
Porter, Dick 34
Portland Beavers (PCL) 186
Potter, Nelson 62
Povich, Shirley 18, 99
Pulford, Don 34–37, 42, 59, 143
Pytlak, Frank 27, 31–33, 37, 41–43, 48, 57, 58, 60, 64, 65, 68, 70, 83, 100, 101, 105, 106, 118, 144, 145, 151

Ramirez, Manny 119
Reed, B.H. 35
Rice, Grantland 18
Rochester Red Wings (IL) 35, 36
Rogers, Packy 32
Rolfe, Red 39, 105, 115
Rongino, Lou 143
Rosar, Buddy 115
Rosen, Al 119
Ross, Lee 81, 96, 113
Rowe, Lynwood 56, 59, 167, 172
Ruffing, Red 29, 35, 39, 67, 73, 126
Ruppert, Jacob 18, 73, 104
Russo, Marius 39, 40
Ruth, Babe 24, 58, 106, 107, 114, 182

St. Louis Browns 6, 7, 25, 44–46, 52, 55, 57, 58, 66, 68–72, 76, 78, 101, 109, 110, 119, 121, 127–130, 133, 134, 142–146, 151, 157, 161–163, 169–171, 186–188
St. Louis Cardinals 15, 35, 37, 39, 46, 77, 79, 83, 162, 168
St. Mary's College 159
St. Paul (AA) 84
Salsinger, Harry 99
Salt Lake City (PCL) 16
San Francisco Giants 69
Schumacher, Hal 44
Seitz, Peter 70
Selkirk, George 39, 67
Sewell, Luke 31, 43, 57, 59, 60, 64, 96, 112, 128, 129, 133, 136, 137, 150, 179, 182, 185
Shibe Park 61, 81, 113, 142–144
Siebert, Dick 113
Slapnicka, Cy 15–17, 27, 32, 33, 37, 43, 49, 70, 78, 82–86, 93, 94, 96, 100, 101, 106, 115, 117, 131, 139, 158, 177, 179, 180, 181, 187
Smith, Al 32, 34, 36, 37, 58–60, 65, 74, 79, 82, 84, 101, 102, 110, 112, 114, 116, 118, 120, 125–128, 132, 134, 142, 155–157, 160, 164, 187, 188
Smith, Edgar 47, 51, 52, 58, 79

Solters, Julius 23, 52, 144, 155
Somers, Charley 7
Southern Association 38
Speaker, Tris 8
Sportsman's Park 76, 78, 108, 127
Stovall, George 7
Stromme, Floyd 33, 36
Sundra, Steve 17, 39, 40, 102
Swift, Bob 129
Syracuse Chiefs (IL) 34

Tabor, Jim 102, 122
Tebbetts, Birdie 132, 173
Terry, Bill 46, 106
Thomas, Luther 60
Three-I League 32, 143
Toledo (IL) 17
Torres, Gilberto 34
Travis, Cecil 140
Trosky, Hal 26, 32, 34, 38, 43, 45, 53, 60,
  61, 63, 65, 73, 77, 78, 81, 86, 87, 89, 90,
  99, 104, 105, 110, 111, 113, 119, 122, 128,
  147–149, 151, 152, 154–156, 158, 168,
  169, 177, 181, 188
Tucker, Tommy 94

Uhle, George 74

Vandenberg, Hy 36
Veeck, Bill 58
Vitt, Oscar 2, 15–27, 29, 34, 35, 38, 40,
  41, 43, 45, 48, 49, 51, 54, 56, 59, 61–63,
  65–67, 69, 71, 72, 79, 81–84, 86–101,
  103, 106, 107, 112, 114–116, 118–122,
  125, 130, 132, 133, 135–143, 146, 148,
  149, 151–153, 158, 160, 161, 165–167,
  169, 170, 172, 176–183, 185, 187, 188

Washington Post 18, 99
Washington Senators 6, 8, 9, 25, 35,
  44–46, 53, 62, 65, 71–73, 82, 83, 97,
  101, 113, 114, 119, 120, 126, 130, 144–
  147, 163, 164, 180, 186
Weatherly, Roy 26, 27, 32, 34, 38, 45, 52,
  55, 59, 68, 81, 90, 96, 111, 115, 127, 144,
  145, 148, 153–156, 158, 161, 163, 164,
  168, 181
Weiss, George 16
Western League 5
Whitney, Eugene 137
Wilkes-Barre 23, 59, 78, 112, 125, 135,
  143
Williams, Joe 161
Williams, Ted 53, 75, 122, 124, 125, 159
Wilson, Jack 65, 135
Wright, Taft 52, 53
Wrigley, Phil 104
Wynn, Early 34

Yankee Stadium 14, 67, 68, 84, 89, 114–
  116, 139, 140, 161
York, Rudy 55, 165, 166, 173

Zuber, Bill 32, 34–37, 51, 58, 60, 68, 82,
  114, 120, 137, 140, 155